Whatever Happened to Daddy's Little Girl?

Whatever Happened to
DADDY'S
LITTLE
GIRL?

The Impact of Fatherlessness on Black Women

JONETTA ROSE BARRAS

THE BALLANTINE PUBLISHING GROUP
NEW YORK

A One World Book
Published by The Ballantine Publishing Group
Copyright © 2000 by Jonetta Rose Barras

All rights reserved under International and Pan-American Copyright Conventions. Published in the United States by The Ballantine Publishing Group, a division of Random House, Inc., New York, and simultaneously in Canada by Random House of Canada Limited, Toronto.

One World and Ballantine are registered trademarks and the One World colophon is a trademark of Random House, Inc.

www.randomhouse.com/BB/

ISBN 0-345-42246-5

Library of Congress Catalog Card Number: 00-102210

Text design by Ann Gold

Manufactured in the United States of America

First Edition: May 2000

10   9   8   7   6   5   4   3   2   1

for Umoja Shanu,

Afrika Midnight,

Jasmine Malika,

and my mother

Contents

Author's note

Sandra Jackson, Helen Minor, Jonathan, and Milton are all pseudonyms used by request. In most instances I intentionally withheld the names of my siblings, hoping to accord family members some measure of privacy. All other names, dates, and episodes that appear in this book are real and accurate, based on my research and interviews.

Acknowledgments

I am eternally grateful to: *Washington City Paper* and its editor, David Carr, for believing in me and allowing me to write the essay from which this book evolved; Meri Nana-Ama Danquah who, with patience and love, helped me craft the book proposal and later read the manuscript, offering words of encouragement when I doubted myself; my literary agent, Victoria Sanders, who eagerly and aggressively fought to move the proposal from idea to book and guided my entrance into the world of the published author. Thanks to Stephanie Tade who helped usher the project to its completion, keeping my anxiety attacks to a minimum. Landing at One World/Ballantine with such an incredibly talented publisher/editor as Cheryl Woodruff was a dream come true.

Thanks also to the psychologists and other experts whose knowledge helped me extend and properly frame my thesis regarding the impact of fatherlessness, particularly Audrey Chapman, Gayle Porter, Maxine Harris, Wade Horn, and David Blankenhorn.

Thanks go also to my friends around the country who have given me decades of support, but especially those who assisted with this project: George Miller, Roy McKay, Judith Scott, Olive Vassell, E. Ethelbert Miller, Jerome Meadows, Michael Rogers, Brooke Stephens, the folks at the Martin Luther King Jr. Memorial Library, particularly the staff in the Sociology Division who assisted me in my research, Jonathan at La Tomate in Washington, D.C., who opened the restaurant to me and my ragtag band of fatherless women; Christine DeCuir and the good people at the New Orleans Tourism Center; the management of the Plaza Hotel on St. Charles Avenue in New Orleans; and my friends at Vertigo Books—Todd and Bridget—who culled their shelves for related materials.

My heartfelt thank-you extends to my daughter Afrika, and to Ivory, Tonya, Meri, Misty, Judith, Helen,* Sandra,* Jerome, and Milton*; they opened their lives for my exploration. Without knowing exactly how I would handle their suffering or their souls, they displayed an enormous amount of courage and trust. I grew because of their immense generosity.

Most important, I'd like to thank Russell for being there.

*Pseudonyms

Introduction

By the time I was eight years old, I had already lost three fathers—Bill, John, and Noel. Each one abandoned me. Each one wounded me—emotionally and psychologically. At an age when I was supposed to be carefree, brimming with happiness and laughter, I frequently felt a deep sadness, an abiding loneliness. Nothing seemed powerful enough to permanently soothe the agony I felt. I had no well of wisdom from which I could draw to communicate any of this. Consequently, the personal narrative I wrote, through actions and thoughts, was laden with grief. What could I do to cope with the loss of these three men?

A girl abandoned by the first man in her life forever entertains powerful feelings of being unworthy or incapable of receiving any man's love. Even when she receives love from another, she is constantly and intensely fearful of losing it. This is the anxiety, the pain, of losing one father. I had had three fathers toss me aside; the cumulative effect was catastrophic.

It was a potent tragedy begun even before I knew my name, one from which I was unable to escape for years.

Despite the weight of this reality and its seemingly intractable nature, I tried to grapple with it, failing more often than succeeding. I didn't understand the reason for my anguish. Then in the late spring of 1988, I received a telephone call from New Orleans asking me if I would be willing to meet my biological father. After spending an afternoon with my father, I began, instinctively, to make a connection between the poor choices I had made and the years this man had spent outside my life. It would take nine years before I could fully understand or articulate what this first encounter with "Daddy" had unleashed inside my soul. Of course, I went on with my life. But my heart and head held tenaciously to one burning question: How had his absence affected my life?

Three years after meeting my biological father, I began to have difficulty with my own teenager, who appeared destined to replicate my experience; she was acting out in ways that defied her nature. She became a foreigner to me. I became xenophobic in response, fearing her future more than I feared her behavior.

I woke up one morning asking myself what had created the change in her, what caused the misdirection? Asking that question about her life made me reflect on my own; what had caused my own misdirection? What was causing it still? Was there any connection, I wondered, between the challenges my daughter was facing and those I faced?

Even then, I saw life as a series of concentric circles. I knew that none of us escapes our own history.

Still, no matter how feverishly I searched, I could not find the common center for my daughter and me—until 1995. That year, things began to come together. Maybe I had grown enough to understand. Maybe I had prayed so many years, the universe had decided I deserved some answers. I can't say for sure what finally put the pieces in place for me. This wasn't an epiphany; it was an incremental awakening.

That year—1995—plans were afoot for a Million Man March. The Nation of Islam leader, Minister Louis Farrakhan, aided by the Reverend Benjamin Chavis and others, decided to bring one million men to the nation's capital. The organizers had asked women to stay away: The event that October was to be a man's thing, a day of atonement for their failure to be the leaders of their families and their communities. Some women, mostly feminists, were angered by what they perceived as an attack against them. They blasted the event as the prelude to a return to patriarchy. Hadn't black women also faced myriad forms of discrimination and sexism? Hadn't they stood shoulder to shoulder with black men against white supremacy? Why now should they be cut out?

I reasoned, however, that there are occasions when men must be alone together, to confront themselves and each other: to celebrate their successes, analyze their failures, chastise misbehavior, call for improvements, and ruminate on the question of what constitutes a well-integrated manhood. In an essay that appeared in the *Washington City Paper*, "Ain't Nothing But a He Thing," I endorsed the march.

During the writing of the essay and as excitement began to build surrounding the march, I began to reflect deeply on my relationships with my fathers—Bill, John, and Noel—other men in my family, and the men I had married and divorced. The need to understand this tangled web of emotions was made urgent by my own daughter's decline. I sensed her desperation, and I recognized the aura of unworthiness beneath her bad attitude.

Underscoring the march was a five-year national fatherhood movement, which aggressively advocated the involvement of men in the lives of their sons. Young boys and men were being handicapped by the absence of their fathers, movement leaders said. Farrakhan and Chavis echoed this sentiment.

I watched these efforts with great interest, observed the fervor of advocates in this fatherhood crusade. I did not doubt their sincerity, nor did I doubt their conviction. As I searched their membership and read their materials, I came to understand the emphasis is on males—reuniting fathers with their sons.

I asked myself, If the absence of a father handicaps sons, what happens to daughters? What role does a father play in the development of his "little girl"?

I looked at my own daughter—the child of divorced parents—and found the answer. Her father and I had divorced when she was five years old. Our separation devastated her. Her hair began to fall out and she exhibited other signs of physical and emotional trauma. While she and her father maintained a relationship, through weekend visits and summer vacations, when he remarried and moved to another state the loss she began to feel from his absence rapidly turned into anger.

For thirty-six years I had stoically struggled to reconcile myself with the loss of my fathers and forged an identity in the face of their absence. I had searched the faces of men looking for my father, the one who existed in my fantasies. I dated older men, hoping for the return of a security I had never possessed. And I feared the departure of or abandonment by any man who befriended me.

One burning question always remained: What kind of person rejects a child?

As I was beginning to grapple and at least admit to myself the role fatherlessness was playing in my life, in December 1995 I received a phone call from New Orleans. Bill had died. I remember the wistful comment I made to my mother's announcement: "Now all my fathers are gone."

Perhaps it was this final blow that forced me onward in my investigation of the issue of fatherlessness. In 1996, I began reading tons of material and calling experts, including psychologists and sociologists. There were more than two dozen books on the topic of fathers and sons in print that year. Less than a dozen books explored the father-daughter relationship; most of them had been published in the 1980s. Even more important, of the books on fatherless women, none was written by an African American.

During my investigation, I camouflaged my own self-interest behind the journalist's facade. I wanted to know if there were others like me. I talked with female colleagues, friends, and perfect strangers and learned the answer was a resounding yes!

Writing has always been therapeutic for me. I started during my troubled and lonely adolescence, finding solace in the characters I created and the poems I wrote. As a writer, I know that like the parables of the Bible, a story told well truly can offer insight for others—even when the tale is not theirs. I decided to compose an essay: "Whatever Happened to Daddy's Little Girl?" which later appeared in the *Washington City Paper*.

The newspapers had been on the stand for less than twenty-four hours when the phones began to ring. I was amazed at the number of people who walked up to me on the street, telling me the impact the essay had had on them, proving that the relevance of the topic transcended my life and the lives of the individuals I interviewed.

Even today women walk up to me on the street, thanking me for writing the article, commenting about how much it touched them, how closely my experience mirrored their own. Some said they cried after reading it, seeing themselves in the words and stories that were told. Even men weighed in, citing unpleasant or difficult episodes with wives or girl-friends that emanate from their fatherlessness. One young woman in a class at American University in Washington, D.C., after reading the ar-ticle, broke down in tears before the entire room of her peers. For all these years, she had thought herself alone. It became apparent to me that after so many years of feeling as if I were alone, unwanted, and abandoned, there was an entire community whose experiences echoed my own.

Although I had written the essay, I knew I had only skimmed the sur-face. I had to learn more. I had to write more. I wanted desperately to heal myself. But equally important, I wanted to heal my daughter. I wanted to know how fatherless girls—young women, through divorce, death, or abandonment—are expected to cope. How do we fatherless women teach ourselves the mysteries of men? The way men shape their conversations and the way men shape their consciousness?

I wanted other women to know that someone understood. I know fa-therlessness. I know the emptiness it creates, the years searching for something to help fill the void, looking for a substitute to make me whole. I know the insecurity; the endless battles with doubts that are re-created with each new relationship—battles that are never won; the pain that resurfaces after each departure of a man in my life. I wanted women to understand the distinct patterns of sadness, insecurity, confusion, and unresolved pain that connects those of us who experience father loss ei-ther through death, divorce, or abandonment.

I discovered this common ground in the months following the Million Man March. In the course of writing this book, I have talked to countless women across the country about their relationships with and without their fathers.

Giving a name to my demons had a powerful effect on me. Not only did it permit me to collect the scattered, damaged pieces of myself, it also permitted me to take control. Suddenly, something that had silently directed much of my life now had definition, reason, and therefore a potential solution. It was no longer a hidden enemy, causing havoc and destruction. And as I began to outline the main factors of what I've come to call the Fatherless Woman Syndrome, my adversary had a name. I knew that the wounds it had inflicted could be healed.

The key components of the syndrome are rooted in the feeling of being fundamentally unworthy and unlovable. Like a spiral staircase without landings, these feelings wind about and lead to chronic rage, anger, and depression that are rooted in our fear of abandonment, rejection, or commitment. Think for a moment: If you feel unworthy or unlovable, and someone comes along and offers you attention and affection, you are certain to fear that this person will leave you. Could this person actually care for you? You don't believe he could possibly commit himself to you. Sooner or later he's bound to reject you. Many seek to salve the fatherless wounds through "sexual healing," engaging in the extremeness of promiscuity or anti-intimate behavior, either of which can worsen the situation.

We are not whores or "heartless bitches." Promiscuous fatherless women are desperately seeking love. Or we are terrified that if we give love, it will not be returned. So we pull away from it, refusing to permit it to enter our houses, our beds, or our hearts. To fill the void that our fathers created, we only make the hole larger and deeper.

The spiral continues downward, leading us to even more destructive forms of overcompensation: Mild to severe forms of addiction—to drugs, alcohol, food, or work—mar the lives of many fatherless women who suffer from such a profound sense of loss that they will take nearly any measures to fill that hole.

While we are hurting inside, we often project a demeanor of being able to "handle it." That is until it all boils over. Then we erupt with rage. Sometimes the damage is external, but all too often the meltdown is internal, leading us to depression, or worse, suicide. How can we bring an end to this insidious cycle?

What I have come to realize is that the causes of the Fatherless

Woman Syndrome are as complex as the symptoms it produces. But healing is possible. And so I have written this book for us, using my own story of fatherlessness as the book's foundation and primary thread. The experiences of other fatherless women are woven throughout my story, accompanied by the perspectives of psychologists and sociologists whose comments connect or further explain our histories.

We are still learning and growing in our awareness of what "fatherlessness" means. Ultimately, I believe the best answer to the question Whatever happened to Daddy's little girl? must be given only by women who know fatherlessness personally. This volume does not tell all of our stories, nor does it offer all the explanations. Nevertheless, it does begin to chronicle the fatherless daughter's journey. And it shares the skills we fatherless daughters have learned as we face ourselves and our fathers without fear.

Most important, this book permits us to speak. It offers us—me, my daughter, and other fatherless women—the opportunity to transcend our loss, to embrace our lost selves with love and compassion, and to forgive. And that is the happiest of endings.

BOOK ONE

Open the world to me

it's been closed
dark, flat
i kept thinking i
would fall off if
i went to the edge
but there was nothing
only a circle, waiting
to repeat itself
and me wondering
why every little girl
needs a daddy
before she can ever
become a woman for
some man to love.

—Excerpted from "Father,"
   The Corner Is No Place for Hiding

1. STRANGE FRUIT

We faced the Gordon Plaza Apartment complex on St. Ferdinand Street. A rust-colored, four-inch band of wood raced around the middle of the mustard-painted buildings, reminding me of the dirty ring my two sisters and I left inside the silver metal tub when my aunt Laurita bathed us all together. During those days in the 1950s we were refugees, finding pleasure in our escape from the New Orleans summer, teachers, watchful grandparents, and an overworked mother. Although the weather in Dallas, Texas, wasn't much better, Aunt Laurita was worth the trip. She had no children of her own and, along with Uncle Cephas, spoiled us rotten.

After our baths in her makeshift tub, she invariably dressed us in identical outfits, as if we were triplets. She pressed our hair down against our heads with globs of Vaseline petroleum jelly, pulling it back into a traditional bun—a symbol, she thought, of southern gentility and Creole aristocracy. My hair was always the most unruly. But Aunt Laurita never surrendered and never failed to bring it under her control—a boot-camp sergeant whipping a new recruit into shape. Years later, partially because of what she accomplished, I came to call Vaseline petroleum jelly black folks' elixir. We used it for everything: unruly hair, ashy legs, diaper rash, and makeup removal. There wasn't a role it couldn't perform. It had magical properties.

Such memories crowded my mind as my older sister and I traveled the perimeter, marching like soldiers in formation, searching for a point of entry into the apartment complex. I had not spoken a word to her since leaving the car. I had become lost in the day that sent me to this place.

Spanish Moss

"Do you want to see your father?" my mother had asked when she telephoned me that day from New Orleans; I was living in Washington, D.C. The incessant ringing of the phone had intruded on my day, and I was slightly irritated when I picked up the receiver. The day was hot, and I was forlorn. Even now I remember that 1988 season as the Summer of My Discontent. I saw nothing in it to praise, except my son's graduation from high school—everything else burdened me. To begin with, my temperamental disposition and legendary temper had gotten me into trouble yet again: I was fired from my job as city editor at the *Washington Afro-American* newspaper, after attempting to quarter the publisher with my acid tongue; I had no immediate employment options. To add to the misery, I had just broken up with my boyfriend. In the middle of all this, my mother called asking what I considered to be the dumbest question.

I couldn't remember the last time I had seen Bill. Latin-looking and short, with shockingly dark, curly black hair, mustache, and a warm brown complexion, which over the years grew pallid with his drinking, Bill was quite handsome. But he never belonged to me. He was the possession of my brother and my older sister. They seemed to worship him, and he them. Once when I was nearly junior-high-school age, I remember his visiting our home. The three of us, my brother, older sister, and me, were in the backyard. They seem to burst out in smiles when he arrived. He had come with another, taller person in tow—his older son by a previous marriage or a similar arrangement, I never learned which. He drew away from me. There was no smile on his face for me as there had been for my siblings. He was cold and distant. I did not know why, but at that moment I felt awful, as if something were seriously wrong with me, as if I did not belong in their family. I was an outsider, with no redeeming qualities. I remained in the corner, removed from the affection, accepting that he was my father but knowing that my embrace would never be reciprocated.

"For what reason? Why would I want to see Bill?" I asked, knowing that my mother, too, must have remembered that encounter.

"No, not him; I mean your real father," she replied casually. I fell silent. The shock reached more deeply inside of me than if I had been told of my best friend's death. I grabbed for a chair, thinking that at the very least I would faint.

Why would my mother deliver such earth-shattering, life-altering news by telephone?

There, with unimaginable ease, as if she were suggesting numbers to play for the lottery, my mother told me Bill was not my father—he was only her husband. She had made flesh and whole my feelings about Bill. I had not imagined the emotional abandonment. The chasm between us during my childhood—it had been real. He had always felt instinctively I was not his—except in name only. Although, for a time, he had tried to make himself my father, he could not. But none of this had been explained to me. All I had known was that I was unwanted.

My mother made no attempt to soften the blow, to explain the complexities and contradictions in which she had wrapped my life for thirty-seven years. If anyone else had been so cavalier, I would have mortally wounded them, releasing a missile of profanities. Instead, I wondered how she could be so remote, so insensitive. How could she not understand the nature of the assault she had just made?

The deception she harbored had its roots in the place where she and I were born; it endorsed this kind of charade. Like the South captured in John Berendt's *Midnight in the Garden of Good and Evil*, New Orleans is a place of layers. All the lines and edges are blurred. There is no way to discern the beginning or end of anything. The Spanish moss, which hangs from trees, is as symbolic as the aboveground cemeteries. Nothing is ever clearly viewed, and nothing is ever completely buried.

Not unlike Berendt's Savannah, New Orleans is a place where deceit is a natural occurrence, accepted, like voodoo, as part of the city's historical and cultural tapestry. To know the facts is not necessarily to know the truth. My grandmother always said that not even what is seen with the naked eye is to be completely believed.

In New Orleans, miscegenation and polygamy are as commonplace as the city's famous beignets and coffee with chicory. Some years ago, after learning the truth about my birth, I discovered another deceitful thread in my New Orleans family tapestry: I learned that two people who I thought were my aunt and uncle were actually cousins. They had challenged a societal taboo and done the unthinkable thing of having a child together.

When I was born, in October 1950, the law required that my mother give me her name. It was Barras—the name of the man to whom she was married. It hurts me to admit this, but my mother was guilty of adultery. And if that is not true, then the man she called my biological father had been guilty of rape. The choices weren't pleasant. Bill and my mother had been married when I was born; four years later, they legally separated. Both of them were Catholic, so they did not seek a divorce. They remained married for twenty-six years—although they had long since stopped living together as husband and wife. None of this history offered comfort or tolerable explanation for what my mother did. These were simply the facts. The truth is slipperier.

"He wants to see you," my mother continued.

He had called my grandfather, asking him to find out where I was and to give him my telephone number. I could not believe my grandfather had been part of the conspiracy that denied me the truth; I nearly worshiped that man. Once, I confessed to my mother that he was the only person in our family over whose death I would shed a tear. I considered him the most honest person I knew. Sometimes an adult doesn't discard a child's vulnerability and gullibility. I plead guilty to failing to discard my idealized notion of my grandfather, which may be why, years later, when my grandfather's own skeletons were uncovered, I was the only person shocked by the discovery.

My mother balked when she received my grandfather's call. But he pushed: "It's the man's child; he has a right to see her."

"So, do you want to see him?" she asked me.

I grew angrier at her impatience. How could anyone be expected to answer such a question in a matter of seconds, and over the telephone? I fell into a real funk, but restrained myself.

If I said no, I thought, then I would close the door forever. If I said yes, I didn't know what Pandora-type box I was opening: Who was this man? What baggage would he bring? Could I handle the consequences of allowing him, after all these years, to enter my life? In reality, fate gave me no choice. I had to say yes.

I was going to Mississippi, via New Orleans, later that month to attend the high-school graduation of my son, Umoja. "I'll see him when I come, then," I said, attempting to close the conversation before I exploded. A note of resignation and disappointment that I was agreeing to my father's request seemed to tinge my mother's voice. But she accepted my answer and hung up. I held the receiver in my hand, the silence filling the room. I was dazed. I seethed over the abrupt appearance of this unexplored past. The longer I sat in the chair at the dining table of my small two-bedroom apartment, the more enraged I became.

I had been subjected to a bushel of lies. I was the victim of unspoken covenants that had kept me in darkness. At that moment, I detested the southern culture that permitted the truth to be carved, diced, and smothered in a thick, albeit sweet, gravy.

For the next few weeks, I gave myself no peace. I wondered about this father I never knew existed: How did he and my mother come to know each other? How will I receive him, and he me? Why did it take all of this time for him to ask about me? What should I wear? What should I call him—Daddy?

Plexiglas (and Other Obstructions)

A row of squat gray and burgundy buildings alongside the Gordon Plaza Apartments constituted the neighborhood shopping center and billboarded the Desire Community Housing Corporation, the Sav-More Supermarket, and Jackson's Beauty Salon. The center teased like an aging prostitute unwilling to accept her mortality. My sister and I halfheartedly yielded to its funky allure, if only out of curiosity. We found in its armpit what we had been seeking: a sign directing us to the main office.

Upon our arrival, we were greeted by a plus-size African American woman who was seated at a desk. She buzzed us through a gate, but not into the office. We were denied the opportunity to see her and to hear her voice without obstruction; the entire office was shielded by Plexiglas.

The bullet-proof plastic has become standard construction material in an America crowded by narcissism and so overwhelmed by the concept of intimacy that it regards Bazooka bubble-gum wrappers, baseball cards, computers, E-mail, and television more inviting than the human touch. Perhaps this too-pervasive reality, more than anything else, is the reason that at the end of the twentieth century there transpired an epidemic of children killing children; children killing their classmates; children killing their parents. Everyone has forgotten how to love.

Once upon a time, we met one another and talked face-to-face; even foes were obliged to confront the human form directly. Those fighting the duel in the eighteenth and nineteenth centuries behind New Orleans's Saint Louis Cathedral stood nose to nose before measuring off the distance and firing their weapons. This was, of course, before the H-bomb, chemical and biological warfare, AK-47s, Glocks, the killing fields of the twentieth century, and the World Wide Web.

Plexiglas. I hate the stuff. I was so disturbed by its presence that day at the Gordon Plaza Apartments that I could not fix my mouth to say anything. My sister took charge. She told the plus-size office attendant who we were looking for. "Is he expecting you?" she asked. When we replied affirmatively, she picked up the telephone either to notify him that we were on our way up or to confirm that we were not lying—I wasn't sure which. "Apartment 235," she said, giving us hazy directions and leaving us even more confused. Nevertheless, showing our home training, we said thank you and took our leave.

We traversed a labyrinth of concrete walkways sheltered by iron fences. New Orleans remains famous for its decorative ironwork, part of its French and Spanish heritage. In fact, the old section of the city, known as the Vieux Carré, or the French Quarter, is infested with wrought-iron balconies and interior courtyards, hidden behind huge wooden gates. But the wrought iron of the Gordon Plaza Apartments lacked the French Quarter quality and personality; this fence served more to keep out the riffraff than to accentuate the architectural design of the place.

The revelation that a man different from the one my sisters and brother called "Father" had impregnated my mother with me branded me anew as the family's black sheep. Like Vietnam veterans whose flashbacks are so real that they are transported, once again, to the Southeast Asian jungle, sweating from the oppressive heat, jumping at the deafening sound of gunfire, and fearful that life may end within seconds, I was mangled by the implicit resurrection of the tale I had heard throughout my childhood: a taunt, whispered by my sisters and brother in our bedroom, drawing blood from my soul, crippling me beyond anyone's understanding. Even today, it bruises me and it anchors me in anguish.

The story went like this: My mother has just given birth to me; the nurses at Charity Hospital in New Orleans, who had tended to her when my brother and sister were born, are the same ones at her side when I arrive. Seeing me all cleaned up in the nursery, they come to warn her that she cannot take me home. They say her husband, Bill, will know I am not his. There are distinct differences between my features and those of my older sister and brother. They have dark, curly hair, which some black people call "good hair." Their Creole skin evidences the mix of white, Spanish, French, and Indian blood that runs through our family. I, on the other hand, flaunt darker skin, nappy hair, and a broad nose.

Years later, after hearing far too many times how different I was, I looked into the mirror and saw only what those nurses saw. I was perplexed by the deviation and believed myself an awful mistake. I wanted to beat myself unmercifully for my ugliness. I tried lightening my skin with bleaching creams; even before that, my mother used a hot comb in my hair, hoping to straighten out the kinks, only to have them return with the slightest moisture. There wasn't any help for my nose. As a young girl, my mother told me not to smash it, which is exactly what I did when it itched. There were times, however, when I went around squeezing and pinching my nose, as if I were victim of a malodorous wind. Sometimes I fantasized about rhinoplasty. Frequently and privately, I searched the faces of relatives, looking for commonality—a mole, a wrinkle, an eyebrow—that said "You belong." I found only loose threads, nothing whole and complete that I could embrace with security; nothing to which I could cling as Linus does to his blanket.

The Circle Circles Back

Having lived many lives and traveled many places, I have come to realize that we tend to walk a similar physical or psychological terrain most of our lives. Only the lucky, those blessed by miracles, avoid re-treading the same ground. We return to where we have been before because we sense that the answers to life's perplexing challenges lay just beyond the edges, along the side of the road, skillfully hidden in the underbrush. Psychologists repeatedly acknowledge that our search for definition and explanation inexorably leads back to our childhood, the wellspring of joys and sorrows. I was struck by this truth when my mother gave me my biological father's address: 3421 St. Ferdinand Street.

The youth that I most fondly remember, and the youth that I most assuredly despised, revolved in the sphere of 4712½ St. Ferdinand Street, where my mother, brother, and I lived for a time in a small, single-story house situated in the backyard of three larger homes. Our place could have been built for in-laws or a young couple just making their way into the world. Later, we moved to one of the larger houses on the street. Both places were owned by a Mr. Francis; he lived in the duplex fronting the smaller house. His daughter, her husband, and their two sons lived on the opposite side. I never knew Mr. Francis's first name. He rode a bicycle with a basket hanging from the handlebars. He killed his chickens with his own hands, and he loved the ground his wife walked on. I felt as if we lived in a small village, protected from the cruelty of the outside world. But that was before we moved to the Desire.

Yes, Desire. Say it softly, and romantic illusions arise. The word evokes sultry, exotic images and thoughts: of some man, bare-chested, walking in tight pants, coming toward me, with a lustful expression on his face; or perhaps of Marlon Brando yelling for Stella. The Desire I knew was none of these; some linguist had played a cruel joke. That the city had planted such a moniker on the place spoke more for New Orleans's sensual imaginings than for the reality of the lives lived in one of the country's most notorious public housing complexes.

A bevy of two-story, redbrick, garden apartments stretched across acres of land, the Desire was a mini–concentration camp, whose residents were sandwiched between an open sewer canal and train tracks. Most of the occupants were low-income, but not all were welfare recipients. My mother, brother, and I lived at 3344 Abundance Street.

There was nothing abundant about Abundance, except in the dreams of all of us who lived there and hoped every day for an escape to something better. Our house was just around the corner from where my mother had lived when I was born. The street and the house had been erased by the government, and were now only a memory. Actually, the area had been razed and its residents relocated to make way for the project, which was supposed to be an improvement. The program to build public housing was, in some measure, the 1940s/1950s precursor of the 1960s urban renewal programs. Those latter versions of urban restoration found tons of federal money sweeping through inner cities, slicing old, poor, or working-class African American neighborhoods in the name of progress. But people had lived and died in those homes that the government called shacks. A certain camaraderie among neighbors had sculpted those communities into extended families. While some may have viewed the project as simply the demolition of buildings, in fact it was the destruction of the spirit and culture of whole communities, many of which were never restored.

I hated moving to the Desire. We had lived with my grandparents in the middle-class community known as Pontchartrain Park. That subdivision of detached houses felt more like a neighborhood; I didn't know it then, but it also had the feel of a suburb. It boasted a new golf course, built mainly for the "Negro" residents of the city; public facilities remained segregated for much of my youth. In truth, racial separation made little sense in a place like New Orleans, which touted quadroons, octoroons, mulattos, and Creoles, long before the concept much less the word *multiracial* entered the lexicon of mainstream America. Most of us in New Orleans associated with nonblacks whenever we wanted. And when we decided to stay in our own little world, we found an unmatched comfort and wholeness.

In Pontchartrain Park, my sisters, my brother, and I played outside in the nearby parks or on the streets until the lights came on, or until my grandfather executed his famous whistle, which sounded through the air with the same clarity as the bells at the St. Louis Cathedral. The public buses stopped operating at ten o'clock in the evening. During those days, virtually everyone had a car, and those who didn't, didn't go out at such an "ungodly" hour.

When it became clear that four children and three adults, representing three generations, could not continue to live in a three-bedroom house—even one as modern as ours—our family split up. My younger and older sisters remained with my grandparents. My brother and I went with my mother. I never understood the reason for their choice, although years later, after some reflection, I surmised it was because my brother was a boy and could spell trouble, and I, well, I was the black sheep.

Early one morning, after we had been in the Desire for a few weeks, I awoke to the sound of tussling outside our second-floor apartment. I raised the window shade to glimpse who was creating the ruckus. A man was ripping away a woman's skirt and tugging at her panties. The woman fought fiercely, punching at his head and trying to pull away. He grabbed her again. Finally, he forced her to the ground and pounced on top. I didn't know what to do. If I called my mother, he might try to do something to her.

If I called the police, I would have to give my name and then he might come looking for me. My mother and I had no man to protect us.

Still, I had to do something: I turned on my bedroom light and lifted the shade, hoping to illuminate the area around the two embattled figures. Frightened, the attacker ran away. All night I wrapped and rewrapped my gown tightly around my body. Later that morning, when I went out for school, I saw the woman's green panties still on the ground, near the shrubbery.

There were good families squeezed inside the hellhole called Desire. But most often, the ones who came in whole and healthy soon caught the disease. My own brother was sucked up by drugs that were sold as openly as all-day-long hand suckers. Children were left alone without food, and death might be found on any corner.

Most of us kids who lived in the projects attended Moton Elementary School or one of the George Washington Carver schools—junior or senior high—which had been physically connected, through a conspiracy designed to keep us isolated and confined, like Native Americans on a reservation. In the mornings, we marched two and three abreast, escaping the confines of our apartments. We darted between parked cars and raced down pothole-infested streets; there were few sidewalks, and trucks, delivering beer and sodas, stole what little curb space there was. Profanities flew from the mouths of some kids the way Molotov cocktails leapt from angry hands years later, after the death of the Reverend Martin Luther King Jr.

A block from the school, we often were forced to take out our handkerchiefs or whatever other protection history and experience had taught us must be raised against the ruthless dust of this desert. We looked like bandits preparing for robbery. But we were the ones being robbed; even as an adolescent I knew that.

I often wondered what was on the minds of the construction crew as they systematically uprooted each tree. Did they ponder the absence of magnolias to guard against the wind and the stench of the canal? Did they consider the nakedness of a playground without even one tree from which boys and tomboy girls could jump after betting who could climb the highest? I wondered if they considered, even as they wiped the perspiration from their foreheads, that the hot, humid July days of New Orleans, without a tree's shade, were merciless; or that mornings without birds perched on branches, chirping and singing enchanting melodies, were lifeless. Even now, I wonder: Did those men know that the dust would become a vulture, circling constantly, then sucking the breath from our mouths? If they knew, evidence proved they didn't care.

Forgive Me, Father, I Have Sinned

My childhood was one long, empty night. I owned an overwhelming sadness and loneliness. A waiflike sentience consumed me. I cannot situate the precise moment I began to have this experience. But it was the very air I breathed, surrounding me and suffocating me with its pollution. Part of me did not want to escape it; I wallowed in this shattered emotional landscape. Years later, I realized that, at least in part, I had attributed my fragmented geography to an episode that remained imprinted on my psyche in unbelievable detail and that had a profound affect: Noel's mysterious departure.

Noel and my mother lived together for several years after her legal separation from Bill. One day he was in our house; the next day he was gone. Years later, upon reflection, I came to understand the depth of my sense of abandonment. By the time I was eight, three men had left me— three fathers: first Bill, who left my mother when I was still a toddler, then John, and now Noel. But it was Noel whom I remember the most fondly, maybe because my cognitive skills had fully developed by the time he came into my life. In other words, I knew him more fully, perhaps, than the others. Consequently, I missed him desperately.

I have replayed one particular frame in my history with Noel over and over again. Recalling, without any aids, the weather, the pose, the feeling of security it offered me:

It is 1956. I sit, poised and comfortable, in my white jumper and sandals, on the hood of a shiny white-and-silver Buick parked outside our home at 2612 St. Anthony Street. New Orleans is saturated with streets whose names are redolent of Catholicism—St. Ann, St. Claude, Elysian Fields. The aroma of fish frying, the sound of church bells, and the sudden appearance of rosaries in the hands of a sidewalk bum testify to the Pope's powerful pull: On Good Friday, for a time, it was not uncommon for some people to visit as many as nine churches, performing aspects of the stations of the cross at each, as if they were Simon, carrying the wooden crucifix. Nearly the entire population would be caught on Saturdays, inside pitch-dark closets, reciting a litany of small and large sins for which penance was dispensed. On Sundays, the liturgy sounded throughout the city. The day after Mardi Gras, people squeezed inside churches to have ashes pressed into foreheads, beginning the ritual of Lent, during which something valuable must be sacrificed. And each year, on the first day of November, cemeteries, resembling miniature cities, were visited; tombs whitewashed, weeds pulled, sidewalks swept, and prayers murmured in hopes that the dearly departed would rise beyond purgatory to heaven.

I know this reverent history even at (almost) six years of age, as I sit in the New Orleans summer heat, my hair neatly pressed and styled into Shirley Temple curls; the nuns and priests had carved it into my brain each day during Mass and Catechism class at Epiphany School, where I made my first Communion.

This afternoon, I am both witness to and beneficiary of a miracle: Noel's long, lean arms wrap around my waist, like a hula hoop or a life preserver. The left side of his forehead brushes mine. My dark skin does not nauseate him. It is black silk; he smiles from its touch. I smile back. One curl, unable to contain its excitement, shoots up in the center of my head. He is Daddy, although I don't call him that. He is the only man I think of that way. I feel protected and loved.

But only a small black-and-white photograph and a weeping heart serve as evidence that Noel ever existed.

After he left, and I realized he wasn't coming back, I frequently made my way inside the confessional at Epiphany, later at St. Gabriel, sometimes at St. Paul. I fell on the wooden floor rest, my bony knees whining from the discomfort. "Bless me, Father, for I have sinned," I whispered as the priest positioned his ear close to the mesh opening, listening for me to begin my inventory of offenses. With the sincerity expressed only by the very young, I muttered that I lied when I said I didn't care that Noel was gone. I lied when I said I was happy. I did not know what happiness was.

There was an internal civil war under way; I was too young to explain the battle to anyone, least of all the priest, who engendered reverence. I wanted God to resurrect me, the way he did Jesus Christ. The term *suicide* was foreign to me then. Now, however, I realize that is the word I would have used in the confessional. Instead, in my timid voice, I begged for forgiveness, believing that five Our Fathers and ten Hail Marys could cure anything; believing that prayers could create and re-create miracles. I believed this because I remembered the stories about Our Lady of Fatima. I remembered stories about how people were healed when the minister and the Reverend Mothers laid hands on them and asked God's blessing at the Rose of Sharon Church my great-grandmother attended.

Initially, I thought to blame my mother for Noel's departure. But then I realized that if I assaulted her, I jeopardized the little love I had. What would happen, I asked myself, if I screamed at her, told her she was the reason he went away? I worried that she might also leave, never to be heard from again. And then, there would be no one there to love me. So, I attacked myself: He left because my skin was too dark, my nose too wide, my hair never stayed down when it was told. Even the space between my teeth was too offensive; years later, my mother suggests we close it. I am the black sheep no one loves.

Father, what prayer should I say so God might forgive my ugliness and send Noel back? There was no answer, only a prescription for forgiveness. I raced back to the pew, knelt, and recited the prayers, eagerly, eating each word as if it were red, juicy watermelon. I knew when I finished, when I had recited the requisite Our Fathers and Hail Marys, Noel would return. But he didn't come back that day, nor the next. I cried.

I continued to cry for three decades. The weeping was all internal. No one understood my sadness; it was impossible to explain. Noel had deserted me. He had made me feel loved; he had made me feel wanted. He was the father from whose departure I would never recover. He was gone. Adding to the injury, God had turned his back on me.

During the 1970s, in Argentina, women marched in the plaza in the capital, holding signs and pictures of their children and loved ones who had been taken away by the then oppressive government and never returned. The women wore lace mantillas on their heads and blank, anguished looks on their faces, as if their vision had been frozen on the day they last saw their family member. They recited prayers or fingered rosary beads as they made their walk around the plaza.

The international media seized upon the sight of these lonely women crying for their children and loved ones—some too young even to have experienced their first romance. They were "disappeared" by their own country's vicious military regime. But despite the worldwide attention that the women's struggle received, their loved ones remained "The Missing."

I have never been to Argentina and I no longer wear the mantilla, but I have felt like those women. The French Quarter of New Orleans was my plaza. Each time I went there, I wore that frozen, distant look in my eyes; the picture of that summer, 1956, was imprinted on my chest. Does anyone know this man? Have you seen him? Do you know how to contact him?

Sometimes I sat at one of the sidewalk cafés; sometimes I sat on a bench or on the curb, like a lost, homeless child. I waited for Noel to drive through, recognize me, and take me with him. On the bus, I searched each man's features; I did not want mistakenly to pass him. It has been years; maybe his hair has grayed. Maybe his face has wrinkled. But his eyes, surely his eyes are transfixed in the same place and the same season as mine: summer 1956, when miracle was my middle name, and he wrote it over and over.

Embracing Punishment and Longing for Daddy

By 1962, at almost thirteen, having failed to locate Noel, I began subjecting myself to austerity: I incarcerated myself in my bedroom after school and on some weekends, permitting few friends and little frivolity. I dressed in uniform, believing adornments served little usefulness; nothing could help me. Nothing would make anyone love me. I wore my little pink, pleated skirt and white blouse two or three times a week, washing the outfit overnight, letting it dry the next day and ironing it—folding and spraying Argo starch on each single pleat. My shoes were black or brown, sometimes white. I ventured to buy or wear colored shoes only at Easter; otherwise, they were much too flamboyant. I did not deserve the glamour, I subconsciously had concluded.

My mother worked two jobs, so her schedule abetted the regimented, solitary life I had begun. Sometimes I prepared my own meals. Sometimes there were leftovers, which I rarely heated. I preferred a sandwich; it was less formal. I hated eating alone. There was no one to tell how good the beans were, no one to whom I could say, "Pass me the salt." No one to argue with over why I was left so little in the pots. These days, I am a little envious as I watch a Campbell's chicken soup television commercial where the three boys are at the table, and the youngest is yelling for his brothers to pass the soup, and not to hog it all. By the time he gets the pot, he is excited to find that there is chicken in the chicken noodle soup. He pops a piece into his mouth: Mmmm. Each time I see this scene, I am reminded of what I missed, all those solitary nights, in our project apartment.

Often, when I was ready for bed, my mother had not yet arrived home from work. I do not remember ever having a bedtime story told to me, either as a child or an adolescent. Frequently, no one tucked me in or kissed me good night. Most mornings, I rose from bed unprompted. I can't remember a time when my mother or any relative shook me from sleep, telling me to get ready for school. While I had a zest for learning, my early rising was motivated more to reseal, in my mind's eye, the contours of my mother's face or the melodious quality of her voice, not yet exhausted from the two jobs she would work that day.

Then, as now, she was a lovely woman with copper-colored skin and a youthful demeanor that surprised me, since she had four children and I was in my teens—old enough to have a baby, as some of the other girls in my neighborhood had done. My mother's auburn hair was long and soft; she passed a hot comb through it, more out of habit than need. Burn marks on each of her slender arms were testimony to the hazards of the job of short-order cook. I imagined myself as pretty as she. But it was only imagination.

At five-thirty in the morning, when the sun had not quite kissed the sky, I walked the few blocks from our apartment on Abundance Street to the Bynum Bakery, purchasing doughnuts and coffee as her breakfast and mine. Often my brother was still in bed; he didn't eat with us. Sometimes he was visiting his paternal grandmother. My mother and I sat at the table, saying few words. Sometimes she gave me instructions for the day: Make sure to clean the bathroom and mop the kitchen floor. Cook the beans for dinner. Or you can heat the spaghetti. She almost never asked me about what I was doing at school.

There was something about my mother worthy of admiration, I found. She rarely exposed her unfulfilled desires. There must have been a time in her life when she dreamed. But she was married at sixteen and had my brother, her first child, when she was eighteen. My sister followed the next year, and I the year after that. My youngest sister happened along three years later.

On those mornings in the Desire project, I wished for a way to keep my mother at the table, drinking coffee or hot chocolate, eating glazed and jelly doughnuts. While I was thirsty for her company, I sipped her slowly—not in gulps. I did not want to spoil the moment with too many words; feeling her presence was communication enough. I knew that in the evening it would be only me, at the window, looking onto the courtyard as the other children jumped rope, or raced after one another, or simply sat on porch stoops cursing and telling jokes.

I was a latchkey kid, although such a fancy, nondescript, emotionless term wasn't used then to characterize my experience. Sociologists coined the phrase years later to describe an entire generation of children who were born into poor or working-class families and left alone while their parents scratched out meager earnings. Back in the early 1960s, I was simply a child with a working mother and no father.

One morning, fully confident in my environment, I strutted, alone and, by now, unafraid, through three blocks of project terrain to Bynum Bakery. I sashayed inside and made my order. Just as I was paying the bill, the owner asked me about bringing him "the case for the trumpet." I was confused: The trumpet in question, for which my grandfather paid two hundred dollars so that I, at almost thirteen, could audition for the school band, had been stolen weeks earlier from our apartment.

Did the baker have it? Did he steal it? How did he get it? "Your brother sold it to me for seventy-five dollars." Liar! I was hurt and infuriated by the conversation.

For a time, I idolized my brother. He was strikingly handsome—soft, golden skin, curly black hair, a chiseled face that would look youthful even as the years ate into him. He was a drummer. I watched him beating, with two blond-colored wooden sticks, the black pad that drummers used when they didn't want to create a ruckus on the real thing. Sometimes I fancied him in a band, like my grandfather, sitting center stage, with all the girls yelling to "give the drummer some," and he—cool, like Sam Cooke—only smiling back. He and I were relatively close for a time, since we were the two siblings living with my mother. We watched *Morgus the Magnificent* on television together, late Saturday nights. The inventive, fictional scientist and his assistant, Chopstick, introduced the horror shows, which I loved and my brother watched with me, despite being frightened. After seeing one of those shows, it wasn't unusual for him to curl up at the foot of my bed instead of going to the living room, where he slept on a sofa bed. His fear of the Indian spirit Black Hawk also amused me. My mother often threatened us with Black Hawk's appearance if we didn't perform as she wanted.

One night my brother awoke from sleep, running through the house screaming that an Indian with a tomahawk was after him. While Black Hawk may have once existed in real life, I never saw his spirit. To this day, I can't say with authority that he actually existed in the spiritual world or merely in my mother's and brother's minds. But I am certain that my brother saw something, somehow, and it frightened him greatly: When my mother caught up with him, he was about to jump from the rail of the second-floor stairwell. She had promised before we went to sleep that Black Hawk would visit the person who stole money from her purse.

Stealing a few nickels from your mother's purse seemed a rather insignificant crime. But it was quite another thing to steal—and sell—someone else's music. The Desire project had transformed my handsome and talented brother into a character from a *Morgus the Magnificent* movie.

I rushed back home from Bynum Bakery, forgetting the coffee, doughnuts, and my change on the counter. Sobbing uncontrollably, I told my mother about the encounter with the baker who had my gold trumpet but not its green case.

"What are we going to do?" I wailed. I felt like that woman whose green panties had been torn from her. We had to do something, I insisted. We should call the police. I was still young, naive, and gullible enough to have faith in the police to right wrongs. Short of the police at that moment, I wished for a father. I told myself, If Noel were here, he would march back down to the bakery and demand the trumpet. He would do damage to the owner. I desperately needed a father—Noel or someone else.

Seeing the movie *A Time to Kill* decades later, I was reminded of the episode in the Desire project. I remember identifying with the little girl who, in the movie, was violated and left to die by redneck hoodlums. As she lies on the sofa of her family's home, her mother is tending her wounds and awaiting the ambulance. Her father, who raced from his job upon hearing that something had gone terribly wrong, rushes in and sits near her on the sofa. "Daddy, I kept calling for you to come," the little girl says, one eye so badly bruised she cannot see out of it. "Where were you, Daddy? Where were you?"

Looking into a Face Like Mine

It is hard to believe that such trauma had visited me within blocks of my father's apartment. The irony did not escape me that day my sister and I went to visit at the Gordon Plaza Apartment complex. I didn't consider for a moment that perhaps my father had not even lived there when my youth became a horror show, interrupted only infrequently by humorous commercials. The thought that consumed me as my sister and I climbed the stairs to apartment 235 was that my savior had been only blocks away, and that my rescue was finally at hand.

We hesitated outside the door. I was nervous, unsure about what awaited me on the other side. We smiled at each other. When I am worried or frightened in public, I have learned to reach for that smile. It is a cultural thing. Most African Americans throughout our history have used humor as a shield, a spear, a salve. If we had not been able to laugh, sometimes at the sheer absurdity of our condition in America, we would have committed suicide, massacred all white people, or been massacred as were Native American nations. I use my smile also as a buffer against intrusions by people who want to know what I am feeling. I don't share my emotions easily. Those I feel deepest remain buried inside—sometimes for decades. I could not bring up my hand to ring the bell. My sister did it for me.

A man, old but lean and hard, opened the door. He wore a receding hairline. His face was long, thin, but not gaunt. His eyes defied the feeble condition of his body; they sparkled, as if he possessed a secret or had just been privy to a joke. His nose was wide, not quite flat. A tube dangled from it and traced to a machine he carted alongside him. His breathing weighed down his energy. It made me tired. A smile that was a mixture of fear and satisfaction appeared on my face. Despite his weakened image, I was excited to see John Asemore, my father. Finally, I had discovered a face that mirrored mine, a temperament that mimicked mine, and a man who unknowingly shaped my life.

He invited us to sit on his green leather sofa. My sister chose the chair. I rested next to him. For some reason, during those first few seconds, I knew he had been sent to rescue me. He was hesitant, seeming unsure whether anything he said would affect a lifetime lived in a swamp of deception. This man with a tube in his nose talked easily; he possessed an infectious laugh, which—as I would soon learn from Mama—camouflaged a mean streak that, if stirred, could not be easily smothered.

Though I was silent, I wanted him to know about the lacerated life I had lived. I wanted to show my war-torn interior landscape, littered with bodies that all looked like me and tears that fell only from my eyes. I was simultaneously the attacker and the attacked, victim and victor. I was the casualties; I had spent most of my life searching for the Red Cross station. I wanted him to soothe this thing I called my soul.

Daddy, Tell Me a Story

"Your mama was separated from Bill," he began, telling our family narrative. "She was living with your grandmother and grandfather; your sister and brother lived there, too. They were Bill's children. You all lived right down the street from where my cousin lived. I spent a lot of time at my cousin's house. Your mama would come to visit and we would talk sometimes. She was a beautiful woman. One thing led to another."

My mother wanted to marry him, but he wasn't ready, and wouldn't have made a good husband. "I don't know if I would've made a good father, then. Maybe I would have, because sometimes when your mama went to work, I took care of you. I fed you red beans and rice. You were still a tiny thing.

"Then one day I came to see you. Your mama had left you at your cousin's house on Bienville Street. I had diapers and milk and stuff like that. But they wouldn't let me in. Your mama had told them not to let me see you. I just left the stuff on the porch. I never saw you anymore, until now."

For months, John tried to persuade my mother to let him see me, but she never relented. Once, she even had him arrested when he approached her on the street. Not long after that, he joined the merchant marines. Although he moved away, he always called my grandfather's house, hoping to get in touch with me.

Upon retiring from the merchant marines, he went to live in Baltimore. Someone told him I lived in Washington, D.C. But because my maiden name didn't appear in the telephone directory, he never found me. His last plea to my grandfather finally yielded the results he'd long sought.

When John's story ended, day had become night. It was too late to tell him my tale. Instead, I left in silence. My sister and I made our way to the car; her mood was as somber as mine. She had shared my life and sensed the awkwardness and the betrayal I felt. It was also her betrayal. All those times Bill had professed I was not his, she had defended me. Now she realized she had built—unnecessarily—a barrier between herself and her father. It was too late to repair the damage.

Back at my mother's house, words—nasty, hateful words—spewed from my mouth like a drunk's vomit. I ranted like a madwoman, enraged that for years she had taken liberties with my life. I realized, too, that my mother had lived a life of deception. Who was she? I wondered. Had anything she'd ever told me been true? Were there other lies waiting just beyond the road's edge to ambush me?

She did not rise to her defense, nor did she permit my sister to shield her against my attack. Initially, she refused vehemently to tell her side of the story. She warned that it was best to leave the door closed. She said it was past. How could a woman steeped in New Orleans spiritualism not understand the gathering of energies that thrust us from the present to the past, and back again?

Mama Speaks

Years later, as I began to investigate in earnest the relationship between my fathers and me, to examine the wound created by the absence of John, Bill, and Noel, my mother telephoned me from New Orleans. She had decided to tell her version of the story about herself and John: The way they fell into bed, she could have accused him of rape, she says! Nine months from the date she had her first sexual encounter with him, I was born. "I wrote it on my calendar when I got home; that's how I knew you were his."

He was a beater; when he drank, he became unruly. He was not a nice man. Once he pushed her through the glass fronting of a department store. The police arrested him. They told him she was too little—only four feet eleven inches tall and about one hundred pounds—for him to manhandle. She stopped him from seeing me because he threatened to take me away and get his mother to raise me.

The story ended abruptly, the way it does when a parent realizes a child has fallen asleep during the telling. My mother knew I had closed my ears. I was not listening. In her version, he was a bad guy. Surely she must have played some role in her own drama. But she did not reveal it; the truth was sliced and diced.

A year later, she wants to know why I am talking about Noel and Bill. "They were all no good," she says. I am sympathetic to her suffering. But I cannot overburden myself with her failed relationships. All I know is that she denied me the opportunity to know these men, especially my biological father. She denies me still.

Each time we talk about this father conundrum, I try to fashion the conversation in such a way that she can understand how important these men were, and are, to my life; how they sculpted me, although they were mere shadows. She can't grasp the significance, perhaps because she didn't live without a father. Even now, as I write this, her father, at almost ninety, is still at her side—a little cranky, but no less alive. She makes no connection between her actions and the dilemmas I have faced as a woman in my relationships—with myself and with others—with men in particular.

I hold the telephone receiver to my ear during yet another conversation; her voice trails off, becoming fainter and fainter. The only thing I can hear clearly is the fatherless song. I sing it sorrowfully, achingly, the way Billie Holiday sang "Strange Fruit."

2. A CHOIR OF THE WOUNDED

The "fatherless woman" song is not only mine; it is subtext in the lives of too many women—particularly African American women: Janet Langhart, the wife of Defense Secretary William Cohen; the authors Bebe Moore Campbell, Gloria Wade-Gayles, and Meri Nana-Ama Danquah; the Reverend Bernice King; the community newspaper publisher Judith Scott; Bill Cosby's alleged daughter Autumn Jackson; college student Helen Minor; human resources director Sandra Jackson; attorney Tonya Butler; art critic Misty Brown; and Malcolm X's daughter Qubilah Shabazz. Walk down any street in America, and there are others to be found; the list seems endless. We are a choir; listen to the dirge we sing:

"Father's Day is a very difficult time for me. I don't show it outwardly. In my childhood everybody had a daddy, except me. To me there is such a stigma attached to it. I feel so ashamed," laments Ivory Nevada Sanders, a thirty-seven-year-old, medium-tall, cocoa-colored resident of Baltimore, Maryland. Her father is two black-and-white photographs her mother gave Ivory one day when she was nine years old. She has never seen him in person, never heard his voice, never felt her hand inside his.

"My girlfriends who have children, those fathers are still involved with their children," Ivory continues. "All my male friends who had children out of wedlock, they spend time with those children. I think, Where is my daddy?"

I know this sentiment intimately. It rides shotgun with me, an ever-present companion even when I want so desperately to kick it out of the car. In New Orleans, when my siblings and I lived on Mexico Street with my grandparents, there wasn't a house that didn't have a father. The Barbarans, the Bells, the Lawrences, the Thomases, the Jacksons, all had fathers. Those were the days when fathers could be seen going to work in the mornings, or sitting on porch stoops in the evenings; or, on weekends, shouting out to the children not to play so rough and to watch for the cars, "or I'm gonna spank your little butt."

"For Father's Day, when I was in elementary school, we'd have to make cards. I would just sit there," confesses Helen. "I was the only person who didn't have a father. My teacher said, 'Make one to your grandfather.' But it wasn't the same.

"The neighborhood we grew up in, my friends' fathers were around. I was different from everybody else. I felt the strain of that, emotionally," adds Helen, a twenty-something college student from the Midwest whose mother is white and whose father is black.

Crystal writes, "I am fourteen years old and my father left when I learned to say 'Daddy.' Even though my father's not around, in my heart he is always here. Every birthday and every Christmas, I cross my fingers in hopes that my father will come home. Does my wish come true? No. But I will never quit looking and hoping."

Where did the daddies go?

"Every second kid in my elementary and middle school, it seemed, had a story about birthday gifts that their separated or divorcing dads promised but which never had arrived in the mail, missing child-support checks, custody visits abandoned for the sake of the dad's vacations, and the dad's new girlfriends, new wives, and new children taking all the money," Naomi Wolf whispers in her book *Promiscuities*, a personal memoir and exploration of female sexuality.

"Today, every time I see a commercial with a father holding a baby, with a child running into a man's arms, with a reunion at a rail station or an airport, unbidden tears come, ridiculous tears," Anne Roiphe confesses in her book *Fruitful*, which brilliantly combines memoir and commentary about motherhood and feminism. In *Fruitful*, Roiphe describes her father as emotionally unavailable during her youth.

"These are not the tears for toothpaste, jeeps, or dog food. If you don't have a good father, you mourn for him always," Roiphe adds.

But Misty Brown does not weep, although she struggles to forget the lyrics of the fatherless song. Tall, deep-dark-skinned and sporting dreadlocks, the freelance writer already has forgotten, deliberately, the color of her father's hair, the shape of his eyes, the size of his lips, how many feet he towered over her when at eight years old she was reintroduced to him.

"I blanked my daddy out, big-time. I don't want to remember his face; he might look too much like me." Merging Samuel Jerome Brown's image with hers traps her with a pain she desperately wants to disown. If she acknowledges its presence, she will be overwhelmed. So she becomes an actress, switching persona and role, never fully disclosing her anger or hurt until it explodes.

"I used to wish he were dead. That way I wouldn't have to explain why he wasn't around. It would have made it easier to say he was dead," confesses Sandra Jackson, a tall, graceful woman who works as a human resource developer and describes herself as a born-again Christian. Her father left the family when she was nearly two.

"What I missed most [after my dad left] were the daily things," confides the writer Meri Nana-Ama Danquah. A deep-dark woman of medium height and build, she is older, intellectually, than her chronological age suggests. But for all the wisdom she conveys, deep inside a little girl cries to be comforted. Her mother and father divorced when she was ten years old.

Meri longed to watch television with her father, to tell him what happened at school, to plead for help with some boy who had gotten out of hand. But her days were filled instead with wondering: Will Daddy come today?

"I used to sit at the window of my bedroom, which faced onto the parking lot of our apartment building, and would look at all the cars coming into the lot. I would just look and I would wait. The first few weeks, I was half hoping, half expecting that he would come home. After a while it just became this huge gaping hole that was occupied with sorrow.

"Sunset is still the worst time of day. When the sun starts to set, it's very disconcerting. I feel like crying, sometimes I actually do start crying. If I am at home, I start looking out of the window. It wasn't until [1993] that I was able to make the link with my father."

In the morning, when she wakes, my own daughter hums the sorrowful lyrics of the fatherless song, like some meditation or mantra she has been taught to repeat over and over. It reverberates throughout the house.

Petite—four feet eleven inches tall and not quite one hundred pounds— she sports an Afro hairstyle. Physically, she more closely resembles her father, a constant reminder of whose little girl she is. She sits on the sofa next to me, her arms crossed over her chest, her eyes fixed in that year when her world went from gray to black. We have been talking about how things changed; how her father used to provide greater physical and financial support for her in school. At one turn she is angry; at another she is hurt. The memories bruise her.

"I feel terrible. I feel like my father abandoned me," she says. "He's been gone too long. Sometimes I wish my mama and daddy would get back together." And then the fatherless-woman song is caught in her throat.

When she tells me these things, I crumble. At this moment, her spirit is much too fragile to withstand a conversation about the ridiculousness of her dream. I sit motionless, riddled with guilt over the destruction I have brought to this young, innocent life. I have committed the sins of my mother. At least I now understand this. But I do not know what can be done about this avalanche of anguish burying us.

I extend my arms to embrace her, pronounce my mea culpas, knowing my daughter's life depends on my being forgiven and on my preventing her from repeating the crimes of her mother. But this is only a temporary fix—a Band-Aid over a gaping wound.

The Wailing Wall

We are legions, a multicolor choir of wounded. Nearly four out of every ten children in the United States live without their fathers in their homes; 50 percent of them are girls, according to the National Fatherhood Initiative. But it is as if there were only one fatherless woman in the world: Our faces are invisible.

All that can be heard in the national fatherhood movement is a cacophony of men and boys. In fact, most of the data on fatherlessness in America captures the effect on boys and men, little of it references girls and women. Experts—mostly men—say it is natural that females are squeezed out of this inchoate movement. After all, they say, only a man can teach a boy to become a man, and later a father.

"If there is anything clear about the Afrikan-American [sic] community, it is that women are having serious difficulty teaching black boys to be men, and, by extension, to be fathers," says Haki Madhubuti, founder of Third World Press and author of *Black Men: Obsolete, Single, Dangerous?*, a collection of essays that explores the status of African American men in America.

"Women, no matter how wonderful, no matter how loving, can't teach [masculinity] to us," asserts Dr. Frank S. Pittman, author of *Man Enough: Fathers, Sons, and the Search for Masculinity*, a book that examines the relationship between fathers and sons and their search for masculinity. "If we don't have fathers, we should have grandfathers, uncles, stepfathers to raise us from boys to men. If the males we know are other teenage boys or the macho heroes from the movies, we may get a distorted, exaggerated concept of masculinity."

The other reason experts give for the emphasis on boys is that the fatherhood movement is an offshoot of the 1980s men's movement, which claimed Robert Bly as its mentor or founder. Back then, men felt the enormous exigency of an antagonistic women's movement, which had begun more than a decade earlier and was led by people calling themselves feminists.

Women leaders were not interested in simply insinuating themselves into what theretofore had been a male-centric society; they wanted a percentage of the booty, including top-level corporate positions and comparable pay for comparable work. They also wanted men to do their equitable allocation of dinner dishes, diaper changing, and dirty laundry.

Here was yet another in a long series of American gender conflicts. But this time, patriarchy was getting the hell kicked out of it. Men were under siege. "How did we become the monster of the feminist nightmares?" asked Pittman.

Ellis Cose, in his critically acclaimed book *A Man's World: How Real Is Male Privilege—and How High Is Its Price?*, which looks at men's concerns about their status in the feminized American society, argued that white men believed themselves the primary target of "male-bashing feminists, diversity trainers, and equal opportunity litigators." Black men saw themselves as an endangered species, and Latinos were told that "their culture is irredeemably sexist."

By April 1999, experts were reporting that one in three young black men was under the supervision of the criminal justice system, and the figures approached 50 percent in some states. About twelve states and the District of Columbia imprisoned blacks at a rate ten times that at which whites are imprisoned. Black males had a life expectancy of 66.1 years, compared with 73.9 for white males. About 74 percent of black men graduated from high school, compared with 86 percent of whites.

"This crisis has broad implications for the future of the race," said Mary Frances Berry, head of the U.S. Commission on Civil Rights, during a 1999 conference on black males.

"Our humanity has been stripped, restored, attacked, defended, impugned and explained . . . more often than we'd like to recall. We have been hyped and stereotyped, valorized and demonized," wrote Darrell Dawsey, author of *Living to Tell About It: Young Black Men in America Speak Their Piece*, a book that, through interviews, offers compelling portraits of African American men in the 1990s and the challenges they face.

There is a great deal of truth in Dawsey's assessment when weighed against author Terry McMillan's *Waiting to Exhale*, in which the female characters try to reach self-actualization mostly by demonizing men. The men are portrayed as stereotypically lazy, shiftless Uncle Toms, good only for sex, and always chasing after some white woman. In the book, a character named John, the husband of eleven years to Bernadine, aspires to be a white man and can reach the penultimate goal only by having an affair with a white woman fresh out of college. He decides to leave his family—wife and children—for the blond bubbly. Then there is Russell, who comes home one day to find that, after discovering he is having an affair with another woman, his girlfriend has moved out all of the furnishings from their apartment. Instead of taking a reflective pause that might inspire him to change his ways, Russell reflexively shifts dependency to the woman with whom he is having the affair. He moves into her place and proceeds to drain her dry of her resources. And there is Michael, the thirty-second man, who leaves his woman wanting in bed. The entire slew of men are irresponsible, pathetic misfits; in truth, the women aren't much better.

But the demonization of black men began well before McMillan. A decade earlier, Alice Walker's award-winning novel *The Color Purple* thoroughly trashed black men. In the book, which charts the development and self-awakening of women, particularly one Celie, Walker casts men as child abusers, wife beaters, philanderers, tightwads, and rapists. Nearly every man is up to no good; those who aren't are considered weak or irrelevant. In the end, Walker either kills off the men or neuters them, making them symbolic eunuchs. A book intended to demonstrate the evils of violence toward women had perpetrated enormous violence against men—mostly African American men.

The gender war of the 1970s through the 1990s produced stories of heroic deeds by women. A sort of resurrection of women's importance to society occurred, which contributed in part to the restoration of women in America and proffered a more balanced history. We learned the names and read the narratives of women like Harriet Powers, Fannie Barrier Williams, Ellen Craft, Mary Church Terrell, Anna Cooper, and Dorothy Height. Their stories of escaping slavery and their remarkable success in segregated, patriarchical America were liberating. But they also produced a fulminating anger over the second-class citizenship accorded women and the abuse—psychological, physical, and emotional—women had suffered.

"The anger was not without just cause but it dominated some women; it blocked human sympathy; [and] it promoted sloppy thinking and silly thoughts," asserts Roiphe.

"Some women were saying that men were responsible for war, misery, and pollution. Women once again were everything nice, environmentally clean, and good. Instead of establishing equality between the sexes, all the banging of the consciousness-raising drum had somehow managed to reverse the polarity. Good was now female and bad was male. This was an improvement, if you were a woman, but not quite the social solution most of us had hoped for," Roiphe added.

Women had hoped their movement would feminize society, making it more keenly aware of the contributions they made, were making, and could make. Also, they had hoped that men would display a softer side; that the structures of their corporations and even their old-boy network might adopt a more feminine strategy of development. At the very least, women could become equal partners.

Initially, black women were reluctant to join a movement ostensibly launched by white women—Betty Friedan, Gloria Steinem, and others; many feared that the movement wore the trappings of a male lynching. Besides, African American women were disinclined to embrace the concept of white women as friends. After all, their ancestors, in the person of "Miss Ann" on the plantation, often had been as brutal and as lethal as their husbands and other male counterparts. Black women understood that they and their men often experienced the same atrocities. And because of the construct of early American society, black women and black men always worked side by side—on plantations and in the master's house—and often for the same pay—next to nothing. What had the black man denied the black woman? Both were victims.

But within the same epoch as the feminist movement two seemingly unrelated things occurred that caused many African American women to abandon their early opposition: Affirmative action and quotas were introduced into the labor market, and black women became commodities that were highly sought after, while black men became dispensable.

Corporations and other employers received special benefits for giving preference to African Americans and for hiring women and other "minorities." Black women became known as twofers. That is, an employer received double credit for hiring a person who was not only a racial minority but a "gender" minority. As a result, sweeping and unprecedented opportunities became available for black women. They had greater access to jobs, job training, and education. The gap that had appeared between them and black males widened further.

Simultaneously, the country shifted from an industrial economy to a service economy. Where once black men could always find jobs working with their hands, fewer and fewer of those jobs were available upon the altered landscape. Further, wages that came with those positions were not keeping pace with the cost of living. Complicating this diminishment was the arrival of hundreds of thousands of immigrants, mostly from Latin countries, who did not quarrel with the low-level jobs; thus, there wasn't any pressure on employers to increase the salaries for entry-level or non-skilled positions. Many black males were without sufficient education and market interest; black men were not desirable employees for corporations looking to score points with the federal government and the market.

Literally and figuratively, African American men were placed on or kicked to the curbside, like old refrigerators or cans of rubbish. Along the way, they naturally developed "an attitude" and became lethally angry about the turn their lives had taken. Some of that anger was directed toward African American women, many of whom were either riding the hog, or had learned to grab its slippery body long enough to pull themselves up out of the mud. The tensions between black men and black women heightened, giving the feminist movement sufficient footing for buttressing their own platform.

Without work—a means of caring for a family—many African American men couldn't or wouldn't get married. Consequently, some black women who engaged in romantic relationships with these men ultimately married the government, which, until recently, proved to be a jealous lover, refusing to permit men to remain in the homes with the children they had fathered, said *Washington Post* columnist William Raspberry. A 1994 report by the Annie E. Casey Foundation, which confirms this assertion, found that the percentage of men between the ages of twenty-five and thirty-four who earned enough to lift a four-person family out of poverty had steadily declined since 1960.

"The powerful correlation between diminished male earnings and employment on the one hand, and the increase in father-absent families on the other, is most unmistakable in high-poverty neighborhoods," said a foundation official.

At the start of the last decade of the twentieth century, almost 5 million children were growing up in neighborhoods where a majority of working-age men had been unemployed during the previous year, according to the Casey report. In these same neighborhoods, more than 45 percent of all families were headed by women—almost twice the national average.

"Young men stopped being as valued as they might be [because they couldn't earn a living]. They became at first useless and then positively dangerous," says Raspberry.

The result was a "convenient rationalization, shared and reinforced by other men in similar situations, rationalizations that reject the institution of marriage," says William Julius Wilson, of Harvard's John F. Kennedy School of Government.

Cross-Dressing: When Men and Women Aren't Equal

The feminist movement exacerbated this predicament by creating a sort of cross-dressing orthodoxy, which advanced the philosophy that men and women are the same, and bequeath the same valuable gifts to the family. This doctrine created an environment where women began to perceive the men in their lives—fathers, husbands, lovers, and friends—as irrelevant.

"Our cultural decision-making created the mythology of the superfluous father," remarks Wade Horn, a clinical psychologist and founder/director of the National Fatherhood Initiative.

This "we can do fine without them" perspective permeated every aspect of society. It spurred the death of the traditional male and created massive confusion about the present and future role of men in American society. Only during the last decade of the twentieth century did women come to realize that in their quest for equality and liberation, they also created a chasm between themselves and their men, and inconclusiveness about their own definitions of womanhood, femaleness, and femininity.

The problem was especially dramatic for African American women. Audrey Chapman, author of *Getting Good Loving: How Black Men and Women Can Make Love Work* and a therapist in private practice who also hosts a weekly talk show, "All About Love," on Howard University's WHUR-FM in Washington, D.C., suggests that black women and girls are "likely to get tremendous support in the development of their masculine side, at the expense of the soft or feminine side." This emphasis by women sometimes means an unconscious devaluation of the feminine, further fueling the assumption that the masculine is all-powerful. It seems a confusing cycle, rife with contradiction.

"There are women who enjoy being girls and there are women who are angry about the limitations and unfairness of their gender roles. Some women are so angry about what they see as unequal power differentials between men and women that they deny having any power at all. They assume men have taken their power and must give it back. Consequently, they emotionally mutilate any man they encounter to get back at him for being so powerful," argues Frank Pittman.

The schism, rooted in a perception that males were all-powerful, was widened by women's demand for the same sexual freedoms and entitlements accorded men. Women wanted to sleep with whomever, whenever, as frequently as they desired. But in order to achieve this "power," women had to remove stated and implicit double standards. Once again, they had to deny some part of their own femininity and place themselves on the same shaky platform that men had long occupied. Thus, opening doors, pulling out chairs, and other "chivalrous" behavior had to be eliminated, or characterized as unacceptable and demeaning.

Women, like followers of Santeria and voodoo who mount garlic on their doors to prevent evil from entering, posted warning signals that, essentially, forced men to discard traditional male behavior or remain outside. Nation of Islam's Elijah Muhammad established whites as devils; and in mainstream America, it seemed that men were being made evils in society.

The Exiled Man

The hostility toward men, and their symbolic castration, became acceptable blood sport. Like rats in a lab, receiving electrical shock upon approaching their cage, those men who were single became increasingly reluctant to get married or to engage in viable, committed relationships.

Women, determining that men were "no good," "shiftless," and otherwise "irrelevant," further embraced the idea of giving birth out of wedlock, divesting that circumstance of its long-held taboo status. Some women came to believe that men were useful only for impregnation, after which they should be discarded, promptly. Test tube babies further ratcheted down (to the level of antiquated) the perception of men as necessary entities in the family structure.

Men came to accept their exiled status. In some instances, those who hadn't already deserted their families left eagerly, believing they held no valued position in their households or in their relationships. By 1996, only 35 percent of black children lived with their biological mother and father.

"It's simple psychology," says Horn. "Anyone who is told the same thing over and over again begins to believe it. For almost thirty years, men have been told that they don't offer anything unique to their families and children. Many men have believed it, and now they're living the myth of the superfluous father."

But individual families aren't the only ones damaged by this notion of fathers as insignificant presences—or outright absentees. In fact, all of American society suffers, as it must snatch from fading memory those snapshots of men as featured characters and moral compasses in their communities. The damage caused by this perception of fathers as mere window dressing: It "undermines families, neglects children, causes or aggravates our worst social problems and makes individual adult happiness—both male and female—hard to achieve," asserts author David Blankenhorn, whose book *Fatherless America: Confronting Our Most Urgent Social Problem* documents the declining significance of men in family structures.

In the end, a "decultured" paternity is born. "A decultured fatherhood produces a doubtful manhood," continues Blankenhorn. "For without norms of effective paternity to anchor masculinity, the male project itself is increasingly called into question and even dispute." That instability, by extension, obscures the female project.

It is not surprising, then, that by 1996, 60 percent of all black children were living in homes where the fathers were absent; 19 percent of whites and 30 percent of Hispanics also were living in households with only their mothers, according to statistics collected by the National Fatherhood Initiative.

"The feminist movement has been so busy blaming, chastising, [and] attacking men that it has barely had a moment to catch its breath, change signals, and call men to come in the home and stay awhile," says Anne Roiphe. "If we weren't always watching TV programs about incestuous dads and fathers who did us dirt by marrying wives younger than we are or abusing dwarfed twin sisters, we could discuss father participation with more urgency."

In the case of African Americans, television, the movies, and in general the national media allowed few images of black fathers and "intact families." Except for *The Cosby Show*, during much of the 1980s and 1990s, when African American families did surface, they usually were filled with drug addicts, welfare recipients, the shiftless, or buffoons-turned-parents. While the black fictional neighborhoods may have become more upscale by the mid-1990s, as in the case of *The Fresh Prince of Bel Air*, the context was very much the same—blacks and blacklike as comic features. And with few exceptions, Fresh Prince being one, most of the shows did not reveal two-parent multidimensional black families. But by 1999 even these were scarce, as the National Association for the Advancement of Colored People (NAACP) lambasted the three major commercial networks for the absence of blacks in any of the new shows of their fall lineup. The NAACP threatened a lawsuit, which prompted the networks to concede that they actually may have erred.

In fairness, some aspects of those negative television portrayals were accurate. Thus, the wholesale destruction of black families and their communities could not be placed solely at the feet of the media and entertainment industries. It had begun even before Daniel Patrick Moynihan's seminal report "The Negro Family: A Case for National Action," issued in 1965. In that treatise he called the black family a "tangle of pathologies," and warned that it was at the "heart of the deterioration of Negro society."

"That whole debate had a chilling effect," said Blankenhorn, founder of the Institute for American Values. "African Americans somehow felt [Moynihan's report] was like airing dirty laundry. And [they believed] that the main issue was not the family structure." Therefore, little real attention was focused on how to arrest the problem. Instead, African Americans argued about the racist nature of the Moynihan report and the whole of American society.

There was a measure of truth in both the report and the reaction to it. There were other ills being suffered by African Americans in the United States that contributed to the destruction of families. They faced debilitating racial discrimination, which often expressed itself as economic and political repression and oppression. Further, the entire African American culture was under siege—every aspect of American life told blacks that how they looked, dressed, and talked was not acceptable; they didn't fit in. Black people in America suffered from residual complex psychic and physical effects of slavery. Owing to the devastation produced by that "peculiar institution," the pain of fatherlessness festers today in black America.

In slavery, neither men nor women were able to determine how long they might remain a couple, and marriage was beyond the realm of possibility. They didn't even know with whom they might have children. Men and women were used as breeders.

"You didn't know and had no control over who was going to be the father of your child. It could be anybody from the master, to the overseer, to Tom who the master said you were going to have a baby by. The only thing you knew, at some level, was that the baby was yours. For nine months you had control," explains Gayle K. Porter, a clinical psychologist and director of the Johns Hopkins East Baltimore Community Mental Health Center.

Slaves who married learned that their survival depended on their not assuming they could remain as a couple. By comparison, Jewish people during the Holocaust assumed they would die as a couple. Their decision to live or die didn't focus on the issue of whose property they were as it did with slaves, but rather on their religion. For slaves the promise of death hinged upon their economic viability, over which they had little control. "When as a people you grow up and you spend two to three hundred years of your life in that kind of environment, it takes a long time to get beyond it."

For a time, this adverse by-product of slavery was offset by the extended family culture reflected in black America. Uncles, aunts, even neighbors served as a secondary support system, extending emotional, physical, and economic assistance where necessary. The feminist movement and the attending economic issues evidenced by Affirmative Action and the shift to a service-based economy eroded this thread of hope and healing, however. Black families and the children therein were torn asunder.

The Fatherless Song Has No Color

Make no mistake, fatherlessness in America is not some black disease. It is boundless, transcending race and class. By 1995 an estimated 24.7 million children were living in homes without their biological fathers. About 40 percent of the children who lived in fatherless households haven't seen their fathers in at least a year; 50 percent of children who weren't living with their fathers had never stepped foot in their father's home, according to the National Fatherhood Initiative.

Only about 3 percent of children born in 1950—the year I was born—lost their fathers through death before reaching age fifteen. In 1992, only 5 percent of all female-headed households with children had experienced the death of the father. About 37 percent had experienced divorce, and 36 percent had never been married.

"Abandonment registers pretty much the same way in all of us. It's America's story. It's the story of many women growing up in America," says clinical psychologist Maxine Harris, executive director and co-founder of Community Connections, a mental health agency in Washington, D.C.

But black America *does* act as harbinger for mainstream America. "We black folk, our history and our present being, are a mirror of the manifold experiences of America. What we want, what we represent, what we endure is what America is," said Richard Wright in his book *12 Million Black Voices*. Wright's cogent commentary is as true today as it was in 1941 when the book was published. Consider this: 51 percent of black teen mothers, and 12 percent of white teen mothers, were unmarried in 1965. Twenty years later, 55 percent of white teen mothers were unmarried. These are statistics provided by the National Fatherhood Initiative and Rutgers University professor David Popenoe.

In 1960, 22 percent of black children and 7 percent of white children were living with only one parent. By 1990, the number of white children living with only one parent had increased to 20 percent.

"Black family life, then, appears to be a precursor of what family life is likely to become for the rest of the population," says Popenoe, author of *Life Without Father: Compelling New Evidence That Fatherhood and Marriage Are Indispensable For the Good of Children and Society*, and head of the National Marriage Project at Rutgers University.

"While African American families undoubtedly face some stresses that are unique to them, they are instructively viewed as prematurely suffering the negative consequences of an American family environment that all groups share."

In absolute numbers, in 1995, there were more fatherless white children—13 million—compared with 6.5 million fatherless black children, says the National Fatherhood Initiative. Whites have gained parity with blacks in the area of family dysfunction. Blankenhorn notes that millions of men "are voluntarily abdicating their fatherhood. Though paternal death and paternal abandonment are frequently treated as sociological equivalents, these two phenomena could hardly be more different in their impact upon children and upon the larger society.

"To put it simply, death puts an end to fathers. Abandonment puts an end to fatherhood . . . death is more personally final, but departure is more culturally lethal," he explains.

To be sure, the United States, which stood as exemplar of the model for democratic government, now stands as the poster child for fatherless families. In the early 1970s, Sweden reported an international high of 15 percent single-parent families; by 1986, the United States topped that with 24 percent. Today, nearly half of all marriages in this country end in divorce. Like kudzu, fatherlessness overruns America.

"In addition to losing fathers, we are losing something larger: our idea of fatherhood," explains Blankenhorn. "Fatherlessness is now approaching a rough parity with fatherhood as a defining feature of American childhood."

Boys for Him, Girls for Her

What is scathing about all of this is the utter lack of attention given by society to fatherless girls and women. Every now and again, a voice that sounds like mine, or my daughter's, or Ivory's can be heard. There is this generally accepted parental paradigm of "boys for him; girls for her," reinforcing indirectly the implicit philosophy of the fatherhood movement.

Hope Edelman, author of *Motherless Daughters: The Legacy of Loss*, inadvertently endorses this equation, as do most Americans. "The loss of a mother is one of the most profound events that will occur in a woman's life and like a sound in an empty house, it echoes on and on," she says, writing in her book about the effects of losing her mother at an early age.

But what about the loss of a father? Is it not as significant or profound? Do not women, who lose their fathers through death, divorce, or abandonment, also witness an indescribable pain that shadows them throughout their lives?

Few people will dispute Edelman's claims of a mother's importance in a child's life. Certainly my own mother made enormous contributions to my development. She helped to shape the woman I have become. Nevertheless, while in many ways a woman sets the standard for society, there still are limitations to a mother's sphere of influence. She can give all of herself to a child and still come up short.

"The male perspective is completely foreign to me," confesses Judith Scott, a writer and thirty-something District of Columbia native whose mother and father were never married and never lived together. "I was very focused on my mother."

I listen to these words and hear myself, describing myself in association with my mother—her hips, her laughter—and other women in my family. Yet as strong as these bonds are with the women in our lives, there is a corresponding weakness in my bonds with men.

Each parent is critical to the child's development. "I don't care how wonderful, how competent, how caring, how great you are as a single parent, you are never going to be able to do as much in terms of caretaking as when you have somebody else who can complement what you do. It's kind of a gross simplification but mothers give kids certain things and fathers give kids certain things," asserts Gayle Porter.

Who would dispute this fact? My own mother worked two, sometimes three, jobs. She prepared the meals, cleaned the house, and taught her children as best she could to care for themselves. But she could not retrieve my trumpet from Bynum Bakery, nor could she teach my brother what he needed to learn to survive the Desire project. "The best mom in the world cannot be a father," Blankenhorn correctly asserts.

Further, a mother's attempts at trying to fulfill the father's role are doomed even before her child is born. Charles Ballard, founder and executive director of the Institute for Responsible Fatherhood and Family Revitalization, says that research conducted by his organization concluded the following: "The child under age one died [more often] when the mother was unattached to the father during pregnancy. Infant mortality is driven by low birth weight, which is driven by the absence of the father. The relationship between the man and the woman directly influenced the outcome of the pregnancies." (By 1995, about 69 percent of black children were born to unmarried mothers.)

Still, some feminists and women's rights advocates argue against the significance of the father. "I've often seen women who make a decision to have a baby outside of an ongoing relationship," says Porter. "It's clear at some level they discount the impact of a father. Because they never had a father, they are not conscious about the impact that this did have on them."

Experts have found routinely that there are important departures between women and men and their child rearing. Fathers help to "individuate" their children. They often permit unrestrained exploration, aiding in the development of a child's strong and confident emotional self. Even before a child reaches the toddler stage, a father teaches standards and principles, and is often responsible for reinforcing sex-appropriate behavior for his children.

Also, "the father is generally the first man the daughter wants to love. If everything goes well, and the daughter is loved by the father, and in return loves the father, then the daughter grows up feeling love worthy and thereby demands that other men in her life live up to the model her father created, treating her with love, respect, encouragement," says Horn.

"The mother teaches specifics of sexual behavior, but in terms of the core sense—how comfortable she is with her femaleness—the father's nurturing seems more predictive than the mother's," he adds.

The absence of a father in a young girl's life predicts her difficulty in adjusting to married life, thus ensuring the continued increase in divorces. California psychologist Judith Wallerstein, who studied the plight of children of divorced parents for twenty-five years, affirmed the long-lasting and cumulative effects of fatherlessness. "Unlike the adult experience, the child's suffering does not reach its peak at the breakup and then level off. The effects of the parents' divorce are played and replayed throughout the first three decades of the children's lives."

Unfortunately, these first three decades are crucial. By the time an infant is three months old, she is able to distinguish between father and mother, assert child psychologists. Moreover, by six years of age, most children have developed most of their value system. Their introduction into the world beyond that age, then, is hampered by the absence of a father. And when a girl begins the ritual of dating without a father to help guide her choices, she is sure to stumble. The loss of a father, at any place along this continuum, nearly guarantees personal, social, and relationship difficulties, if not failures.

Because women, through the paradigm of the feminist, are being taught to mask their feminine needs, they articulate, by their actions, a comfort with the absence of fathers, choosing to project a tough, masculine exterior. They do not expect the availability and involvement of their own fathers or the fathers of their children.

The *New York Times* columnist Bob Herbert recalled a meeting in 1997 with a group of seven African American women in East Orange, New

Jersey. He asked how many had children. "All but one of the seven nodded or raised a hand." How many were married to the father of their children? This time none raised a hand. How many had been to a wedding? Only one of the women answered affirmatively.

The most disturbing aspect of Herbert's encounter is that none of the women seemed to believe her experience abnormal. We are all wounded. We all have been forced, either through our own or others' choices, to make our way alone, as I did those mornings in the Desire project. I deliberately walked with a bravado that masked my internal pain. Yet while I swaggered, I knew, as we all know, that I was not okay.

Singing in the Choir

If it is true that a "decultured fatherhood produces a doubtful manhood," as experts like Blankenhorn have concluded, then cannot father absence produce a comparably emaciated and conflicted womanhood?

If it is true that a father helps to develop his daughter's confidence in herself and in her femininity; that he helps her to shape her style and understanding of male-female bonding; and that he introduces her to the external world, plotting navigational courses for her success—then surely it is an indisputable conclusion that the absence of these lessons can produce a severely wounded and disabled woman.

And, if we can pass along various genetic disorders, can we pass along to a subsequent generation the effects of fatherlessness? Tonya and Afrika offer an unequivocal yes. They are inheritors of intergenerational fatherlessness—both their mothers grew up without their fathers. It is a phenomenon not unlike that reported during the 1960s and 1970s with welfare recipients, where the mother received government assistance, then the daughter, and soon the granddaughter. Will the fatherless circle be unbroken?

To understand the deadly effects, we must concede that the *hand that rocks the cradle really does rule the world*, especially in a society like that in the United States. In this respect, women set the standard for society;

what happens to them, happens to everyone. Many of the older women around whom I grew up in New Orleans, Louisiana, had fathers, who indirectly transmitted this message to them. These women forecasted their values-encoded yardsticks not only by how they carried themselves and what they expected from themselves, but also by what they were willing or not willing to accept from men. They considered themselves not subordinate to men, but different from them. They could articulate those differences because they clearly understood them; they were taught their meaning by their fathers and mothers, who learned them from their fathers. And while these older women had relationships with men that, sometimes, were less than perfect, they were more confident in the handling of those rough patches when they surfaced.

But what happens when a woman is reared and comes into parenthood without the benefits of these early lessons taught by her father? She may be quite capable of transferring to her children lessons about issues related to women, but she is unable directly to translate for her children the mysteries and secrets of men. It's comparable to blood transfusions: If you have blood type A, you can be a donor to another person with blood type A—but not to a person who is O. With the decline of two-parent households, the base of information and knowledge previously developed by women about men also diminished: If we were running a blood bank, we would have declared a state of emergency and issued a call for donors.

As we have discovered, the cycle of fatherlessness doesn't stop with one woman. Her children may eventually head fatherless families. Now there are women rearing fatherless girls and fatherless boys. These women must communicate, to both genders, skills that she has not learned. Thus we arrive at where we are today: with boys and young men challenged by the definition of masculinity. Girls and young women, however, are doubly handicapped; they are challenged both by the definition of masculinity and by the definition of femininity. A woman surely learns some things about her femaleness from her mother; but as Horn asserts, her core self is strengthened by her interaction with her father. Further,

her understanding and engagement in a male's world can only be provided by her father as chauffeur.

More precisely, fatherless women who become mothers are unable to properly translate, for either their male children or their female children, the legends that describe the terrain of manhood. They cannot adequately explain the uniqueness of either sex. At best it is difficult—at worst it is impossible—for a fatherless mother to aid her daughter's understanding of how men communicate, or how their linear thinking sometimes clashes unintentionally with the circular consciousness of most women. Fatherlessness has made it nearly impossible for both women and men to be fully versed in the myriad complexities of manhood.

This struggle for meaning is not the sole possession of men. Young girls are caught in the throes of trying to create their own workable definition. If a boy buys Pampers for his young child, then isn't he a man? If he pays for his girlfriend to visit the hair salon, isn't he a man? If he purchases a gold chain for his girlfriend's neck, surely he must be a man? If he dresses in a three-piece suit, works on Wall Street, but then goes home and beats his wife, does that make him any less or more a man than one who is unemployed, spends his days on the corner, and returns in the evening, passively sitting in front of the television until bedtime? The complexities of manhood confound fatherless women.

"If my father had been around, he could have been a buffer. He could have educated me. I didn't know how to act around boys, except my brother. I still have trouble trusting men," admits Sandra Jackson.

"When a girl cannot trust and love the first man in her life—her father—what she is missing cannot be replaced by money, friends, teachers, social workers, or well-designed public policies aimed at helping her," explains Blankenhorn. "She simply loses."

Fatherless women know this, although sometimes they are not adept at accurately describing what is missing. "There's the sense of this great mystery," confesses writer Judith Scott. "And I'm not privy to the answer; I can't unravel it."

3. NOONDAY FIGHTS

John Asemore's arrival catapulted me into a deep reflection, causing me to concede certain facts: The cardinal nexus between us and the lives of others is always subtle—a wisp of a thing even when the relationship is intense. Yet, it is powerful enough to direct us through time immemorial. Each seemingly remote choice ripples; nothing ever stands fully detached. But because the effects of many decisions are often obtuse, their interconnections and their links with those made by others escape us.

Was the Charity Hospital story, which centered on my anomalous physical appearance as an infant, the family's way of telling me the truth surrounding my birth? I had been abandoned by Bill, then John, and finally Noel. How had this triple abandonment affected me? Had it changed my impression of the world, altered my vantage point? Had my fathers' absence shifted my value system? Had it changed the way I crafted a sentence? The way I combed my hair? If they had been around, would I have worn that same pink pleated skirt and white blouse so many days in junior high school? Am I the woman I have become because they were the men outside my life, forever on the periphery, apparitions sculpting my world?

I had no answers that summer of 1988 when I met my biological father. I certainly didn't know about the research by Ballard's organization, nor had I any inkling that a child can differentiate between mother and father as early as the age of three months—and that therefore, once making such connections, that child knows when one or the other parent is absent.

But this I did know: The first three decades of my life had been troubled in ways that buttressed the findings of Wallerstein's study. I had spent those critical years searching endlessly for something I could neither define nor describe. If someone had asked what I wanted, I would have stood slack-jawed, unable to articulate any of its features, even the most prominent.

I had a child out of wedlock at eighteen; a year later, I was pregnant with the second. I dated older men and feared the departure of any man who befriended me. I went through two marriages and several relationships, barely escaping a couple of them with my sanity intact. And in between all those episodes, I tried to find some beauty in myself that I felt was worthy of celebration. I tried to make myself whole; there were periods where I believed I had succeeded: *"this mind/has stopped/its noon/day fights/it is/peaceful here/i smile/in the mirror/at my wide ass/spaghetti thin legs/ I have no doubts/of who/i am, i am/a believer/in myself!"* When I wrote at twenty-five the words to the poem "Peace," I believed the worst of my despair was over. But it had only just begun.

Why had I had such a tumultuous life? Was the commotion connected in any way to my older sister's pregnancy at thirteen years of age, or my older brother's plunge into juvenile delinquency and later drugs? Why, and with whom, was I angry? Had I unconsciously blamed my mother for Noel's departure, despite my young determination not to? Did I unknowingly blame her for John's? At more than one juncture in my life, I considered suicide; was that related to my fatherlessness? Why did I hurt so much?

Before John Asemore's return, I believed that the answers to those and other questions were glued to my mother. She was the one constant between me, my sister, and my brother. I was convinced that if I could more adequately chart and navigate the channels between my mother and myself, I could know some measure of peace. I could discover myself— not the public persona, but the soul and spirit of me.

My timid effort to expose the reasons for my behavior and the fault lines of my life chased me back to the trivialities of dates and facts. And because such minutiae, evaluated in a vacuum, offer no useful insights, I claimed no wisdom. Consequently, believing I needed to take some course of action, I redoubled my crusade to separate myself from my mother. I wanted to live my life beyond her boundaries. I wanted to shape a world different from the one I knew hers to be. This, I was sure, was the prescription for my recovery.

What ailed me was not my mother. It was my fathers. It took me more than three years after John's reappearance to understand that, and another four years for the revelation to fully redirect my life and to right my relationship with myself.

Those years taught me that fathers fashion their daughters as expertly and as powerfully—or as haplessly and unfortunately—as they do their sons. And when no caring father's hands are available to shape his daughter, the result is as certain to emerge askew as a bowl denied the potter's touch before it is placed in the kiln.

The absence of my father—even one I had never met—wounded me. It motivated the image I crafted of myself as a woman—an African American woman. It determined the challenges I faced and the suffering I endured. And although I did not know it when I met John Asemore, I know now that much of my life has been spent trying to reconcile myself with the loss of my fathers—all three of them.

It is difficult to articulate pain as you are suffering. Your entire being gets wrapped around the hurt; you can't stop for a second to determine what is causing it. The drive is to extinguish the pain—not to analyze it.

"The saddest, most insidious implication of unresolved father loss is that for most, the loss becomes unconscious, and is therefore unnamed and unknowable," says psychologist Beth Erickson, whose father died when she was an adolescent.

Even as I knelt on the wooden floorboard in Epiphany Catholic Church agonizing over the loss of Noel, I could not fully describe the interior damage his departure caused. Nor could I tell anyone how I blamed myself for his leaving.

"Children have no story, no organizing text with which to process their loss," says Maxine Harris, author of *The Loss That Is Forever: The Lifelong Impact of the Early Death of a Mother or Father.*

"In the same way a child is likely to create a myth about the parent who has died, he or she may create a set of false beliefs about the self. . . ."

I did not understand the myth of madness I sculpted with my words, thoughts, and actions. I simply knew far too intimately the pain of loneliness and wanting. I lived a misdirected life as I sought to avoid the hurt, never understanding that all my avoidance techniques were leading me into deeper trouble—the gaping wound grew only larger.

4. WHAT IS THIS PAIN I FEEL?

I wanted desperately to heal the wound. But how could I when I had not fully defined it? Was the pain localized? Did I feel its throbbing only when I came into contact with men, in an intimate relationship? Or was this thing a constant in my life—there when I awoke in the morning and when I went to bed at night? Could I write it off as some generalized ailment, as people do when they have high blood pressure and can eat only certain foods, drink only certain drinks, and must avoid stressful situations? Could I point to fatherlessness as the reason I am such a voracious reader? Could I use it as the cause of my loner status? Also, did it matter how I became fatherless; was a girl who lost her father through death in a better position than I?

These questions overwhelmed me. There seemed too many puzzles to solve, so many paths to travel. For a time I hesitated, afraid of what I might discover. Or more accurately, who I might discover. Yet I had come too far to turn back. I had to continue the journey.

In my pursuit to name the pain I felt and to fashion my own healing balm, the first thing I learned was that the *way* a girl becomes fatherless is extremely important. What I felt as a fatherless woman was different, albeit in minor degree, from that pain suffered by Beth Erickson or the Reverend Bernice King when they lost their fathers through, respectively, an untimely death and a death that was at once untimely and violent. Did their losses leave fewer scars and fewer social dysfunctions?

More often than not, fathers who die are kept alive by the family through photographs and shared memories. In the case of King, the entire nation honors her father, the Reverend Martin Luther King Jr. Thus, she came to know her father didn't leave voluntarily; he didn't walk out on her—as all of my fathers did. She couldn't necessarily equate her father's absence with some unexplained defect in herself, as I had done for over twenty-five years.

But even in the case of absence by death, I learned it is dangerous to conclude that one size fits all. Psychologist Audrey Chapman tells the story about a woman in one of her therapy groups whose father died of a heart attack when she was five years old.

The woman questioned, " 'If he knew he had a heart problem, why didn't he take care of himself? He didn't love me enough to take care of himself. So as a result of [his] not loving me very much, I must not be lovable. Therefore, no other man will love me,' " says Chapman. "She has yet to have a relationship with a man. She is thirty-four and still a virgin; she has all of these conflicts."

If we can be so conflicted when a father leaves through no fault of his own—when he is called home to his Lord—what happens when our first male love is pushed away by divorce, or simply chooses to walk away? "Often in situations like that, women have an intense reaction to males who represent a 'father.' They either are overly invested, or often are very clingy, or they can be distant because they're so afraid that this is going to happen again," explains psychologist Gayle K. Porter.

Once again, however, the fatherless daughter's response is contingent on the kind of relationship she had with her father and on her perception of what will occur after the divorce. "When there is a divorce and it isn't clear how the relationship is going to continue, often what you have initially is a great deal of displacement toward the mother," continues Porter.

In other words, the daughter points the finger at her mother, as I did for a brief period toward my mother, as both Meri Danquah and my daughter did with their mothers. As far as Meri and Afrika were concerned, their fathers were near-perfect—the light of their lives; their mothers caused their fathers to leave.

"I'd say mean things. I would tell [my mother] 'I don't like you. I want my own space.' I was angry because she was the reason my father had gone away," confesses Afrika about her reaction toward her mother and toward her own fatherlessness.

Perhaps as a coping mechanism, the fatherless daughter concludes that if the mother had been a decent wife, the father wouldn't have left. This perception takes root and over time shape. It forever alters the daughter's understanding of what makes a relationship work. Later, as an adult woman, she is likely to focus on creating, by any means necessary, the ideal relationship.

"In other words, having the opposite of what her mother had. But she doesn't grow up with these bitter feelings about men; she might have some trust issues, but they are not severe. And, she'll probably look for men who are more reliable," adds Chapman.

But the so-called "reliable" father figure may not have any basis in fact. It may be all illusion, since the fatherless daughter's perceptions about her father's responsibility for the divorce are clouded, weighted against her animosity toward her mother.

"If the father and daughter have had a loving relationship, then the daughter can at times be reluctant to hold a male accountable for what he needs to do in a relationship," continues Chapman.

On the other hand, if the daughter realizes that the difficulties between her parents were the result of an abusive father, she "can sometimes develop a generalized anger toward all men. Ironically, the girl may repeatedly find herself in abusive relationships as she unconsciously attempts to undo the effects of her father," adds Porter.

Often a daughter is unable to discern exactly what is happening between her parents. Yesterday everything seemed fine; today Daddy is carrying his suitcase out the door saying good-bye, and she is crying on the sidewalk, pleading with him to take her with him, as did the little girl in the movie *Hope Floats* when she realized the separation between her mother and father was final. "Please, Daddy, take me with you, take me with you," she cries, suitcase in hand, running alongside the car.

The fatherless girl doesn't know why her parents are separating, snatching away the man she loves. All too often, her mother, hoping to comfort her, mixes a concoction of half truths and half lies and serves it generously. "As the daughter gets older she has to deal with something else, she has to deal with the uncovering of a lie," explains Harris. "That is an extra wrinkle in the fatherless woman's story."

And so it wasn't strange that my mother had kept her terrible secret all these years. Or that she had refused to discuss the details. Nor was it abnormal that I harbored animosity and anger toward the liberties she had taken with my life, the lies and deceit in which she had wrapped it. What mothers don't realize is that, for the fatherless daughter, such lies create layers of trust-based issues. She doesn't know whether to trust her mother, especially if she believes her mother wholly responsible for her father's departure. And she doesn't fully trust men—the first one walked out on her. She is caught in a quagmire.

She must have her mother; and, later in life, she comes to believe that she must have a man. Alas, she gravitates toward men who are not dependable, reaffirming her earlier experience of loss. "It's called the abandonment syndrome," explains Chapman. "You grow up with this message in your head—to love is to lose. So, unconsciously, you open yourself up to people who are going to leave."

It's illogical. The syndrome is further complicated for women like me, who knew their biological fathers very late or never, and were reared in a household dominated by women. In many instances, we develop an unconscious disdain for men, but at the same time we feel a tremendous need for them.

"It's a terrible dilemma. It's a double bind," says a sympathetic Chapman.

Sometimes we harbor an attitude that men are unimportant—an attitude exacerbated by the women's movement, although it is on the wane. Sula Peace, the protagonist in Toni Morrison's novel *Sula*, finds men good only for using. She has grown up in a house of women who maintained conflicting relations with men: Her grandmother Eva Peace "tested and argued with her men, leaving them feeling as though they had been in combat with a worthy, if amiable foe." Her mother, Hannah, "rubbed no edges, made no demands, made the man feel as though he were complete and wonderful just as he was." Sula, on the other hand, used them and tossed them aside. "She went to bed with men as frequently as she could. It was the only place where she could find what she was looking for: misery and the ability to feel deep sorrow," Morrison writes.

But the hunger for affection—or, in Sula's case, simply to experience some emotion, even pain—is not the only telltale sign of father deprivation. Research by the National Fatherhood Initiative indicates that children who live without their biological fathers are likely to be poor, and to experience educational, health, emotional, and psychological problems. They also are likely to be the victims of child abuse, and to engage in criminal behavior more often than their peers who live with their married biological mothers and fathers.

"When fathers leave, children generally feel discarded, expelled, and unlovable. This especially goes for abusive, addicted, or traditional fathers living in the home but who might as well occupy the outer ring of Saturn," says Erickson. "And even in the case of abandonment by natural causes, children are left with a fierce hunger that is difficult for them or for anyone who loves them to satisfy."

5. MANIFESTATIONS OF PAIN
The Fatherless Woman Syndrome

How does a girl or woman know whether she suffers father deprivation? Like a cold, which often can be identified by a runny nose, wheezing, and an achy body, there are common symptoms that denote a fatherless daughter. Over the years, I have developed my own dictionary, warning signs, and help stations. These are the things I have learned through reflection of my life; I do not come with a bushel of pat answers or solutions—I can offer only a few valuable stepping-stones that I discovered on my journey.

Although we wear a mask, hoping to prevent our discovery, there is no hiding the Fatherless Woman Syndrome. Grouped in five somewhat overlapping categories, the traits are as follows:

- **THE "UN" FACTOR.** Frequently the fatherless daughter believes herself unworthy and unlovable. She has decided that she is the reason her father left. When Noel walked away, I blamed myself; I reflected on my physical appearance—dark skin, kinky hair, and flat nose: Who could love such a face? This notion roots in the fatherless daughter's subconscious, infecting her with incredibly low self-esteem. Fatherless women are sure, absolutely sure, no one would really want them, no one could love them. When it does appear that they have won love, the triple fears (which will be discussed next) kick in. They believe themselves unlovable, so there has got to be some hitch; it's a trick. After all, what have they done to earn the love? And because they believe that the only excuse for anyone's loving them is that they have done something spectacular, they engage in fits of driven activity, hoping to guarantee that their lover or mate remains; instead, they run the person away. They are living their self-fulfilled prophecy.

Don't think it matters that fathers, who are leaving the family because of divorce, say that the children are not the cause of the breakup. Few children believe the hype. Fatherless daughters speak their fathers' names, see their fathers' faces, and desperately try to recapture their fathers' love with every man they meet. They do these things without realizing they are doing them, with a reflexive response as involuntary as blinking; I searched for thirty-three years. I never realized that, in fact, I perceived myself as unlovable and unworthy of love. I never realized I was on the hunt, never realized I was trying to solve the mystery of which Judith Scott speaks.

- **THE TRIPLE FEARS FACTOR** (professional clinicians call this the abandonment syndrome). The fatherless woman is a fireball of fear. She fears rejection. She fears abandonment. She fears commitment. The questions repeatedly posed in her mind in any situation, but most especially in male-female encounters, are these: If I extend myself, will I be accepted; will I be rejected? Will this person or these groups of people one day walk away and leave me alone? Should I commit myself, knowing there is always the possibility that this person, or these people, will leave? Why bother getting close; it won't last anyway.

  Because a fatherless woman knows the pain of being left, of being told implicitly that she is not wanted, she both repels and attracts relationships and circumstances where she is liable to duplicate that experience. "Daddy's sudden and untimely death caused me to choose men who ultimately will abandon me, emotionally or literally," confesses Beth Erickson in her book *Longing for Dad: Father Loss and Its Impact*, which explores the impact of father loss on her and her clients. "Unfortunately, being abandoned feels familiar and 'right' and probably accounts for my divorce. And yet, I am terrified of being abandoned."

There are times when the fatherless daughter wants desperately to have a mate. But the triple fears ride her like a bad dream. She reaches out for someone. Unconsciously she has reached for the person she instinctively knows will leave; something in her psyche already has forecasted that person's departure. When the announcement finally comes, a part of her is relieved. The veil of fear has been pulled down again until the next time.

"After a while you come to accept that any relationship you get near will fall apart or the other person will leave. Then you start to feel not so sure about yourself, a bit insecure," says Chapman. The pattern repeats itself, and the fatherless woman develops a complex.

"Usually what these persons will do is to play it safe to protect themselves; they will not put themselves in situations that are going to be intimate. They will be highly social, sexual, intellectual, but not intimate."

In playing it safe, the fatherless daughter frequently determines that it is best not to stay and fight for any relationship or any situation where there must be some emotional investment. We all face this dilemma: Is it worth the hassle? But the fatherless woman responds to real or imagined threats more strongly and sooner and, in most cases, by fleeing. She fears that she will lose the battle and so she runs away; often her decision to flee is precipitous, but it is better to leave than to be left, better to determine the circumstances and timing of loss than to have someone impose it on her.

Consequently, in many respects the fatherless daughter becomes a dilettante, someone who passes through—floating but refusing to be touched deeply, because touch means involvement, and involvement means commitment. All of which trigger the triple fears, deeply rooted in the fatherless daughter's self-image.

• **THE SEXUAL HEALING FACTOR.** Sexual expression can be a primary indicator of fatherlessness in a girl or woman. The behavior can range from promiscuity to an aversion to intimacy. She wants to be close but is afraid. She determines that she cannot be intimate unless she is in control. She wants to be the one who decides the positions for making love; she wants to be the one to decide when or if she and her mate will get physical. She decides if she will have an orgasm, regardless of how long the man may perform hoping to bring her to a climax. Because all of this places her in control, she does not confuse love and intercourse. She presents an impenetrable, cool, or unaffected demeanor. But these are merely defenses.

Too often, women who are wounded by the loss of their fathers through death, divorce, or abandonment go from man to man, from bed to bed, calling sex "love" and hoping to be healed by the physical closeness. "Hannah simply refused to live without the attentions of a man, and . . . had a steady sequence of lovers, mostly the husbands of her friends and neighbors," Morrison tells us in the novel *Sula*. Like me, Hannah was a fatherless daughter, reared in a house of mostly women and visiting men.

Teen girls who grow up without their fathers tend to have sex earlier than girls who grow up with both parents; a fifteen-year-old with only a mother is three times more likely to lose her virginity before her sixteenth birthday than one living with both parents, according to statistics provided by the National Fatherhood Initiative.

Sometimes sex isn't enough. Fatherless girls develop an obsession with having a baby. A baby is a defense against loneliness, against abandonment. In our fantasies, we try to believe that the man we have chosen to love us will not leave—as our fathers did. But we half expect him to; we program ourselves for his inevitable departure. The baby is a feature of that programming. At least when he leaves we will have someone—we won't be alone. In fact, we'll still have him, because we have his baby. It is ludicrous, but, nevertheless, we cling to this reasoning; it is our life preserver.

- **THE "OVER" FACTOR.** The fatherless woman is determined not to allow anyone—man or woman—to discover her wound. She develops myriad masking techniques. She may "overcompensate" in loving relationships by doing too much; she sculpts herself into the perfect mate. Dinner on the table, chilled champagne glasses, and great jokes. Another facet of the "Over" Factor casts the fatherless girl as the archetypal "overachiever." The superwoman—able to leap tall buildings in a single bound. Ready to kick ass and take names. It is the fatherless daughter's way of announcing, to the father who left her, that it is his loss; he will miss out on claiming her as part of his family. We are at the top of our class. We break the glass ceilings. We spend endless days and nights working. We are the most decorated, the most awarded, the most rewarded. In many ways, fatherless girls and women adapt a masculine identity. But it is simply a shield, a tool designed to prevent anyone from getting close enough to see the despair.

When perfection doesn't produce the desired results, we "oversaturate" our lives with food, drugs, alcohol, sex, or work. We consume them in large quantities; these are anesthetics. Sometimes, however, we punish ourselves, denying ourselves food and other nourishment; the result can be anorexia, of body and of soul.

A study of 22,000 children ages twelve to seventeen found that those living with single parents or stepfamilies were 50 percent more likely to use illegal drugs, alcohol, or tobacco than were children living with both their biological or their adoptive parents. Adolescent girls in the same study who lived in mother-only families were found to be nearly two times more likely to use those substances than girls living with both biological parents, according to data provided by the National Fatherhood Initiative.

- **THE RAD FACTOR—RAGE, ANGER, DEPRESSION.** The fatherless daughter is a fount of unexplained anger and rage. Sometimes it is on the surface; other times it seethes out of sight, but within range to burst on the scene at a moment's notice.

Rage can take the form of addictions—drug, alcohol, food, sex.

Sometimes it presents itself as a fierce drive to succeed. Other times the anger takes the form of depression, which is nothing more than rage turned inward. "One woman in five can expect to develop depression or manic-depression sometime during the course of her life," say Drs. Donald F. Klein and Paul H. Wender, authors of *Understanding Depression: A Complete Guide to Its Diagnosis and Treatment.* If untreated, depressive illness can lead to personal, familial, and social disasters. U.S. Surgeon General David Satcher in 1999 characterized suicide as a "serious health threat." For young people fifteen through twenty-nine years old, suicide was the third leading cause of death, exceeded only by unintentional injury and homicide. Between 1980 and 1985, the surgeon general said the incidence of suicide among black youths ages ten to nineteen doubled from 2.1 per 1,000 to 4.5 per 1,000.

But depression may be the natural outgrowth of anger. Yet sometimes when anger ceases to be an effective weapon for confronting danger or for removing perceived obstacles from one's life, a sort of apathy sets in. A person begins to feel that there is no useful method for meeting the inequities of life. Depression sets in. It can take the form of crying, having a chronic state of the blues, being unable to get out of bed.

Sometimes, however, the rage becomes a violent external expression. It isn't an accident that more and more women are engaging in criminal activity. Nor is it coincidental that over the past ten years the incidence of child abuse and neglect perpetrated by women has skyrocketed.

There is a direct correlation between the increasing number of women taking drugs, being diagnosed with clinical or bipolar depression, being found guilty of child abuse or some other criminal violation, and the number of fatherless women. More than an attack on society, these are representations of the fatherless woman's self-hatred.

Only Make Believe?

Aren't these the issues with which most women contend or suffer? The answer is both yes and no. Certainly, since the 1960s sexual revolution, women have been promiscuous, although a study in 1998 indicated a recent drop in sexual activity among teenage girls. And some of those women, hopping from bedroom to bedroom, had their fathers right there in their homes all their lives; the fathers are still there.

Some women are filled with rage, not because their fathers split but because sometimes being an African American woman on your own in America can be a hard, mean experience. And yet many daughters of divorced parents do go on to lead very successful lives.

"We're always talking about elevated risks. We're talking about probabilities, not certainties," clarifies psychologist Wade Horn. He cites an example: Two airplanes are scheduled to leave at the same time and get you to your destination at the same time. You get the same seat on both planes, and the ticket price for both is the same. Which plane do you catch? Suppose one flight has a 99 percent chance of getting you to your destination without the possibility of crashing; the other only a 90 percent chance of not crashing. *Now* which plane do you catch? "That is the issue with the fatherless daughter; she has an elevated risk of bad outcomes," continues Horn.

Further, the symptoms of the Fatherless Woman Syndrome often are expressed not individually, but rather as a group of symptoms found in fatherless girls and women. Think of the syndrome as a quilt composed of separate, distinct scraps of fabric, all stitched together to create a bed cover. For example, a fatherless woman's assessment that she is unworthy and unlovable fuels her expression of the triple fears—abandonment, rejection, and commitment. Often these feelings of being unworthy or unlovable combine with the triple fears to produce promiscuous sexual behavior because she is desperately trying to prove that she is worth loving. But when she fails at her efforts to lasso a man who will validate her worth, she often resorts to self-medication and oversaturates with drugs or food to soothe her suffering. When such overcompensation spins out of control, it frequently produces full-fledged substance addictions. Or she hides her suffering and desperate effort to prove she is lovable by becoming an overachieving superwoman. When none of the over-compensation pays off, the unexplained anger and rage often spiral downward into into rage's twin—depression. So it is the confluence of these symptoms uniquely stitched for each fatherless daughter that makes her circumstance critical.

These are real symptoms: I *know* the syndrome. I have lived with it in varying degrees all my life. I live with it now. As someone diagnosed with high blood pressure or diabetes, the pain of fatherlessness *is* constant. Still, healing and self-reconciliation are possible. Achieving them is not an easy feat. But I and the other women whose stories I tell offer testimony that peace of mind can be achieved. The first steps that must be taken are to confront our fears, to recognize our anguish, and to call this disease by its proper name—Fatherlessness.

6. A SELF-EXAMINATION

You think this Fatherless Woman Syndrome has nothing to do with you, although you grew up without a father. You believe yourself to be well adjusted. Maybe you are. Maybe you're just fooling yourself. Maybe you've adapted to the dysfunctional behavior for so long, you no longer view it with an appropriately jaundiced eye. Answering these questions will help reveal whether you're hiding something from yourself. Best of all, it will provide a moment for directed reflection.

1. At what age did you have your first sexual experience?

2. What was your chief motivation for entering that relationship, or those relationships?

3. Do you distinguish sex from love, or are they the same thing to you?

4. Did you ever consider having a child, although at the time you weren't married? If yes, how old were you and what motivated the desire?

5. If you have children, what is your relationship with them—are they used to fill the empty space in your life; do they serve as a weapon for keeping your partner in line, etc. If you do not have children, do you still have a strong desire to have them; what is your motivation?

6. How and why did you end your last relationship?

7. How strongly do you respond to criticism from a mate? Even when the criticism is valid, do you sometimes find yourself worried about whether the comments mean he is about to break off the relationship?

8. Do you prefer dating men who are married, have another girlfriend, or are intensely involved with their work?

9. Do you sometimes find yourself in a good relationship but still feel uncomfortable about it?

10. How often have you ended a relationship before the man whom you were dating, living with, or married to decided to end it?

11. When you look at yourself in the mirror, what do you see? Are you comfortable or uncomfortable with your body image?

12. How many times have you tried dieting or gaining weight over the past three years?

13. Have you ever suffered bulimia, anorexia, or any other eating disorder?

14. When you are hurt, angry, or lonely, do you frequently head for the refrigerator or the stove, or for that bottle of wine?

15. How often do you head for work, either in your house or at your office, when things are going badly in a relationship?

16. Do you lash out at others for no apparent reason?

17. Have you within the past five years been the first to attack, physically or verbally, your male partner?

18. Do you sometimes become so angry with yourself that you deny yourself certain niceties?

19. Do you sometimes spend days in bed when you are not physically ill, find yourself tired when you have exerted very little if any physical energy, realize you can't get yourself motivated?

20. Have you ever thought that you would be better off dead, ever thought of committing suicide, ever attempted suicide?

21. Do you sometimes bend over backward in a relationship, attempting to please the other person, even if it means sacrificing your own pleasure and happiness?

22. Do you invest more time in helping a man improve his life than you do in improving your own?

23. Are you frequently overly conscious of how people perceive you?

24. Do you feel that you never measure up to others?

25. Do you believe everything you do has to be perfect?

BOOK TWO

—there are flowers lining

the porch's edge
tilting over
trying not to die. . . .

—Excerpted from "Someone Could Get Killed,"
  The Corner Is No Place for Hiding

7. SEARCHING FOR MY FATHER'S IMAGE

"Please, dear God, let me have a baby," she prays. Then she constructs altars—small ones, large ones, square ones, circular ones—in the bedroom, in the bathroom, in her studio; they are all dedicated to the conception and successful delivery of a baby. She burns candles, lights incense, meditates. I do not know the names of the deities she worships. Sometimes she sings songs in a language I do not know; perhaps it is nothing more than an untranslated version of the fatherless woman's dirge.

Who taught her this?

My daughter thinks a baby will fill the void, the great big hole in her heart left by her father's departure over seven years ago. "I felt my father didn't love me anymore. I felt lonesome. I didn't have a boyfriend," she tells me. "A baby will change my life. It will be something of my own. A baby will show me love. A baby will love me in all ways."

The "baby as mythic rescuer" narrative written by fatherless daughters is pronounced and dramatic. It is their primary vision, a preoccupation of mammoth proportion. The baby is seen as the surrogate savior, the knight in shining armor, come to erase the hurt, to bring rainbows, sunshine, and love.

As the problem of fatherlessness has escalated, so has the problem of teen pregnancies. In 1960, 5 percent of births were to unmarried women. Today, it is an alarming 31 percent. Some experts predict that in the year 2000 as many as 40 percent of all American children will be born out of wedlock; 90 percent of minority births will be out of wedlock, according to data provided by the Fatherhood Initiative.

According to the National Centers for Disease Control and Prevention, in 1994 the birthrate for Hispanic females ages fifteen to seventeen years was 74 per 1,000 women—more than three times the rate of 23 per 1,000 women for non-Hispanic white females of the same age. Among eighteen- and nineteen-year-old Hispanic females, the birthrate of 158 per 1,000 women was more than double the rate of 67 per 1,000 non-Hispanic white females. Teen pregnancy rates among black adolescent females are comparable to rates among Hispanics, 76 per 1,000 females ages fifteen to seventeen and 148 per 1,000 females ages eighteen to nineteen.

"Teen pregnancy is to girls what jail is to boys," says Joyce Ladner, a sociologist and fellow at the Brookings Institution, a think tank in Washington, D.C. Fatherless boys frequently engage in violent and criminal behavior as a way of demonstrating their masculinity and as a scream for help.

Still, not all fatherless girls who want babies are acting out. Pulitzer Prize–winning journalist and author Leon Dash, who in the 1980s spent over a year charting the lives of young girls in the poorest communities of Washington, D.C., observed, "Many teenage girls have sex, often reject birth control, get pregnant, and have children—not because of ignorance—[but] because they see those actions as ways to keep a vital relationship alive, to escape from families or poverty, or to achieve something *tangible* (Dash's italics) in lives filled with poor education, joblessness, failure, violence, and a penetrating uncertainty."

"Those who have [experienced] loss try to fill that space; they befriend a child or foster a child," says Meri Danquah, mother of a preadolescent girl. "It is human nature to try to heal ourselves, to unwittingly fill that space." But danger awaits children born to temporary unions out of wedlock. Experts say those children are at greater risk for developmental delays, difficulty in school, and antisocial behavior.

Still, the child as rescuer remains an obsession—not just with fatherless women. In her book *Motherless Daughters*, Hope Edelman implicitly draws a parallel in the lives of girls and women who have lost their mothers: "Motherless daughters often say they feel whole again when they have a child of their own.

"They say the type of intimacy they lost when their first mother-child bond broke returns when they reenter the relationship from the other side. And they say becoming a mother allows them to reconnect with their mothers, and in doing so regain a small part of the original mother-daughter relationship."

Fatherless daughters are looking for healing, a way to repair the parental bond that was torn asunder by their father's departure. "Fathers try to say to kids things like: 'It's not anything wrong with you. I'll love you forever.' It's a very shallow reassurance," explains clinical psychologist Wade Horn.

Initially we believe it. We wait at the telephone as Afrika did. We look out the window, as Meri did. But the days turn into weeks, and the weeks into months. Before long, what began as a small sore has become infected—an infection so large that it can't be cut out—it reaches to the core. We are desperate for a cure. We reach for a baby.

"I always wanted a family, from the time I was a teenager," confesses Sandra, the human resource developer and born-again Christian. When she went to Washington, D.C., right out of college, she thought maybe she had found the man who would help her start that family.

He was her age—twenty-two. They both worked part-time in the evenings for a telemarketing company. At first their acquaintance was just conversation. He was married to a non-American woman, who, he says, didn't understand him; it was too hard. He thought he should leave. Finally he did; he also talked about getting a divorce. That's when he and Sandra became an item.

Now, she thought, she had found the guy ready to make a commitment. After all, he had already made one once, what's to stop him a second time?

"We got into this hot and heavy relationship. I had my own apartment. We would spend a lot of time together. I dated him for about two years; it was a very rocky relationship. We were both emotionally unstable. I was so clingy.

"Eventually he went back to his wife; he said it was a matter of convenience. But we still carried on this relationship. I was so unhappy and sad. We argued all the time about the situation. I couldn't even go visit this man at his house. Me and the wife would have conversations where we would be screaming at each other, because he led me to believe I could call there whenever I wanted to.

"By this time, I discovered I was pregnant."

Instead of the marvel Sandra thought pregnancy might be, she found herself alone and unhappy. Six weeks later, he took her to have an abortion. She was devastated, and vowed that everything was over with him.

"But he would still try and show up and be in my life when he felt like it." And she would let him.

Then one day, trying to find some things to occupy her life, to expand her social reach in the city, she went to a screening sponsored by the then Black Film Institute at the University of the District of Columbia. He was there with his wife. "I felt like I had been kicked.

"And after, I couldn't eat. I couldn't sleep. I felt like an empty shell. At one point I tried not to feel. I tried to drink; but somehow, stepping into the world of alcoholism was a place I didn't want to be. I felt extremely alone in the world. I was devastated, and then to have the guilt of the baby, too.

"I did think about suicide. I had such a great guilt. Not only had I had this abortion, but I had been involved with a married man. My future looked kind of bleak.

"I felt this great empty void that I was trying to fill—fill with love and doing everything I could to get it and keep the love. I thought by giving, giving, giving, that's how I was going to keep it."

What Is Happiness?

I understand this desperation. Once, the "baby as mythic rescuer" was my creed. Then, I was only fifteen and dreamed of having nine boys; I would never want for male companionship. Eventually I gave birth to two sons; one died, and the other was taken away during my quest for a man to mask as my father. I had a hard time telling my daughter that she, too, was part of that drive toward "mythic rescuer," although by the time she arrived, I was satisfied with a baby—regardless of gender.

On the evening of my twenty-sixth birthday, Tommy, my second husband, asked what I wanted as a gift: "A daughter," I replied. Nine months to the day, she was born.

If someone had asked during those early months with Tommy and Afrika if I was happy, I wouldn't have been able honestly to answer yes. I never expected to be happy; I had not been for most of my life. I didn't believe I deserved that emotion. As long as there wasn't any confusion, and there was a ready companion, I was satisfied. Freud says happiness is the absence of emotional pain; I did not know any other definition, although, in hindsight, I have come to understand the flaws in his definition.

Tommy and I doted on our daughter. Until she was a teenager, she remained a constant companion of one of her parents or her paternal grandparents. I took her to poetry readings and community meetings. Sometimes, I even took her to work; years later, as a daily reporter with irregular hours, it wasn't uncommon to see her at the back of some meeting room, reading, doing her homework, or drawing and coloring.

Her father was just as smitten: The child almost never left his side. He was there when she spoke her first words, when she took her first step, and when she ventured successfully up the stairs of our town house to her room. Wherever he went, she went. There are pictures of Tommy and Afrika at the park, at home reading the newspaper, in the chair listening to music.

But five years later, just before my thirty-first birthday and after her fifth birthday, I decided to leave Tommy. The special relationship he and Afrika had developed never entered the equation. My perspective then was that the separation of child and parent was a nonevent. I suspect it was the same view my mother held when she and Bill separated, when she and John separated, when she and Noel separated. Each time she did not hesitate to remove me from the reach of those three men—my fathers.

A child's adaptability is universally asserted. Ask anyone if a child can fully adjust to the disappearance of a parent, and the answer is sure to be yes. Certainly, I subscribed to that belief. I didn't think for a second that irreparable injury might visit my daughter.

Afrika had tasted the sweet water from the well of the father-daughter relationship. The unexpected drought became excruciating. The past became an oppressive shadow from which she found no peace. It was always there, forcing her to measure it against the present, the way Bebe Moore Campbell did each summer: "I can't remember when this waiting for my father began," she says in *Sweet Summer: Growing Up With and Without My Dad.* "All I know is, it became an end-of-June ritual, an annual event, something I could set my clock, set my heart on. I don't know whose big idea it was to divide up my life the way they did. Summer. Daddy. Winter. Mommy . . . Gradually it began to dawn on me that their division had me lopsided, and lonely: a girl who sat on the steps in June and waited for her daddy."

When Afrika separated from her father, she was too young to articulate any feelings—although now, in hindsight, I am sure she must have felt the same way I did when Noel left. What happened; why did my world collapse? I asked myself repeatedly. And while I did not hear her questions, I saw in the tears she shed nearly every night a futile search for answers. I wept with her—and for the same reason. She missed her father; I missed mine. But then I didn't understand our grief intertwined.

One day, the internal stress and trauma took an external expression: A huge clump of Afrika's hair fell out. I thought it merely the result of changes in her diet and the hectic schedule we now lived. I hadn't been able to prepare food that was as fresh as I once had. And where once we simply jumped in the car and headed for school, we now had two buses to catch. Still, I didn't connect any of our circumstances with fatherlessness.

I concocted my own homemade remedy for the hair loss, increasing dosages of vitamins A and E, which she took internally. I also placed vitamin A on the bald spot. Her hair grew back. But the topical prescription did nothing for the internal devastation.

Afrika retreated inside herself, leaving little room for anyone to enter her world. Her schoolwork began to reflect her anguish and dismay. It was the same action I had taken in the Desire project—sentencing myself in a private world, afraid to reach out to anyone, believing that if I did, if I allowed myself to love again, the same thing would happen. That person would abandon me. But who could be inside Afrika's head or heart? Who could know her hurt?

Tommy and I took her to a psychologist; he suggested regular therapy. We didn't follow through. I can't remember how we convinced ourselves such visits would be useless. There was something about the doctor's being late for an appointment, something about the quality of the staff. I think we were afraid to hear what might be said about us and the havoc we had wreaked in a young life. She plodded along, never fully returning to her once-bubbly self. Even when there were glimpses of her past self, they were fleeting. The somber mood returned.

"[Then] my father met a new woman and he went to live with her; they moved to New York," she says. She had entered high school, but her father's move was the seminal event that shattered her fragile life. As she tells the story now, she is caught in the moment: the day she helped to load the van and drove with her father to the Brooklyn apartment. She watches as he and a group of men from the neighborhood unload it; she stands guard, ensuring that no one runs off with their property. But she is unprepared, someone does escape with *her* property—the new woman, and later her two younger brothers, have captured her father.

"I felt he didn't love me anymore," she continues, tears falling off her cheeks onto a waiting tissue, the third since she began this narrative of loss and love. "I had been around and I did things with him. Having a wife meant he couldn't do as much as I wanted him to.

"She stole him from me," Afrika says, contradicting the impression she gave when she first met the woman. Then she pretended to like her;

she even took to calling her Mama. Later, however, after it appeared her father's new female friend was a permanent fixture and couldn't be conned into leaving nicely, "I would spit on her and climb the curtains to get away from her. I didn't like her, especially when she moved him away from me." Afrika's soft voice suddenly turns hard, tinged with anger.

"I didn't do anything for him to leave," she says. "I wanted what every other daughter wants: someone who will love her, someone who will guide her, and someone who will put her on the right path. I wanted my father back.

"I ask God, What did I do to make my father not love me anymore?" The melancholy that Afrika possesses now arrived at her door when she was thirteen; today she is twenty-two. Loneliness captures her eyes and her voice. Sometimes it takes recess, but most often it holds a tenured position in her life.

Magic Elixir

She thinks a baby the cure-all, the cure-all elixir I thought I had in Vaseline petroleum jelly. Although I understand it, this baby thing drives me crazy—maybe it takes me too deeply into the alcoves of my own past. I look for some reason for this obsession and conclude that the new boyfriend Afrika has found is encouraging her behavior. I am sure of it.

Not long after he came, the altars began to be assembled. He seems a nice guy, but neither he nor she is ready for parenthood. I try to impress upon them the demands of children. Try to make sure that he understands there is someone who is going to protect her and that he cannot take advantage of the situation. I emphasize that she is going to make something of herself; she will not repeat the mistakes of her mother and her grandmother.

But I have been talking to the wind. One day he leaves a telephone message saying he has taken her to the emergency room of the hospital. I don't know which hospital; there are a half dozen in the city. I am frantic.

Finally they arrive home: She has been subjected to a half dozen tests. She goes straight to bed. The next morning she tells me that they also went to a family-planning clinic and had a pregnancy test performed. I hit the roof, and rant something about a baby not coming into the house without a wedding license, ring, and father attached to it.

She isn't listening; she is a concrete wall, one constructed with tears and years of absence. I try to take a sledgehammer to it.

Weeks pass before she finally says she no longer wants children; she has broken up with her boyfriend. "Nobody loves me." I tell her I love her and her father loves her. She cries herself to sleep.

Three weeks later, no new boyfriend materializes. But the altars are up again. There are pictures of babies all over. When I ask her about them, she smiles. I hold my head and recite a silent prayer.

Love in All the Wrong Places

This search for a baby, this quest for unconditional love, often leads fatherless girls to all the wrong places. We think every man wears our father's face. This one has Bill's dark, brooding eyes. This one Noel's melodious voice. This one is tall and lean like John. This one touches my heart. God help us. The search is relentless. Obsessive. Destructive. Pathetic.

I go from house to house, from bed to bed, from wrong man to wrong man—sometimes a right man but for the wrong reason. I am impatient and intolerant. Absolutely confused. I proclaim victory where there has been none. And I declare defeat far too prematurely; it is a case of the "un"s— "unwanted and unlovable." This unlove song is backed up by the constant chorus of the triple fears. This wisdom is, of course, sculpted from hindsight.

Until a few years ago, I did not understand the impetus for my incessant running. Psychologists and therapists say fatherless women are notoriously promiscuous—not because they are so fond of sex. "If they can attract other men, then surely the reason their fathers left isn't because of some defect in them," explains Wade Horn.

"The father's departure created in many women my age a feeling of cynicism about the durability of the bonds of commitment and love and an almost blind religious faith in the strength of the bond of sex," says Naomi Wolf.

The physical connection that comes from sex creates a sense of belonging, of being loved. Although most often the fatherless girl believes she wants to be loved, she frequently runs from that emotion. Or she doesn't know what love is. She mistakes the sexual bond for the real thing. At least for that moment. And the moment is all she expects. The fatherless girl comes to believe that love is fleeting, a sort of apparition that never can be captured. The best she can hope for, then, are brief episodes. Fits of love, if you will.

If fatherless daughters' pursuit of unlove were a business, we might call what we do "limiting our risk—if not our exposure." Only it isn't that logical. It more closely resembles what junkies do when they try to recapture the power and impact of that first high. But it doesn't come the second time they shoot up, nor the third time, nor the fourth. They continue shooting up, believing that the euphoria they felt that very first time will arrive in the next bag. They are willing to risk their lives, just to get back that feeling. Sometimes they die in the pursuit.

But while the junkie can name, describe in detail, offer in vivid color the ecstasy that came with the first injection, fatherless girls and women, especially those who were abandoned, are without references. We don't know exactly what we are looking for, but we think we will know it when it comes, if it ever does. All we really know—and only subconsciously—is that it has something to do with our fathers. We are hoping to restore that feeling of well-being, of security, of worthiness we felt in our father's presence. It was there even when our fathers were less than perfect, even when they spent an inordinate amount of time away from our homes. If we had even the merest of relationship with them, they still maintained a sort of legendary status.

"The strongest presence that I feel is my father's absence. It clings to his places and possessions," Deborah Tannen says in her essay "Daddy Young and Old," about the times when her father left for work and she remained at home. "I spent hours typing letters to my father telling him what happened to me during the day and laying out grievances against my mother. I can't have any grievances against him, because he isn't there.

"My mother is a continuous arc," Tannen continues, "my father is a series of snapshots that I take with me where I go."

When our fathers leave forever as Bill, John, and Noel did, we repeatedly, albeit subconsciously, pull those photographs from the pockets of our hearts, comparing them to each man who enters our lives. Running to the next man, hoping he matches more succinctly. And when we think we have him, we want to be held. Sex becomes a balm.

A 1994 study of eight hundred African American and Hispanic adolescents, conducted over a five-year period by Carolyn Smith and reported in the *Journal of Social Work*, found that boys and girls who did not live with their biological parents were significantly more likely to engage in sexual intercourse than were their peers.

This reliance on sex begins so instinctively. Like many other symptoms of the Fatherless Woman Syndrome, it is initially unnoticeable—like a colorless, odorless gas. Its imperceptibility makes it all the more lethal.

My chase began innocently, in junior high school, a season when a girl is a bundle of confusion, conflicted by almost everything with which she is presented. The teen-year dynamics are exacerbated by fatherlessness. The girl without a father is without a daily resource from which she can draw to help her interpret a boy's flirtations, advances, or conversation. She isn't sure how she should behave in this new male-female environment. We are navigators without working compasses. Even now, I sometimes find myself searching for meaning in a male companion's actions. I am not sure how to discern if a man loves me, without his saying it.

My search for that guide, that compass to replace my father, began with Jerome. He whispered sweet words in my ear as we walked the campus of Carver Junior High School. I was thirteen, enamored of his good looks and his two-parent family. He bought me a ring, the kind with an adjustable band. It was my birthstone. I wore it proudly, as if we were engaged. The girls at the Carver Junior envied me; they couldn't understand how a girl from the Desire project could land a guy like Jerome; equally, I considered myself unworthy of the prize. So the love affair did not last long. I ran to the next one: Henry. Then Antoine, Arthur, and a half dozen others, whose names I have forgotten with time. There wasn't any sex—just petting, kissing, warm feelings, and fantasies of having a baby.

I was a senior in high school, with plans to attend college, when I started up with Donald. Twenty-four, tall and slender, he wore John Asemore's body. I didn't know that consciously. But somewhere in my mind, I had imprinted the image of my biological father, although he had departed from my life before I could speak his name.

Donald treated me nicely. My mother allowed him to take me on dates to nightclubs. One day, about four months before my graduation, Donald invited me to his apartment. I accepted the invitation, although on previous occasions I had resisted. He convinced me to climb in bed. I didn't enjoy our singular experience and thought that he had taken advantage. I quickly dropped him.

But even that disappointment didn't stop me from running. Maybe I ran harder because of it. I met Curtis, the recreation-center coordinator for the Florida Avenue public housing complex. At thirty, Curtis was dark, with a chiseled body. He was Noel, and so I melted inside his embrace. I had returned to the summer of 1956, when everything was magical. Curtis displayed a maturity that I had never glimpsed in Donald. I could count on him to teach me the mysteries of the world and protect me from the evils that existed therein. The boys at the center, hunching over pool tables and slamming Ping-Pong balls, were no competition for him.

Each Thursday, after school, I went to the center, participating in conversations, demonstrating my intellectual agility, feigning the need for assistance. Having objected to engaging in sex with Donald, I flirted shamelessly with Curtis, hoping to seduce him. One evening, after the center closed, I climbed into Curtis's brown Mustang; we headed toward Chef Menteur Highway and the Sands Motel. I made no demands that night or any of the other six nights I spent with him, save for companionship. Curtis made no promises. I was not in love. To love is a dangerous thing; I was sure of that.

"Now that I'm older I can have sex if I want to. And sometimes I do," says Makeba, in Alexs Pate's *Finding Makeba*, a novel about a father's desertion of his family and his unexpected reunion with his daughter after she stumbles upon, and reads, his book.

"But," Makeba adds, "I don't think I'm going to have a love story happen to me. People like me don't have love stories. I have no patience. I have never met a man worth believing."

As much as fatherless women look for love in sex, some actually look to get even. They want to find a man who will fall in love and who will want to make a commitment. These women will maneuver until every duck is in its proper place, and then set the man up for major disappointment. Now the father substitute feels what his daughter once felt.

"What better way to attempt to fill the empty space inside; to draw men in while casting them aside; to be touched in ways that masquerade as love; and to express anger at and mistrust of men all in one fell swoop?" asks psychologist Beth Erickson.

Yet we are the ones who end up hurt and bruised by these games. Too many of us fatherless girls become Edie, whose name I found scrawled on a sidewalk in Washington, D.C.; she had won the title of "Pussy Giver of the Year." I had never met her, but instinctively I knew her and was prompted to write these lines: *"She could not pass the American standardized test/repeat/her flat feet pounded/the neighborhood pavement/in search of friends/there were none./'kiss/a subtle grind/maybe one time/be nice/she wants to be liked/wants to attract friends/wants to be the one/who will get a man/any man/popular at fifteen/she paints her pain/with awards/her clitoris receives.' "*

The prize slips through our hands. Like a fine spring rain, before we have time to hold it, savor the feel of it, it is gone. Misty Brown understands this. She ticks off the names of men whom she left or who left her: "Michael was a guy I just liked; I never kissed him. Albert was just somebody I thought was fascinating because he was three years older; I didn't feel he was my boyfriend. Robert came after Leonard. Robert was my boyfriend for three years. I had sex with him; I started having sex at sixteen. We never did break up; we just drifted apart.

"To tell the truth, I didn't know what a boyfriend was back then. I would think you're my boyfriend because we're talking on the phone, and I find out you're not my boyfriend."

Misty is a woman disconnected from herself. The division between the real and the fake makes it difficult to gauge her true emotions. The authentic Misty is illusion. Although born in Independence, Louisiana, she is as much a product of her adopted New Orleans as my mother and I. Her love of film is emblematic of her penchant to construct opaque screens, obstructing both the view in and the view out. Even at forty-something, she devises labyrinthine tales whose intricacies and ornamentations would confound even Gabriel García Marquez. These stories aim to misdirect any attempts to probe the depths to which the fatherless song has made her plunge. Her narrative is reborn with each telling. First it is one way; then it is another. And then it circles back onto itself. Sometimes even Misty is unsure of the road to herself. The obstacles are less barriers against an insistent traveler than they are shields, self-protection.

Like the woman at the Gordon Plaza Apartments on St. Ferdinand Street, Misty can't remember a time without Plexiglas. It is necessary for her survival, the way the glass bubble was for the boy born without a functioning immune system. Her fatherless wound is still unhealed; any slight touch excites long agony.

Although blind to definitions and behavior, at nineteen Misty shifted from boys to men—older men. Horn explains: "If you're trying to reassure yourself, 'My father did not leave because of some defect in me,' if you're eighteen, better to prove that with somebody who is twenty years older, than with somebody who is eighteen. The older man is much more the equivalent of the father."

That Calvin was twice Misty's age did not faze her. "I didn't see anything wrong with it. I thought older men were more mature, more intellectual. They adored me."

A man of Jamaican and Chinese heritage, Calvin wore a bushy mustache and a ponytail. Finding him attractive and needing the attention of a man—any man—Misty brazenly flirted with him whenever she went into the shoe repair shop he owned. It wasn't about sex, although, if he had shown the slightest interest, she would have dashed to the bedroom, ready to reciprocate.

Mostly, she wanted to sit on his knee, hear his stories about shoe-making and the people who came in with their heels in disrepair and their boots leaning to the side, reflecting the crooked ways they'd walked. She needed the security he could offer.

"He was a teacher-type person; I was the youngest person who hung out at his place. Then I developed an attraction for him. He felt he was too old to be involved with younger women. We weren't sleeping together because he was married."

Misty had never known such a closeness with a man. She repelled her stepfather. She lost forever her biological father. Calvin was a refuge; she did everything she could to keep his attention, his adoration. She even picked up another older man—a record-store owner—planning to use him to stir jealousy in Calvin because he wasn't responding favorably to her seduction.

"Calvin thought the only thing women wanted was to get married and have babies." He wasn't wrong in attributing this desire to Misty, and because he wasn't forthcoming, she eventually moved on to foray in other fields. There was Russell, an older white guy who owned a theatrical group. There was also Teddy, the father of a female friend, who served as a another surrogate "dad"—not a lover.

In 1975, she met George. He was all bad news. Still, she wanted a family and was ready to settle down. He was a journalist. She thought that meant that he was capable of taking care of her financially, that he could be trusted; that he would make a commitment. Things went along fairly decently until he lost his job.

Then the bills started piling up, and everyone needed an attitude adjustment. George didn't want to invest his unemployment check in the house, and he wanted to control Misty. There was a role for her, even if he wasn't fulfilling his role. "He was a Muslim, and he was talking all this bullshit, all this macho stuff." Still, as badly as he treated her, Misty wasn't ready to give him up. The fatherless girl sometimes believes she deserves abusive treatment. Hadn't her father walked away from her? Surely that meant she is worthless, and if she is worthless, why should she expect anyone to treat her well? So while George lathered himself in machismo, he and Misty were unable to meet their financial responsibilities. "If I had had a father, I would have got him to kick George's ass out of my apartment." Instead, she borrowed money from her mother. Tensions only increased. "George dogged me. He took my money; he ruined my credit." Still she refused to let go of him voluntarily.

Then what Misty had been praying for happened. She discovered she was pregnant. Part of her was elated by the news. The other part of her was worried as hell. When George learned of her condition, he blew up. He already had three children with another woman. He didn't want any more. Misty was devastated. "I had my first abortion."

"He was becoming just like my father. He didn't want to work; he didn't want to take responsibility for his children." She speaks these words years later, still not realizing that she *maintained* her relationship with George because he *was* just like her father.

Three years later, Misty went looking for her father again. This time she found Ottway. He was a tourist, rebounding, like Misty, from an unhappy relationship. They dreamed together of possibilities. "I was burnt out. It was a very bad year. I was tired of people taking and not giving." Ottway offered a change of pace. He moved her to Washington, D.C., and after some prodding on her part, he married her. Although their relationship lasted over ten years, it was tumultuous. They fought constantly; often Misty passed the first lick. Ottway frequently put her out, forcing her to pack her clothes and move in with friends. For a few months she even moved into her own apartment. But whenever he asked her to come back, she went. Toward the end, the fights became more serious, more dangerous. They both had had enough; they divorced.

William, Joe, Reginald, and Ed all followed. Each as bad as the previous relationship. "All of the relationships were dysfunctional because I wasn't choosing men for the right reason." She says now, whispering in low tones about the guy she's currently dating, "This time it's different."

Each time we begin, it's as if we have amnesia—we forget the past—all except, of course, the smell of our fathers, real or imagined. The dreams we had of their holding us, nurturing us, telling us we are beautiful. And so with the first guy who comes along to mimic what we imagine, we fall under the spell and into his bed.

When I was under the covers with Curtis, it wasn't love or how he moved that captivated me. It was the warmth that enveloped me. The way he whispered reassuringly in my ear that I was the best and that he would give the world to me if I asked. I did not ask; the moment was enough. To ask for more is to threaten what you already have and to move into the realm of chronic distrust about which Makeba speaks. Demands guarantee loss.

Besides, it made little sense, I convinced myself, to become attached to anyone. I had received a four-year college scholarship and in a few months I would be off to school. Except that by summer's end, I was pregnant. It wasn't Curtis's, because we had been using condoms. It was Donald's.

I had dreamed of being married and having nine boys. They would be the security I needed. With their love I would never worry about eating alone, or slipping into bed without anyone to tell me good night. Now, as my dream dared to come true, I was scared to death.

My older sister, living at home with three children of her own, must have understood the tragedy of the moment. Here I was, the first of my mother's children to finish high school, the recipient of a full scholarship, and pregnant. My sister kept my secret for weeks, trying to help me find some way to abort. Abortions weren't legal then; a woman risked her life if she desperately sought out a coat-hanger operation. My sister and I tried a mess of concoctions, including quinine, which had worked for her but only made me sick. Finally, left without escape hatches, I told my mother and sparred with her over whether to marry Donald. Who would marry someone like Donald? He had been a friend; I had never envisioned him as a husband. Besides, I imagined he would leave eventually; I wouldn't take the risk.

My first son, Al, was born February 22, 1969. He was a speck of a thing. He wore his father's face. Instead of being my mythic rescuer, the baby made me know, even more profoundly than before, that something was missing. Now I didn't have a father and neither did my child. Not quite a year after his birth, I went on the hunt once again. I left Al with my mother. With only ten dollars and one suitcase of clothing, I set out with a girlfriend in her Volkswagen bug to explore the South and join in the civil rights movement.

We went to Hattiesburg, then to Jackson, and finally landed in West Point, which is where I met Michel. He was an artist who made jewelry and furniture, and painted and took photographs. He talked with a confidence and walked with a swagger that convinced me I didn't have to worry, that a man with a shield and sword was in my midst. I relaxed and fell into bed. Again, I wasn't happy. I didn't know the meaning of happiness.

Some afternoons, I found myself at a pay telephone, making a collect call to a former paramour. On more than one occasion he'd send me money to come home. But no man could guarantee that home would be where he was. I stayed in West Point. Michel provided instruction and translation for how a man's world operated. I became emotionally, physically, and financially dependent on him. He liked the dependency. I was the little girl, and he was daddy.

Sometimes during the first year that we lived together, I discovered with the rest of West Point that Michel was having an affair with a married woman who worked with him. Her husband found out about the relationship and beat his wife on the street in front of a crowd of people. Weeks earlier, I had become suspicious of Michel's relationship with the woman; he denied there was anything. Now it was clear he had lied. Translated to my psychic language and my vocabulary, his affair with that woman spelled irreversible rejection of me. But I was afraid to leave.

Soon afterward we left West Point and headed for Natchez, Mississippi— his hometown—and discovered I was pregnant. First Michel and I lived with his aunt and uncle in a shotgun shack with an outhouse. Then we moved to his mother's house. I sent for Al. But not long after his arrival, Michel's mother and I got into an argument about milk spilled on the hardwood floors. Insulted, I told Michel I couldn't stay there. We moved to the house shared by his father and paternal grandmother, who was far more pleasant than her daughter-in-law but who had a wicked habit of turning down the heat at night. It was in the dead of winter and Al caught a cold. I took him to the doctor, received a prescription, and for a time he seemed to improve. But I couldn't get Michel's grandmother to understand the importance of maintaining a consistent temperature in the home. I was at her mercy. It was her house. I decided to go home to New Orleans.

When we arrived in the city, my mother was at work; she'd left the key for me. The Greyhound bus ride had been long. I was tired and so was Al. I decided we both needed a nap. I placed him next to me in bed. About an hour or so later, I woke up. He was still asleep. I began unpacking our suitcases. I was nearly finished, and the child still had not awakened.

I went to check on him. I called his name, tapped him lightly. But he didn't move. Finally, I picked him up; he was as limp as a rag doll. He wasn't breathing. I called 911. The paramedics arrived and went through the motions, trying to revive him. But there wasn't anything they could do. He was dead. They covered his tiny body and rolled him out on a stretcher. I sat on the edge of the bed for what seemed like hours, dazed, disbelieving what had happened. Finally, I called my mother and Michel, who had developed a close bond with the child. If Michel had been in the same room with me that day, he would have killed me. Instead, he bludgeoned me over the telephone: What happened? What did I do? What did I give him to eat? What did I give him to drink?

My own face was a mass of tears and snot. Michel's inquiries captured what I knew people would think: that I had killed my child. I had. I deserted him, leaving him in the care of my mother. I dragged him from one unhealthy environment to another, all because I wanted so desperately to hold on to a man. I had killed the child as surely as if I had placed my hands over his mouth and stopped him from breathing. Michel took the next bus to town. My mother raced home, arriving with her own barrage of questions, none of which I could answer satisfactorily.

There I was, experiencing the death of my first child—who was only thirteen months old—and pregnant with a second. God help me. I didn't deserve the gift.

At the funeral, I couldn't even look into Al's face as he lay in the tiny white coffin; I almost had to be dragged to the front of the church where the casket rested. Michel broke down and cried; he didn't speak to me for days. The doctors said Al had pneumonia—walking pneumonia. My mother, caught in New Orleans spiritualism, said the child was destined to die—he had been born with two teeth.

For years I dreaded February. When the month arrived, a melancholy descended; I would be rendered immobile. I became so pensive and reflective that no one could connect with me; I had no interest in connecting with them. I would replay the entire event.

I don't know why Michel and I thought we could salvage our lives and our relationship from the ruin of a child's death and of infidelity. I knew he felt sorry for me. In fact, he told me as much just a few days before our wedding. I had had one child out of wedlock and faced the prospect of another. The marriage, regardless of the reason we entered it, meant I had not been rejected; it meant that someone wanted me—black sheep or not. Maybe he didn't wear the face of my fathers, after all.

After the wedding Michel went back to Mississippi; I remained in New Orleans, living first with my mother and then moving in with friends from the civil rights movement whom we'd met in Mississippi but who now lived in the city. Six months after Al's death, I gave birth to my second son, Umoja. I was one month shy of my twenty-first birthday.

After Umoja's birth, I moved back to Michel's mother's house in Natchez. Michel went to Jackson to look for work. He sent money home each week, but the chances of our living together as husband and wife seemed more remote with each day. I was being abandoned. This time, however, I could do something about it. I packed our things in a huge black trunk, dressed my baby, and took the Greyhound bus to Jackson. When we arrived, I called Michel: "Come pick me up. I'm in town."

Still, the marriage could not be rescued. After two years of pretense, I filed for a divorce, refusing, despite my attorney's advice, to ask for alimony or child support. I believed then, as I do now, that a man should not need a judge to determine the level of his financial or emotional support for his child. I was content just to depart with the little sanity I had left after three such tumultuous years.

Michel wasn't. He nearly caused me to have an emotional breakdown. He called me an unfit mother, repeatedly reminding me what had happened to Al. "You killed one child; I'm not going to let you kill another." It was psychological warfare, all designed to win him custody of Umoja. He was successful.

Anyone knowing my life's story up to this point would have been convinced that I had learned my lesson. One child had died and another had been taken away from me because I had been compelled to search endlessly for this mystery man who would become the father I never had.

But instead of quitting, I intensified my efforts. It was a compulsion beyond my feeble control. My need was unmistakable and real.

Taking Before We Give

We are so gullible, so hungry, so vulnerable. Is it any wonder that fatherless girls are more likely to be the victims of sexual abuse and assault? A 1995 national survey on family growth found that of the women reporting their first sexual intercourse was not voluntary, 13 percent had lived with a single parent, 9.4 percent with a stepparent, and 6.4 percent with both biological parents.

Misty was only eight when the first incident happened to her. It was one of those evenings when she and her brother were at home alone with her father. Samuel Brown had only recently arrived. Before he made his appearance, she had heard disparaging remarks about him: He had been arrested in Independence, Louisiana, at the hospital where she had been been born in 1955; he was peeping in on nurses. "Samuel the Peeping Tom." Misty's maternal family called him wacky and talked openly about his troubles with the military police: Sometimes he ended up in the stockade; sometimes he refused to return to the base after days on leave. He did strange things to convince army personnel he should be discharged. Because of these stories and the effect they had on her, Misty had halfheartedly awaited his arrival.

Her mother had decided to take a second chance at making her marriage work. "I'm going to try to work this thing out with your daddy. Children need their daddy," Misty remembers her mother saying.

"Every man in my family that I loved was with his children until he died. Our family wasn't about divorces." Nothing about Misty's first meeting with her father is glued to her psyche. She remembers he was with them only for a few weeks. He tried mightily, albeit in an unorthodox fashion, to bond with his children. He took them for long walks, making the two line up in single file and march in formation to the river, shouting military songs all the way. He relaxed their diet, feeding them candy and sodas, which previously they had been forbidden to eat. He played hide-and-seek with them in an old refrigerator outside their home; they had been taught they could die in one of those things. He placed Misty on the family's armoire, telling her to jump into his arms. If he caught her she would trust him, he reasoned. But nothing he did resonated with his two children. Misty was repulsed.

He got a job but rarely went to it. Her mother worked the late-night shift at the train station, leaving the children home with their father. This particular night, Misty and her brother were on either side of him, a scene one might imagine would encompass storytelling or something else innocent and warm. Instead, Samuel fondled them—first one and then the other. Then he masturbated. The children were supposed to be asleep. But Misty remembered slimy stuff on the front of his clothes that looked like mucus. Her brother instinctively knew something bad had happened. Neither he nor Misty reported it to their mother, until one day when they heard a most amazing story. They were on their porch with a seven-year-old girl who was a friend of their family. The little girl's mother operated a boarding house, and Misty suspected that she was doing nasty things with the men who lived there. She was. One of them was Misty's father.

The news shattered Misty and her brother. They told their mother what they had heard and confessed their own experience. A posse, comprising Misty's mother, a couple of uncles, and a family friend, quickly formed. They went looking for Samuel; they weren't empty-handed, either. He made himself scarce. Misty never saw him again.

When she was twelve years old, a neighborhood boy, under the guise of teaching her martial arts, knocked her to the floor and pounced on her: "He put his penis on top my vagina and he kept pushing and trying to get in. I hit him and he fell off me. I ran. When I opened the back door, everyone in the project court where I lived was listening," she confesses. Who could come to help her? Not her father; he was no different from the boy who had won her confidence only to abuse it.

"I ran to my house. I tried calling my mother at work, but the line was busy. Some children knocked on my door. The girls told me they would kill me if I told anyone what happened. I knew people who got killed in the project. I didn't do anything."

Weeks later, the boy rapist pleaded with Misty to let him become her boyfriend. She didn't know what to do. If she said no, she could get killed. Maybe he would come after her again. She said yes.

Misty was without a protector, without someone who could mend the wound as Deborah Tannen remembers her father doing when she got a splinter in her finger. Only he had the magic to heal the injury: "When my father takes out a splinter, he elaborately sets up an operating table: lays out alcohol, matches, pin, tweezers, and a razor blade. He holds the point of the pin to a burning match, then sterilizes both the pin and the razor blade with alcohol. Then, he turns to the operation. . . . It never hurts," Tannen says in her essay "Daddy Young and Old." "I insist on leaving the splinter in place until he gets home."

Meri's father doesn't come home. She can't tell him that when she got dirty playing football, she went to Wayne's house to clean up. She liked Wayne and thought it nice that he cared enough about her appearance that he invited her to his house. He led her to the bathroom and disappeared. Meri can't tell her daddy that when she came out, she looked for Wayne. He had been waiting coyly in the bedroom. He ambushed her. She tried to leave but was confused about what to do. She liked the attention Wayne gave her; she liked the way he kissed her. But she didn't like the way he hurt her. The way he pushed himself inside of her. She wanted him to stop, but she didn't want him to be angry with her. She did not know how to please a boy and protect herself at the same time. She didn't even know if it was possible. She told Wayne she just wanted the hugging and kissing—not the other part. Wayne didn't listen; he said something about her being a virgin and that in a little while it would feel fine.

"I stayed and said nothing as he continued to kiss me, nothing when he laid me down on the bed, not even when he took off my pants. Nothing at all," Meri says. When it was all over, she walked over to her house. She felt dirty, again. She washed up, again. But the memory remained. She was only thirteen; her father wasn't there, so she confided in her mother's boyfriend, Jonathan, asking if it was possible to determine just by looking at someone that they were having sex. She told him the entire story of her visit to Wayne's house. He told her sex wasn't supposed to be that way. Meri thought she had found a friend.

Jonathan reached down and hugged her; he comforted her. He smiled, and then he finished what Wayne started. "What kind of man uses his erect penis, like the pointed glistening tip of a blade, to butcher the trust of a child?" asks Meri.

She never told anyone about Jonathan.

Sandra didn't tell either. She was only four years old when she found herself in a neighbor's backyard and the lady's nine-year-old nephew assaulted her. He pulled Sandra to him; they fell to the ground. He pulled at her panties. She fought him. "Girls aren't supposed to take off their underwear in front of boys," she remembered telling herself. Finally, Sandra broke free and ran home crying. "I was ashamed. If my father had been there, I never would have been at that lady's house."

The Cure Isn't Another Man

If the effects of the "sexual healing" symptom of the Fatherless Woman Syndrome are to be reduced, proactive engagement must be the theme. It doesn't help to sit back and play the role of victim. "To stay mired in victimization is to not recover," says clinical psychologist Maxine Harris.

Achieving true sexual healing sometimes means abstaining from sex. Far too many women confuse love with sex. Fatherless girls and women are the most guilty. Because someone holds us as tightly as Curtis held me those nights at the Sands Hotel, whispers in our ears, and tells us sweet stories, we believe all the hurt will go away. We engage in a dangerous fantasy.

After Sandra finally broke with her telemarketer, she went to another man and then another, each new one as unhealthful as the previous. "I felt

I was having this string of broken relationships because of my nonrelationship with my father. I would be so heartbroken because these things didn't work out."

Distinguishing who was right and who was wrong, what she was feeling, exactly, with each man, and what he was feeling for her was difficult to gauge. Without the dictionary a father provides, Sandra couldn't translate the language of love and sex that men speak. Sometimes she wasn't even sure about the one she spoke.

Since we know that we mislead ourselves when it comes to physical intimacy, fatherless girls must learn to hold the reins on ourselves until we have learned enough about the person we are dating, or at least until we are fairly capable of discerning the difference between sex and love.

"I decided there was nothing wrong with waiting," says Sandra about her decision to choose abstinence.

"The purpose of love is to find a partner we can grow with, through the barriers that keep love at bay to the center of the universe that exists inside all of us," proclaims Marianne Williamson. "Getting past the barriers, those walls that surround our hearts, means hanging around long enough to get a look at what they are."

There is nothing wrong with purely sexual encounters, if that is your taste. But for your physical and emotional well-being, don't play games with yourself or the other person, if what you're seeking is something more substantial; fatherless girls and women always want and need more. After all, sex isn't everything; we need to learn this, otherwise our lives are endless circles and dead-end streets.

"The need is real; the emptiness is real," says Harris. "But sleeping with two hundred people is not going to fill that need."

Substitution is a wonderful weapon for those girls and women like Sandra, my daughter, and me, who find themselves obsessed with the desire to have a child, say psychologists; but the need to fill that hole with a human being is real. Eventually my daughter took down her baby altars and found satisfaction in a day-care program where she could teach and play mother to young preschoolers. Afrika serves as their surrogate mother and they as her surrogate children. The exchange is satisfying for all.

Learning to maintain sex-free friendships guarantees the fatherless girl or woman a treasure—an opportunity to better understand the male species, to feel comfortable in his world, and to distinguish a male friend from the father whose singular love she craves. Often our sexual or physical response in a relationship is unconscious. Before we know it we have become close, romantic, physically intimate, because we are seeking the reassurance that we are desirable, that we are okay. One man's approval is as good as any. If we can't get our fathers to sanction our femininity and desirability—to dote on us—then, as Wade Horn notes, any man will do.

The problem is that any man really *won't* do. We want and need our fathers. But if our fathers can't be found, then what we seek is "fathering," which a male friend can provide—if we choose well. I have learned much about men and myself from the half dozen close male platonic friends I maintain. And, when I have needed protection, the kind we expected as little girls from our fathers or big brothers, these men have come to my rescue. Our friendships have worked well because I didn't permit them to become misdirected by sex, although there were more than a few times when I longed to be held and cuddled.

These platonic relationships also gave me a much-needed commodity—time—time for reflection. If we took the time to reflect between relationships, the time to chart the patterns in our sexual encounters and failed relationships—why we entered them, when we entered them, and how we entered them—we would come to understand the misdirection of our behavior.

My daughter's father, not long after our divorce, said to me one day, matter-of-factly, "Jonetta, you know you didn't give yourself any real time between when we broke up and when you got involved again." His comment came after seeing me fall in and out of three relationships, which may be too strong a word for what I actually experienced with those men. Nonetheless, his point was well taken. Allowing time for reflection is not to assess blame, or ensure you have the latest HIV test before moving on, but to have a wholesome dialogue with yourself about what you are actually seeking and why. After a while, you come to know yourself.

"I know what kind of man I'm attracted to, and I know what kind I should stay away from," says Maxine Harris. It was only after reflection that Beth Erickson realized she kept connecting with men who were likely to leave her, or those from whom she could easily walk away. A committed interior journey can help prevent an exterior catastrophe.

8. STAY, GO, STAY, GO, NO PLEASE...
The Triple Fears Merry-Go-Round ᵛ

H e was an anchor at a local television station. He read and reported the eleven P.M. news. I met him one afternoon as Marie
Ory and I stood outside the Mayfair Apartment Complex holding
a news conference. We had launched the first rent strike in the
history of Jackson, Mississippi; it was big news. As we packed things up
after the press event, he flirted; I, still on the hunt, responded in kind. He
was tall, handsome, articulate, funny, and warm; he fulfilled all the
dreams I had possessed about the kind of person with whom I wanted to
spend the rest of my life. In hindsight, I can say there have been only three
men I have loved in my life; Willie was the first—although I had been
married and had had other encounters before I met him.

The first time he asked me on a date, I couldn't believe he chose me. I
didn't see myself as befitting his stature. I was only a community orga-
nizer, fresh from a divorce, and still unconsciously on the search for my
fathers. I accepted his invitation, thinking all the time that maybe this
one, maybe this time, maybe everything would finally turn out right. Not
long after that first date, we began seeing each other regularly.

When his car pulled into my driveway late at night, after his news
show, I flew through the front door, rushing to meet him, jumping into his
arms the way little girls did on television when their fathers arrived home
from work. I'd never had the opportunity to be that little girl. Whenever
my father Bill visited our home, his aloofness and coldness sent me, rejected and shivering, into the corner. Once, I happened upon him at a
soda stand near our apartment in the Desire project. He was cordial, but
there was a distance one usually reserves for strangers. He acknowledged
my presence, but nothing in his tone of voice or the way he pronounced

my name suggested he longed to take me in his arms and hug me as a father might a child whose presence he has missed for many years. It wasn't the first time he had outlined by his actions the boundaries in our relationship. I knew better than to violate the no-trespassing signs he posted, and did not attempt to move any closer. I smiled and walked away, a tear quietly drifting down my cheek, betraying the reality that even then, years after he and my mother had separated, he still had the power to affect me. I quickly wiped my face, hoping no one had glimpsed my humiliation.

Still, somewhere in the back of my mind, I relished the opportunity to pretend to be that once-unworthy little girl accepted at last. When I raced into Willie's arms, I knew he wasn't Bill, but he responded the way I wished Bill had. Each time, Willie encircled me as if it were the first time, or as if we had been away from each other for years and he had missed me more than he had ever missed anyone.

It didn't matter what time I had gotten up in the morning; I was fresh and alive by the time he arrived. I lived for his visits, despite the seemingly ungodly hour at which they occurred. Sometimes I set the dining table with candles and wine for dinner. Other times I packed a basket and we headed out for a romantic midnight picnic at the reservoir. Those nights seemed the nearest to heaven I had ever been. I was a child, wrapped in a warm quilt, his voice a soothing lullaby, assuring me that no harm would ever reach my door.

But Willie never liked staying away from home all night. He lived with an older aunt who had reared him. He worshiped her and felt it disrespectful and insensitive to leave her alone in the house all night. So invariably he left my bed early in the morning. Each time he left, I panicked and hurt, as if something were being torn from my body, without my permission. Each time, I worried that he might not return.

The first time he rose out of my bed to leave, I simply asked him not to go. I'm sure he was flattered, initially, by my desire to be with him all the time. Later, the softly spoken plea was laden with tears and desperation. Sometimes he would have to peel me away from him, the way someone might a leech. He pleaded with me to be understanding. But I couldn't;

each time he left, I felt as I had that day when I discovered Noel wasn't coming back.

I was totally lost. Alone. Blaming myself for his departure. I wondered what I did wrong to make him leave. I retraced the entire night, trying to figure out the mistake I made. Was it something I said? Maybe I hadn't been a good lover that night. Was it dinner? I prayed to God to point out the error in my ways so I could quickly correct it. I didn't want to do the same thing the next time he came. But would there be a next time? Was he gone forever—like Noel? I was a bundle of nerves until the next telephone call or the next visit. And then, when it was time for him to leave, it would start all over again.

The fear of abandonment, rejection, and commitment is all powerful and all consuming in fatherless girls. These triple fears too often dictate our response in nearly every situation. Sometimes we are too afraid to offer our friendship, fearing it will not be accepted. We are reluctant to pledge membership in any group. Commitment requires the investment of time, intellect, and, most of all, emotion; the investment of emotion leaves us vulnerable to rejection. It is a vicious merry-go-round on which we place ourselves.

In romantic relationships, however, the conflicting cycle is far worse. We are drawn to intimate encounters because we desperately need their affirmation. We race inside as close as possible, often unconscious of the threat they pose to our fragile emotional stability. It is a classic approach/avoidance dynamic that we cannot control. Even as we attempt to get comfortable, even as we recognize how much we enjoy a relationship, in our peripheral vision we are plotting an exit strategy. Our fear can be overwhelming. Either we hold on too tightly, smothering our mate and our relationship, as I did with Willie, or we run as fast as we can, as if our life depended on a swift escape.

Clinical psychologist Maxine Harris explains that a child who loses a parent, through death, divorce, or abandonment, sees love and loss as dancers performing an intricate routine; their movements are so synchronized we believe them one—inseparable. For the fatherless daughter, to love means to endure loss. The concept becomes so ingrained, it might as well have been inborn.

I remember that on Mexico Street during the 1960s, in front of my grandparents' home, there was a wonderful garden filled with all sorts of flowers. I often pulled the weeds out of it and generally tended it. My favorite flowers then, as now, were roses—yellow, white, red. Sometimes, at the end of the day, I'd pluck a rose and take it to my special place on the front patio.

There, in a quiet space no one could enter, I'd pull one petal: *He loves me.* I'd pull another: *He loves me not.* Another: *He loves me. He loves me not. He loves me. He loves me not.* I kept picking roses and kept pulling petals; each new rose wore the name of a different boy. If the game ended with *He loves me,* I didn't stop. I'd play until it ended on *He loves me not.*

Although I could not articulate my conviction, I believed even then that love and loss were entwined. Not unlike clinical psychologist Beth Erickson, I chose men who were destined to effect that loss, to abandon me. When they didn't, I convinced myself that they would, eventually, and so I left first. I fashioned some excuse: I didn't like the way he talked; he wasn't well read; I didn't like his clothing; his nails were too dirty—don't laugh. I actually did break up with a dear, sweet guy because his nails were frequently unclean. I needed these petty grievances to assure myself that I wasn't acting irrationally. As outlandish as it seems, I was typical: the norm, among my anxious kind.

"Part of the task [of the fatherless daughter] is to attract the guy to prove it's not some defect, 'I am attractive,'" explains Wade Horn. "But once the guy's even there, there is this continued anxiety: 'Is he going to leave?'

"What some will do—because they are deathly afraid that the guy is going to leave, like the father—they will look for any sign of abandonment. If there is any sign of emotional withdrawal, they will cut off the relationship quickly," continues Horn.

"Better to leave, than to be left."

The Pas de Deux

Judith is on the telephone telling me she has broken up with her boyfriend. It is the third, maybe fourth, time she's called it quits. Her reasons seem as foolish and as irrational as mine when I was twenty-something and madly in love. She thinks that her boyfriend should not look at other women, that he doesn't need any other female friends. He was supposed to take her somewhere but called to cancel. She thinks she doesn't need the headache. Whenever there seems to be a change in his emotional response to her, she fears he is sending a signal that he no longer wants her, doesn't love her, is planning to leave—at any moment. Playing the game of one-upsmanship, she runs first. Good-bye.

One day, after one of those let-me-get-out-of-here discussions with her boyfriend, she was ready yet again to run, believing he was on the verge. He surprised her with an embrace. And quietly whispered a bit of news she had never before heard: She could not leave each time they had a disagreement. Love didn't work that way; relationships weren't built that way. He knew something about that, he said, and pointed to the fifty-year marriage of his parents.

On the surface Judith relaxed. Beneath the surface, the urge to run, to look for answers elsewhere, remained strong. Almost obsessive.

It's not anything a fatherless daughter plans, it's all reflex. Before she knows it, she's out of the door, moving through the crowd, not looking back, too afraid even to think about what could have happened. In her mind, what could have happened is that she could be on the curb. And that is a most frightening thought.

"I was always very shy. I never really wanted male attention. I was uncomfortable with it. I always felt I wasn't pretty," says twenty-one-year-old Helen, whose African American father and white mother never married; he wanted her mother to have an abortion, but she refused.

"I wouldn't say I had boyfriends during junior high school. We'd talk on the phone, or go places. I didn't really want boyfriends. I didn't want to be connected. I had real problems getting to know people, regardless of sex. I am not trusting of people. It takes a long time for me to get to know people and to feel comfortable.

"The boyfriend I have now, he and I went to the same junior high school. He's my first boyfriend. We dated on and off throughout high school. He says I drive him crazy," she says, admitting that, like me, she doesn't like good-byes. "I always want him to be with me."

Part of her trouble comes not just from her father's absence but from an experience with abandonment that was at once imagined and, yet, very real. "I remember as a little girl thinking that my father was there all the way through the pregnancy and then when I was born that's when he left." Helen squeezes the words from her mouth as she tries to keep the tears from leaking out her eyes.

"I didn't understand how you could not love a baby; how you could not want a baby."

When she was seven years old, her mother sued her father for child support. The court ruled in her mother's favor, and because Dad now had to dole out cash, he suddenly became interested in the little girl he had left behind.

"I started visiting him. I was a little scared but more excited about seeing him. Finally I would be able to say, I have a dad.

"I remember in the beginning I didn't want to tell my friends, because I had not had a father for so long and because I had told some people he was dead," Helen says.

Every other Sunday, she dressed in her finest attire and waited for her father. He had married, but his wife couldn't have children; she took a special interest in Helen, buying her clothes, making her dolls, painting a bedroom lavender. Her father and stepmother never went to school events. The life she had with them was separate from her "real" life.

"Then all of a sudden the visits stopped. He just missed a visit. The next time my mom canceled it. I really don't know what occurred," she says. "I felt he didn't like me. He didn't want me, there's something wrong with me."

When her father tried years later to reestablish contact, Helen was too fearful. She couldn't experience another rejection. Even now, she works hard at avoiding any such experience.

"Every once in a while my boyfriend and I will have a conversation, I'll tell him, 'If you think you don't want to be with me, let me know right now.' He'll say, 'What are you talking about?' " continues Helen, who admits that a feeling comes over her, an overwhelming feeling, that maybe she's not wanted, maybe she'll be alone; maybe she only deserves to be alone.

Diane Weathers, an editor of *Consumer Reports* magazine, understands Helen's fears. "The overriding theme, of course, was fear of rejection, a dire dread that being left by my daddy had marked me for life, doomed me to eternal abandonment. . . . Eventually I became expert at rejecting me before they found me out," she wrote in an essay, published in *Essence* in November 1998, which detailed the effects of her fatherlessness.

"I was clueless when it came to men. . . . I felt more comfortable with types who were at best ambivalent and at worst indifferent, emotionally or physically remote, living in another state or another country, moving in another orbit. Such men could have been dead ringers for my absent dad. . . ."

The Absence of Trust

The triple fears—rejection, abandonment, and commitment—often boil down to the basic issue of trust. As much as I loved Willie, I couldn't trust him to return the next day. I couldn't trust that what we shared was enough, that he could really make a commitment to me and mean it. After all, my fathers had made a commitment, hadn't they? Didn't Bill promise to love my mother forever? Didn't Noel say he loved me? Hadn't he just walked away, never to be seen or heard from again? A child accidentally burns herself on a stove; she is less likely to go back to it. She believes it will hurt her again. The fatherless daughter is afraid to trust any man, believing him capable of doing the same thing as her father—abandoning her, rejecting her.

"If you don't trust, then you have enormous fear," says therapist Audrey Chapman.

At twelve years old, Doris Duke, the daughter of a tobacco magnate, became a millionaire. In bequeathing his considerable fortune, her father told her to "trust no one." Not only did his death cause her great agony throughout her life, Duke was never able to bond with any man. Her father's misanthropic advice foreclosed a happy and lasting relationship with anyone. She died a childless multidivorcée.

"Fear is the biggest stumbling block in the process of self-discovery," says Chapman. "Often it is not only sadness that people fear discovering but also anger. They don't want to get in touch again with childhood betrayals or disappointments—and they are afraid that their anger will be so huge that they won't be able to handle it."

But while we are unable to trust men, we also can't be without them. In our minds, being without a man signals our undesirability. We need them for validation. Our fear sometimes encourages us to stay too long in destructive relationships and not long enough in those that *do* work. We are caught in an extraordinary dilemma.

Clinicians see fear of abandonment and rejection as two sides of the same coin. The fear of commitment and the inability to be intimate also are the flip side of each other. Often, those of us struck by the triple fears resort to various measures to protect ourselves, to ensure that we do not become too attached, too intimate.

"They will be highly social, sexual, intellectual, but not intimate," says Gayle Porter, a clinical psychologist. "If you're a woman and you say you want to settle down and find someone to get married to and you can't be intimate, you have a complex."

A complex is an overreactive psychological condition issuing from repressed but persistent memories and desires. It starts as a pattern of behavior that then prompts another set of responses, which also becomes a pattern. In this case, that of the fatherless daughter, she begins to believe that her relationship with everything she goes near, particularly her love relationships, will fall apart and the man will eventually go away.

"Usually when women come in to see me," explains Chapman, "I ask, 'Why are you here?' and they will say, 'To find out why I keep choosing the wrong man.'

"They think the pain they have been experiencing is because of their choices, and it is," Chapman continues. "But what they don't understand is that they have this self-fulfilling prophecy going on around this abandonment case."

Often, the fear that fatherless women experience is of our making. It is more imagined than real. Still we respond more strongly to this perceived fear than most do. Some people may think this a wonderful survival skill; our antennae always at attention. Nevertheless, we miss out. We can't evaluate when a group situation or a relationship is worth fighting for, and when we should surrender and walk away. In nearly every case, we flee. In the end, that's what I did with Willie—although I made it seem as if he had left me. Somehow, his leaving seemed right.

One of those very early mornings, as he climbed out of bed, I issued an ultimatum: Stay or don't come back. He left. It was foolish of me, I know that now. But I wanted to be rid of the agony I felt each time he left.

A year later, he left Jackson, Mississippi, to work in New York. I left to work in California. We didn't see each other again for twenty-five years. When we happened upon each other at a conference for journalists, he was still in New York; I was closer now, in Washington, D.C. We couldn't restrain ourselves; we were so excited to be reunited. Nothing happened, partly because I still couldn't stand saying good-bye. The word seems so permanent.

Putting Fear on the Shelf

To begin to conquer the Triple Fears Factor, the fatherless girl or woman must unlink Love and Loss. Perhaps as an exercise we can go back to the room where Harris showed us the two dancing. Instead of seeing them as a couple, we must now see them as solo performers, each in his own costume, moving to his own orchestration. Then we must see ourselves joining the dancer called Love, holding his hand, moving across the ballroom floor, fluidly, without any stumbling, as sure of his rhythm as we are of our own names.

Once we are sure we have discovered the right partner—that we really are dancing with Love, and not with its surly sibling, Loss—then we can begin to negotiate through difficulties, rather than allowing fear to force us out of the door.

Think about what happens when you're at a nightclub or a party and someone asks you to dance. Even if you know the tune, you try to locate the other person's rhythm, hoping to establish that you are a couple and not simply two people caught on the dance floor at the same time. After all, you can dance alone anytime you want. But if you've agreed to dance with someone, it becomes a pas de deux. To ensure that no one steps on your toes and that you don't step on anyone's toes, you negotiate those first awkward seconds.

In this same fashion, the fatherless daughter, too, must negotiate the problems, confusions, and missteps that will occur, and that, more often than not, are internal and self-instigated. The awkward feeling that overwhelms and then consumes her about her place in a relationship, the fear that sooner rather than later even this tenuous position will be jeopardized, must be approached practically.

Sometimes, when I feel fear breathing down my neck, whispering in my ear, I find myself at the mirror asking myself fifty questions, probing my queasiness to find its reason for being. I ask myself: Am I creating the end of the story before finishing the first chapter? It's a version of the count-to-ten theory that some people recommend persons with quick tempers employ before exploding.

Harris warns that the "adult survivor of early loss must develop a strategy of how to love in a world where loss and abandonment are ever-present dangers."

"We can't expect solid, wholesome relationships until we have the courage to permit a man to enter our lives. We have to give a man the opportunity to demonstrate to us that not all men are no damn good. Only by recognizing what you do to chase guys away can you start to engage the men so that they demonstrate there are some really good guys," says Horn.

If women are as honest about the effects of fatherlessness as they have become in recent years about premenstrual syndrome, then they can discuss candidly with their boyfriends or husbands what to expect in a relationship with them. They can confess that fear of abandonment or rejection might rear its ugly head at any time in their relationship. They can ask their partners to forgive them and understand the disappointments, which sometimes revisit, that they have experienced throughout their lives. This way a couple can "separate out whether this is a problem with us or whether this is a problem I'm bringing to the table," says Horn.

I learned as a young girl watching television with my great-grandmother and my grandmother that problems arise every day. It's our response to them that determines their power over us. Each day those two women watched, without fail, *As the World Turns*. I have never been a fan of soap operas, but I was always fascinated by them. Each day there was some traumatic episode to report. Some woman had run off with another woman's husband; someone had lost a job; a cousin in the family had lost a baby; someone died; and on and on. Yet each day the same cast of characters appeared, affected but not destroyed by the tragedy.

The message I received, however subliminally, from those dreaded soap operas is that even the best persons can expect woes to descend upon them. Sometimes the difficulty was not of their making, but they would be called upon to manage the problem and rise above it.

The same is true for us fatherless daughters. The trauma we feel from the loss of our fathers is not of our creation, but we can learn to handle it effectively if we remember that regardless of what occurs, the world still turns. There is another day to remake or repair. And when the remedy truly isn't possible in a relationship, then we can rediscover. But above all, as Judith's boyfriend, whom she later married, reminds us: Not every argument, every misunderstanding, every change in the rhythm of a relationship should engender fear, should mean that we have to run for the exit signs. Change is part of the world's turning.

And in our daily evolutions we sometimes find ourselves alone. But Marianne Williamson once remarked that it is "better to be alone than to be living at half throttle." As Gwendolyn Brooks, taking the same perspective in her book *Aloneness*, reminds us, aloneness and loneliness are not the same.

I learned this lesson during one of my attacks of fatherlessness nearly a decade ago. I had just broken up with yet another boyfriend. I didn't give myself time to discover fully who he was before I had started clinging, afraid he would leave. I wasn't in love; I just needed to know that someone wanted me, even if I didn't really want him. The thought that he might not want me was what frightened me, foolish though that notion seems to me today. The guy was really a jerk, selfish and not very warm. I was engaged in this very intense tug of war: Should I let him go, tell him to hit the road; or should I hang in there? What is the reason for hanging in there? Although I never answered the question, I knew part of the reason was that I was afraid of being lonely. I wouldn't have anyone. This feeling of being rejected or abandoned would come crashing down. I needed to keep it at bay, which meant always, always having a romantic male presence.

Then I read Brooks's simple but profound book. In it, she takes the reader through the differences between being alone and loneliness. For a long time after reading it, I wondered for whom it had been written. Had her own daughter come down with a fit of panic? Had she, too, confused aloneness and loneliness? Eventually I learned the difference Brooks tried to illustrate. I came to appreciate and relish my aloneness, and understand exactly what I wanted and needed to manage that loneliness: Not a jerk, like the guy I couldn't release, but a true friend and lover.

9. FEEDING, DROWNING, WORKING

When Sandra was eleven years old, she carried 140 pounds on her five-foot, three-inch-tall frame. She had a voracious appetite. Chicken, Kentucky Fried—straight from the Colonel—was her favorite. Biscuits. Potato chips. Sodas. You name it; she ate it. She gorged herself.

By the time she entered high school, she resolved to fix herself—to lose weight. She hopped on the roller coaster. There was the grapefruit diet one week. A fast the next. Then something would happen, throwing her off her diet, and she would start eating all over again. Then she'd return to the grapefruit diet. The fast. She'd slip, and the pounds would be back—with a vengeance.

Sandra was running in circles, trying to get away from herself. She believed she was ugly and unattractive. Conflicted by her body image, desiring the attention of boys but getting very little, and missing her father, she made food her salvation.

"I was feeling bad, feeling lonely. I needed my father. There was this void in my life by not having him there. All the excess eating I did was to fill that void," she explains. "When you eat a lot of food, you don't have to feel. It takes your mind off what you're thinking."

Sandra has had a lifelong battle with obesity. She has been to four different therapists, and has suffered a string of failed relationships. She calls herself a "pleaser" and admits to low self-esteem, which brings with it fits of insecurity and doubts about her worth. She knows all of this is linked to her father. She can describe the rancid smell of fatherlessness, begun when she was a little girl living in the public housing of northern Pennsylvania.

"I felt we were different, especially when I started school. People would talk about their father's car and what their father did for them and where their father was going to take them that weekend.

"I didn't have any of that to talk about. So I would jump in there and talk about, well, my granddaddy took me here and there. But it wasn't the same," she says. "A part of me felt bad because I couldn't talk about my father."

I know her torment. I know the role fatherless women sometimes hope food can play in seducing our despair, even if only for a minute. For a long time, I relied on candy. One Easter, I devoured nearly two boxes of gold brick chocolate candy—in the same day. I didn't have an answer for my actions—at least not then. I was left alone at home, and as I walked the empty rooms, I ate one gold brick and then another, until they were all gone. I knew I would be disciplined for not following the orders my mother had issued, forbidding me to touch any of the candy, but it didn't matter. Those chunks of chocolate melting in my mouth brought me enough peace that I was willing to risk a few strokes on my butt. Throughout my youth, I sought the comfort of candy. It was my meal of choice—over red beans and rice, fried fish, and macaroni and cheese.

I believed no one would care if I missed a meal or two. In fact, I was sure no one would care if I disappeared. I was always on the periphery. I was the frayed hem of the garment made for my siblings.

Chocolate candy brought a satisfaction too delicious to share or de-scribe. In my room alone, when I nibbled on a Hershey's chocolate with almonds, I felt arms encircle me. When I sipped on a red soda, I could hear words in my ear—someone whispering, "I love you." For years, candy was the daddy I had never known but missed terribly; it was my lover, the warm caring husband I had sought. It was my protector keeping at bay those men who couldn't be trusted. What man would want a woman fifty or sixty pounds overweight; or one so underweight she was scrawny, with a spread of bad teeth? I didn't care.

"This is a powerful strategy for hiding your sexuality, attractiveness, and personal power from yourself and from others," explains psychologist Margo Maine, author of *Father Hunger: Fathers, Daughters & Food*, which explores the war young women wage against their bodies to cope with the inner emptiness of father absence.

Geneen Roth, in her book *When Food Is Love: Exploring the Relationship Between Eating and Intimacy*, tells of meeting with several women called the Breaking Free group. One day each woman was asked to bring in her favorite food. All twelve women brought chocolate in some form— cookies, candy, ice cream.

"Many women said they associated eating sweets with being with their fathers, with the way they were treated by their fathers. . . . The sweets didn't satisfy them; they needed something more substantial."

Some of the phases Sandra and I went through were part and parcel of the normal body changes and attitudes toward our bodies that visit adolescent girls, particularly African American girls. We were confused about what it meant to be pretty and were burdened by self-doubt. We also were affected by the very female notion of wanting to please men with our bodies. But with the fatherless daughter, the battle to achieve growth with some measure of confidence is more pronounced.

Oversaturating and Overcompensating

When Sandra reached for that bag of potato chips or the extra helping of the Colonel's chicken, and I reached for my candy, we didn't know we were exhibiting the "Over" Factor of the Fatherless Woman Syndrome. Many women attempting to deal with the pain and loneliness brought on by the absence of their fathers tend to *oversaturate*. They will use any substance or addictive process—food, drugs, alcohol, sex, or work—as an anesthetic.

The same strategy is at work when a fatherless girl attempts to starve herself as Sandra did with her fasting and unhealthy dieting. The eating disorders bulima and anorexia are simply other expressions of the oversaturation symptom. In 1994, nine thousand people in the United States were diagnosed with bulimia when admitted to the hospital. Experts estimate one out of three adolescent or young women suffer from the disease. That same year, eight thousand people were diagnosed with anorexia, according to the Centers for Disease Control and Prevention.

"By taming their hunger for food, they hope they will also tame their hunger for Daddy, for love, and for acceptance from men," says Maine.

African American women have a unique relationship with food. Much of what occurs in our culture occurs around meals and attending rituals. The Super-Sunday meal, with fried chicken, candied yams, collard greens, corn, and a host of other items, remains a familiar and treasured event even in many of today's African American homes.

Few black men, even during this age of interracial dating and marrying, desire rail-thin women. Consequently, some black women believe that in order to catch a man, they must maintain ample hips and ass. So when a girl eats, her hips become round, her face plump; no one raises any questions. No one worries that she's had too many helpings of peach cobbler, or that instead of eating a real meal she's putting away a pint of chocolate-chip ice cream.

As a cultural group in the Americas, our own attachment to food may have well begun when we as slaves were ripped from a patriarchal society in Africa and transported to foreign lands. In order to cope with the absence of our biological fathers and the African society dominated by compassionate yet strong men, we reverted to food as solace. It became the instrument to bring our families together, to help us forget those who had been sold away from our arms, those who had simply run away—unable to bear the tortures of bondage any longer—and those from whom we had been separated in our native lands.

Our attempt then, as now, wasn't to become compulsive. The attachment to food is more a coping mechanism, a way to survive, to keep from growing crazy. Some psychologists call this a kind of compulsion, a deep emotional despair.

While food may be good for the soul, as the old axiom reports and

many African Americans believe, it certainly has not healed our wounds—
either ancient or contemporary—of fatherlessness.

From Coping to Addiction

Where food fails, some women hope drugs—marijuana, heroin, cocaine, or a host of prescription drugs and other chemicals among the
plethora now available in the United States—will succeed; these women
turn to these substances to kill the pain. When a tooth hurts you use
Orajel or some other medication; you may shun the dentist until your pain
gets so unbearable that the over-the-counter drug is of no consequence.
Similarly, the fatherless woman uses that double shot of Chivas Regal or a
thin line of the white powder for medicinal purposes. Not unlike the
Orajel user, or Sandra and me, the fatherless woman continues to use
these substances, believing that she is adequately coping with her emptiness and suffering.

For a time, as Sandra testifies, the hurt is held in check. The fatherless woman who oversaturates feels warm, safe, and secure. She sees her
method as effective. Consequently, her reliance on these transformative
substances continues through every broken relationship, every disappointment, every perceived rejection, every real pain, until what started
out as a method for coping with the hard edge of life becomes compulsive
and addictive. And still, the specter of fatherlessness haunts her.

The National Institute on Drug Abuse (NIDA) reported that in 1998
9 million women had used illegal drugs during the past year; 3.7 million
women had taken prescription drugs nonmedically during the past year.
Almost half of all women age fifteen through forty-four had used drugs at
least once in their life. Of those women, nearly 2 million had used cocaine
and more than 6 million had used marijuana within the past year. Most
women drug abusers used more than one drug. *Surprisingly, twelve- to
seventeen-year-old females surpassed males of that same age group in the
use of cigarettes, cocaine, crack, inhalants, and legal drugs.*

Misty Brown began her dance with drugs when she realized that she could no longer contend with the ravages of fatherlessness. She and her stepfather had a strained relationship. She had satisfied herself with the comfort of a male friend of her mother; she called him her "play daddy." He died when she was sixteen, and her world caved in. She became chaotic, belligerent, and angry. First she tried to commit suicide and failed. Next, she took up with the Black Panthers while simultaneously entering the world of drugs with high-school classmates.

Who really paid any attention then? The country in the 1960s and 1970s was in the throes of a cultural revolution. Seemingly, everyone was having sex with everyone, regardless of gender, race, or color, and when they weren't shacked up in bedrooms, they were stoned out in living rooms, experimenting with hallucinogenics like LSD, PCP-laced marijuana, and mounds of cocaine. But not all of these people were experimenting with drugs and chemical substances for the sheer hell of it. Some, particularly the women, did it out of desperation.

In his book *Rosa Lee: A Mother and Her Family in Urban America*, Pulitzer Prize–winning journalist Leon Dash charts the lives of one female-headed family, in which the mother, who was fatherless, gets involved with drugs, and the children, also fatherless, follow her lead. One daughter was fifteen when she began using cocaine.

That fatherless girls and women often get caught in the cycle of addiction is not difficult to understand. Much of American society— increasingly, a dysfunctional society of singles and divorcées—has resorted to some method of anesthetizing its pain. For some, television is the drug of choice, bruising the intellect with mindless babble and fast-cut, jittery images until the viewer is unable to engage in quiet, analytical reflection. The demons and ghouls are not all inside ourselves; they appear outside on television and in the movies. We sit there before the screen as oblivious as a heroin user nodding out. This is legalized, societally accepted addiction, and yet as lethal as illegal drugs.

Any review of the number of new pharmaceuticals hitting the market— to lower cholesterol, to control appetite and therefore lose weight, to control

acid, to control the urge to smoke, to improve memory—demonstrates
that the government through the Federal Drug Administration (FDA) has
become a bona fide dealer; the FDA certainly isn't your garden-variety
street-corner hustler with an undercover Magnum, but it is no less
dangerous. Like fatherless boys and men, fatherless daughters find their
own suppressants.

Maxine Harris, who works with women suffering from trauma, suggests that coping techniques are commonplace but extremely dangerous.
Often what the average person perceives as a defect, or even a developmental issue, could be a survival method acquired years before. Take for
instance an eight-year-old girl being raped; she might imagine herself
someplace else, not in the body on the bed that is being pounded by a man
four times her size. She engages in dissociation. If she is confronted with
the same danger, she may use the same dissociating technique. After a
while, she dissociates even when she isn't threatened; it has become a
habit. The woman has so internalized the coping mechanism that it has
become a part of her permanent persona—unless she is able to recognize
what has occurred. Most of us don't.

Medical and health professionals have acknowledged the validity of
dissociation and other coping techniques. Except among a few dissenters,
like Harris, little official connection has been made between fatherlessness and the increasing drug use and general substance abuse among
women and young girls. Nor has the establishment bothered to connect
the use of drugs to the growing incidence of obesity, eating disorders, and
the rising rate of divorce in America.

Leaping Tall Buildings and Damn Near Killing Ourselves

Those of us who have had to face the challenges of growing up without
fathers know there is a definite link between women who are super-
achievers and women who have lost their fathers early in life. Often, that
achiever and that fatherless woman are identical—one and the same

person. These women also suffer the "Over" Factor of the Fatherless Woman Syndrome. They overcompensate in their personal relationships and in other aspects of their lives.

Not unlike Sandra, the overcompensator tries to please everyone all the time. She bends over backward, attempting to be all things to her mate, responding to his every need or perceived need even before he asks. At school and work, she aims to be on top. She is the one who takes assignments home, hiding herself throughout the weekend under tons of paper. No task is too great for her.

These are the superwomen, the Amazons, strong as any man, and able to leap tall buildings. They attempt to demonstrate that they are untouched by father absence; they assert that the men who walked away from them, whether through death, divorce, or abandonment, lost more than these fatherless daughters. The fatherless girl never wants to be dependent.

"It's just too dangerous a position," says Maxine Harris. And so we make sure we are fully self-contained units, like those lunchable snack packets for children that come with the meat, cheese, crackers, and dessert.

"You don't need anybody else because you can't count on anybody else. He can pick up and leave, whether by death, divorce, or whatever," she adds. This desire to be our own person, while being driven by the Fatherless Woman Syndrome, can have a positive effect as evidenced by the push to succeed. Yet beneath the surface, the "flawed" motivation—she wasn't good enough for Daddy—is alive and well.

The twin to the Amazon woman is the Kewpie doll, so fragile that the slightest touch will break her in two. She must be taken care of; she cannot handle adequately any of the normal tasks of life. Consequently, she relies quite heavily on a man. This is the role she plays to cast herself forever as the daughter; and her male companion is always, always the daddy she didn't have as a child but now has as an adult. Eventually, like the Amazon, this role proves destructive.

Still, many African Americans assume the role of Amazon; it has to do with the cultural imperative. "As a group we have had to survive. We have not had options. Because your mate was sold, you couldn't die and not take care of your kids," says Gayle Porter.

"There has been a cultural press on us to be Amazon women that is different from white women," continues Porter. "Even when we no longer have to act as if we are Amazon women, the cultural habit and the immediate habit are so great that we continue to act as if we have to.

"Our ability to negotiate the role is affected by the relationship we had with our daddies. If we didn't have a positive relationship with our fathers or had an abandonment issue, our ability to be interdependent is going to be compromised: We are still apt to act as if we are not in a relationship even when we are, or we are apt to act as if we don't have a relationship with ourselves—only with him."

My daughter's new boyfriend is in town. She has gone shopping at the supermarket, buying all the foods he likes. Later, she prepares a meal of his favorites. He sits in the living room, reading, waiting for the table to be set and the food to be served. He does not volunteer assistance. This continues for a week. I am getting worn out just watching the routine: prepare breakfast, clear away the dishes, prepare lunch to take for work, get dressed for work. He does nothing. Finally, when he has gone back to his hometown, I ask why didn't he prepare a meal. "I tried to get him to do something," she tells me, "but he didn't. I didn't want to push it.

"Maybe he would get upset and leave," my daughter adds. Sometimes, the Amazon woman sees men as weak or impotent, or reacts against his use of power. She takes the power for herself, burdening herself with the attending issues of control, responsibility, and duty.

Very early in my life, I was like my daughter, trying to please every man—even if he didn't deserve it—and promising to remake myself—a newer, more nearly perfect Jonetta Rose. I muted my southern drawl, dissociated myself from the poverty of my past, learned proper dress and etiquette. I swallowed books, reading everything I could get my hands on, polishing my mind the way high-priced call girls are trained by their madams. I returned to college three times before I finally got my degree.

In the interim, I proved that I didn't need anyone: I became a magazine writer, a newspaper columnist, an editor, a political analyst, and an author. All the time, I repeated a line in a Nina Simone tune: "That'll learn ya!"

I wanted to teach my brother and sisters, the nurses at Charity Hospital, the man who was my mother's husband, Noel who left without a word, the others who came and left with more words than I care to remember—I wanted to prove to them that walking away from me, underestimating me, was their loss, not mine. I was every fatherless girl or woman, who, late at night, made a pact with herself to "show them, show them all."

I wasn't different from my daughter, or Ivory serving in the military, beating boot camp, running through rigorous regiments, shining brass, imagining the arrival of her father, Eddie Calhoun—a private—saluting her superior status. Or Tonya, shouting "I'm okay," holding up a law degree, two mink coats, and a Victorian home as proof.

"Earlier in my life, [fatherlessness] was great motivation behind academics and my need to excel. I remember thinking [Ben Knight's] going to be sorry," says Tonya.

"There is the belief that you will be such a star that he will find you and return," explains Maxine Harris. "You are no average daughter; you are an exceptional daughter and for you, he will come back. It is a child's fantasy. It may be that kind of powerful self-assertiveness grows out of that."

Too often, society encourages us. Our overachieving, overcompensating, workaholic tendencies are embraced. We are labeled the new, modern woman. We present the image of a woman in total control. But while we exhibit turtle shells, inside we are, still, screaming with pain.

Ending the Cycle

No one will hear us until we hear ourselves. The first step toward ending the cycle of oversaturation and overcompensation is understanding that food's main purpose in any life is to provide nourishment for the body—not the mind or the soul. A girl like me, coming from New Orleans where eating, as in the French culture, is an event, can become carried away with the importance of a meal even when she isn't suffering from a bad relationship. It took Sandra and me years to learn that it didn't matter how much food we loaded onto our plates or how many gold brick candies we ate in one day; our father hunger could never be satisfied by eating.

Conversely, if we starved ourselves—to death even—we would never instigate the attention we wanted from our fathers, nor could we control the pain we felt. We redefined food's role in our lives and found ourselves the better for it. Sandra enrolled in Overeaters Anonymous. Me? I just grew tired of trying, unsuccessfully, to use candy like caulking; the cracks remained.

So much of the "Over" Factor that fatherless girls and women experience as part of the syndrome is related to control—trying to gain it or lose it. We become compulsive. "Compulsion is despair on the emotional level," says Geneen Roth, author of *When Food Is Love*. "Compulsion is the feeling no one is home. We become compulsive to put someone home.

"Compulsive eating is a symbolic reenactment of the way in which we distorted our feelings when we began eating compulsively: we swallowed our feelings, we blamed ourselves; we felt out of control; we believed we couldn't get enough," continues Roth. "If we allow ourselves to get sidetracked into believing that food is our problem, we will never heal the wounds that we became compulsive to express."

Releasing our need to control and curbing our addiction are the twin motivations needed to deal with our compulsive behaviors, including the use of drugs. Any viable twelve-step program, like the one Sandra chose, is helpful. Naturally, substance abusers of all persuasions need treatment, followed by enrollment in the appropriate program. The key element of most twelve-step programs gets to the crux of the control issues affecting fatherless daughters—that is, that there are some things outside our powers. And that the one true Supreme Power is God—not us. We cannot make our daddies return, cannot force them to love us, do not have the power to alter the past; it already has been lived.

What is in our control, however, is a decision to reconnect to our femininity. Far too many fatherless daughters find themselves trying to father themselves. They try to rebehavior themselves as men. They try to provide all the things for themselves that they wished their fathers had provided, when doing so is nearly, and most often wholly, impossible. They arrive at the assumption that they don't need anyone and certainly not a man. When a man does try to enter their lives in a relationship, they have so completely and dysfunctionally adapted their lives to being without men that they cannot relinquish that position. They fight for control (there's that word again); they are determined to be the leaders. They are determined not to let their guard down, for one minute, for fear that their mate or partner will abandon them or reject their request for assistance: That rejection is *always* interpreted as a rejection of them.

"The Amazon neurosis is the way we have all learned to play the man: to go to him before he comes to us, to call first, to make the first move," notes Marianne Williamson. "The love a woman receives in response to [her Amazon neurosis], if it was love at all, is not the love that warms the night."

Audrey Chapman warns that "a girl's masculine and feminine sides must be in balance in order to allow her to enjoy future emotional interdependence." African American women must be ever vigilant. Everything in our communities denies us the right to be women. Even now, as I write this, my own struggle for equilibrium is constant.

In 1998, a lump was discovered in my right breast during my first mammogram. I panicked. I was afraid because I recently had heard horror stories from friends about their bouts with breast cancer. What's more, I didn't have any health insurance. The financial aspect was easy to resolve. The Authors' Guild provided some cash, and a local program affiliated with the American Cancer Society bridged the gap. When I went into the hospital to have the lump removed and a biopsy performed, I was determined to go it alone.

My boyfriend wanted to take me to the hospital; I refused. He wanted to pick me up from the hospital; I still refused. And so, after spending all day at Providence Hospital in Washington, D.C., I stepped out alone to the curb to catch a taxi to a pharmacy to purchase painkillers; then I caught another taxi home.

My actions clearly indicated that I had determined the bruising from the surgical procedure was much more bearable than permitting myself to be vulnerable, to be at the mercy of someone else, someone who could disappoint me or, God forbid, abandon me. It wasn't that I was the Amazon, or Iron-Jonetta. The truth is, I was exhausted, and because I had made the choice I did, at the end of the day I felt extremely lonely. But for me, being lonely was much more bearable than being rejected.

My response to the medical emergency was a relapse. I had thought I had fully relieved myself of the need to be all things, and certainly of the fear of reaching out for assistance or accepting offers of help from men. But it proved I had not fully reclaimed my femininity, nor had I fully disabused myself of the sins of my father. Instead of becoming frustrated, I simply reminded myself that not every no is a rejection of me, and if a person is a few minutes late, I should not begin to determine that the message of his tardiness is that he is untrustworthy, sure to abandon me just as my father did. Human beings have human frailties, which in many cases have nothing to do with me. And, yes, it is okay for me to be soft, gentle, a woman in the traditional sense. Femininity is not a synonym for weakness. We women have a different kind of strength. If you doubt it, ask any man; he can describe it for you.

I am learning that I can eliminate some of the survival techniques I developed years ago in response to the trauma of fatherlessness. Some of those coping skills Harris talks about and of which, for years, I was completely unaware. I don't have to pretend I'm not present to handle the fears; I don't have to resort to any substance to anesthetize relived traumas; I don't have to play the role of emotional cross-dresser. I can be myself; I can be a full woman and celebrate what that means.

10. WHAT'S ALL THAT SCREAMING ABOUT?

"Young lady, why are you so angry?" asked Joe Black, a vice president of Greyhound Corporation. We were in a restaurant bustling with the more prestigious members of the Jackson, Mississippi, black community. Back then, during the early 1970s, on Saturday nights the place would be packed with sweaty bodies shaking off the turmoil of a week of work and the demands made by white business owners who cared little for the plight of their employees and greatly for the profits they reaped. On those nights, no one was impressed by professions, positions, and the parlance of the petit bourgeois; a black man or woman trying to act hifalutin could find himself or herself being escorted out, as surely as could someone with the wrong attitude looking to fight the first person he heard talking.

That afternoon, there was a greater tolerance: The restaurant was filled with pastors, university professors, community activists, businessmen, and would-be politicians—mostly men, and definitely the petit bourgeois. They gathered each month for lunch and conversation about how best to improve the status of African Americans in the city. Their discussion that day centered on establishing a more equitable distribution of state funds for education. I listened patiently to the timidity of the people who called themselves leaders, and my blood slowly boiled.

Finally, I couldn't contain myself. I pounced on them for their failure to fight the establishment, for ignoring the plight of people I saw daily. If I had been a dog, foam would have been oozing from my mouth. Instead, my voice connoted disgust and severe disapproval. I told them that while it was great to be concerned about lofty issues, there were more severe conditions in Jackson affecting people's everyday lives that had to be ad-

dressed, and asked when they were going to do something about the slum-
lords, about the denial of rights for welfare recipients, about the lack of
jobs for blacks.

I dismissed Joe Black as another of the so-called leaders who wanted
to cover his butt and didn't like being upstaged and uncovered by a young
black woman; years later, we became friends. But that day in Jackson,
Mississippi, I had no answer to his inquiry; that answer arrived nearly two
decades later. By then—after witnessing my arguments with taxi drivers,
bus drivers, politicians, and perfect strangers—dozens of other people including my own daughter had asked the same question in sundry ways:
"Why are you mad all the time? Do you have to be so mean?"

If I do not speak out, who will? I reasoned that my anger was appropriate. Righteous indignation had become an invaluable commodity in a
world where people accepted injustice far too quickly.

Privately, I probed for an answer: Who, and what, had given birth to
such expansive hostilities? The response to that unrelenting, yet silent,
inquiry almost certainly led me to a corner where there was only the
shadow of a man. I begged him to step into the light; told him he shouldn't
be ashamed of knowing me, of being with me; laid out my accomplish-
ments in chronological and fairly detailed order. Were not these works of
which anyone would be proud—black sheep or not? But he remained in
the corner, hiding, unwilling to acknowledge me.

Most mornings, before heading for work, I unconsciously mixed a
Molotov cocktail of anguish and determination. I carried it with me,
tossing it at the slightest provocation. Sometimes I was caught in the ex-
plosion, confused: Who was the real culprit—a man I wanted to call
Daddy, my mother, or me?

Shouting and Stabbing the Hurt Away

For years, I unwittingly exhibited the Rage, Anger, Depression (RAD)
Factor of the Fatherless Woman Syndrome, which wears myriad faces
and speaks multiple languages. Sometimes the RAD Factor presents

itself in oversaturation/overcompensation conduct. Most times, however, it presents itself as a searing violence, frequently perpetrated against the absent father or the present mother; it can also be, as I demonstrated in my behavior, a generic assault on anyone bold enough to enter the fatherless girl's hemisphere.

"I was five when my father was assassinated, so I had no concept of who my father really was. I had been told, but imagine trying to really understand or put it in its proper perspective at that age. When it finally became clear to me around fifteen or sixteen, I was angry at him because he left me. So I didn't want to have anything to do with my father," the Reverend Bernice A. King wrote in the April 1998 issue of *BET Entertainment Weekly*.

Carolyn, a thirty-something fatherless woman who wrote to me after reading one of my essays, said, "I was fifteen years old when my father died. For over a year afterward, I walked around in a kind of a daze. I felt that I had only known him for two years; he left my mother with five children to raise alone when I was five years old. My six-year-old sister had just died.

"I did not see him again until I was thirteen, when he came home for my mother's funeral. She had been killed by a jealous ex-boyfriend; he decided to stay to help my grandmother with us as much as he could.

"He and I became very close in those two years. He was a friend, my buddy, my dad. We would talk about anything together. It devastated my world when he died. How dare he come back into my life, become my friend and the father I never knew, and then die!"

Carolyn's anger, and that of most fatherless daughters, came because she lacked an appropriate outlet. Frequently, the remaining parent, or in Carolyn's case grandparent, cannot take the time to guide the child in the release of that anger and rage, or in proper grieving. Consequently, the pent-up frustrations morph into RAD.

Qubilah Shabazz was four when, in 1965, she witnessed the assassination of her father, Malcolm X, at the Audubon Ballroom in Harlem, New

York. In 1995, she was accused of plotting the assassination of the man nearly everyone believed, although without evidence, had been responsible for Malcolm X's murder. Her hopes to have Nation of Islam minister Louis Farrakhan killed were thwarted when the person whose help she sought in that quest turned over evidence to the FBI.

But Qubilah's troubles didn't begin in 1995; they almost certainly began with the untimely death of her father and the unarticulated anguish she felt. As an adult she found herself traveling from relationship to relationship, dependent on substances and generally disoriented, absent the emotional anchor a father provides.

At the time of her arrest on the murder conspiracy charges, she told the *Minneapolis Star-Tribune* that her mother, Betty Shabazz, told stories filled with such passion that for years she and her oldest sister, Attallah, believed their father still alive.

"I didn't understand that he wasn't coming back until I was six," Qubilah said. No doubt when she made this discovery, there was some unspoken anger toward her mother, which seethed for years, especially since she related to her parents dichotomously. Her mother was the taskmaster. She called her father the "soft" parent.

"He almost had me convinced that I was made up of brown sugar," she said. "Every morning, he'd take my finger and stir his coffee with my finger. He said it was to sweeten it up. I'd wait up at night for him to come home.

"Growing up, I was always angry he left me behind," she said. "I resented the fact that he was not a grocery-store clerk. My rationale was if he were a simple store clerk, he would still be here."

She was so angry over her father's death that she abandoned his religion and the lifestyle he had fostered when he was alive. She left Islam and became a Quaker.

Although she may not have wanted to be known as Malcolm X's daughter, to carry the baggage that came with such an acknowledgment, she wanted to be someone's daughter. She wanted to belong. Yet all the men she chose were like those Beth Erickson claims to have selected. Two years following her arrest for murder conspiracy, Qubilah married a meat salesman, who, she claimed, beat her. Eventually, they separated. Shortly after that her son, whom she had named for her father, set fire to his grand-mother's apartment, where he had been sent by the courts to live. (Betty Shabazz subsequently died from injuries sustained in that fire.) Malcolm X's grandson, his namesake, also was fatherless. The cycle of fatherless-ness and anger had been passed on, all too successfully.

For years, after that chance soda-stand encounter with Bill, whenever his name came up, I steamed inside. What gave him the right to dismiss me as lightly as some dust rag? I was tired of fathers wounding me, then walking away. If I couldn't make the culprits pay, then other men—their surrogates—would bear responsibility for their actions. I even exhibited a passive anger toward Bill's mother, who for a time had lived with us in the Florida Avenue public housing complex. I tossed my anger at my mother, demonstrating a flippancy and total disregard for her authority. When I was fifteen, I ran away from home, staying with friends for over three days and then daring my mother to react to my reappearance. She had taken Noel away years ago, and now I was old enough to let her know, however impulsively, how I felt about her theft.

The generic anger toward my mother and men in general wreaked havoc on my romantic relationships. The slightest provocation not only sent me running, struck by the triple fears, but also prompted me before I left to slam a bushel of profanities and insults into the head of my mate. Sometimes, even when there wasn't any instigation of my rage, I somehow resorted to this behavior, using it as an effective weapon to keep anyone from getting too close; close was dangerous.

"For some, the only way to keep a safe distance from loving relation-ships is to adopt an angry and confrontational demeanor. If one is suffi-ciently prickly and hostile, one can be assured that no suitor will get close enough and no loss will ever occur," explains psychologist Maxine Harris.

Says Audrey Chapman, "Anger is as much a defense as the super-achiever [mode] is a defense. The fatherless daughter is saying, 'I don't need you. I don't need nobody. I never wanted to need you and I don't care if you don't ever come back.'

"[A fatherless daughter] gets involved with men she can fight and argue with, and act out some of her anger that she's feeling about men in general. In this case it's like all men become an enemy. Or she wants to parent all of them," continues Chapman, citing as an example a woman she first saw in her practice in February 1999. The woman's boyfriend couldn't pay his bills, so she assumed responsibility for them. Then, he almost lost his town house, so she began to make the loan payments for that. "I haven't gotten all of her history yet, but I can bet somewhere in there, there is some father stuff."

In the case of her client, Chapman says there doesn't seem to be a problem, because the man then assumes the role the client would have assumed as a daughter, and the client becomes the father she wished she had had. "But it's dysfunctional; at some point she's going to get tired of it because he's continuing [to be dependent]."

This anger and uncontrollable rage projected by the girl who has lost her father through either death, divorce, or abandonment is not always expressed in shrieking and shrillness; it can be as benign as habitual tardiness; forgetting or losing things; perpetually bemoaning the state of things to the point it becomes whining; withdrawing from a partner sexually; or simply refusing to talk with anyone. While I was pissing off everyone with my belligerence, I employed several of those approaches. There was a time in my early life when I was frequently late or simply didn't show up for an event, although I had made the commitment. My friends started calling me "Shaky."

I laughed off the nickname as another of my many peculiarities held over from the 1960s. I came to understand, however, that when I arrived late for an engagement, it was because I didn't want to be there, or I was angry with someone involved in organizing the occasion, or I didn't want to jeopardize my safe haven by letting anyone in my space. Mine was passive-aggressive behavior.

At the root of this kind of angry expression, and perhaps of the entire

RAD Factor of the Fatherless Woman Syndrome, is the desire for control. The fatherless daughter must be the decision maker. She has to believe that she is causing things to happen—they are not happening to her. She will determine when a relationship ends. She will determine when to drop her membership from a group. She will determine if she comes late or skips a meeting. Early in life, too many other people had control over her life, and look what happened. She carries invisible, yet painful scars. Therefore, it is not unusual to see the fatherless girl as a control freak.

One minute the fatherless girl seems harmless; the next she is ready to carve out someone's heart. In the mind of the victim, the response exceeds whatever infraction there might have been. In the mind of the fatherless daughter she has already cast the offender as her father. She will make sure he never hurts her again; she whips him to near death with her rage and anger, or uses her hostility to construct an impenetrable, cold, steel-like wall.

Still, in most instances, the anger and uncontrollable rage of the fatherless daughter are not premeditated. They are involuntary responses, lurking just beneath the surface, waiting to present themselves at any indication of rejection, the threat of abandonment, or the unspoken presumption by others of a fatherless girl's unworthiness.

Inside Out or Outside In?

Initially, fatherless girls camouflaged their rage, giving it a universal aura and keeping it hidden in personal relationships or inside their homes. Now, following the lead of fatherless boys who over the past two decades have increasingly terrorized society with sordid brands of violence, ravaging communities and creating death tolls that rival small wars, some fatherless girls have taken their hostilities to the street. They have turned their anger onto society, becoming involved in drug sales, gangs, murder, and general mayhem.

The number of women in prison tripled between 1985 and 1997, rising to 138,000, according to a report prepared by Amnesty International USA. The increase in crime among females represented faster growth than in the male population in the nation. Women's incarceration rose about 11 percent each year between 1985 and 1997, while men's rose nearly 8 percent. In the District of Columbia, the nation's capital, the number of women in prison jumped by 72 percent, from 400 to 712. Many of the women were products of female-headed households, and at the time of their arrests many had become heads of their own households.

"Children of single mothers are twice as likely to drop out of high school and significantly more likely to end up in foster or group care and in juvenile justice facilities," according to the Annie E. Casey Foundation in its 1995 Kids Count report.

"The relationship between family structure and crime is so strong that controlling for family configuration erases the relationship between race and crime and between low income and crime," say William Galston and Elaine Kamarck, authors of an essay entitled "Putting Children First: A Progressive Family Policy for the 1990s."

The National Center for Juvenile Justice reported a 125 percent increase in violent crimes committed by girls between 1985 and 1994. Further, female gangs are sprouting up throughout the country, especially in urban centers. Contrary to the *West Side Story* image wherein girls in gangs were basically cheerleaders, girl gang members are far more violent.

In the August 1998 issue of *Essence*, twenty-seven-year-old Isis Sapp-Grant told her story of life in a New York gang. She was fifteen when she entered. Her mother was a social worker. She talked of consistent violence, coming home with blood on her shoes and clothing. But the element that connected her with nearly every other girl gang member in America was that her father and mother were divorced.

Lowell Duckett, a retired lieutenant in the D.C. Metropolitan Police Department who worked in the Special Emphasis Unit, a unit that focuses on gang activity, says the majority of the girls in these gangs come from single-parent homes, suffer low self-esteem, and have a need to feel safe or protected. He says that while most female gangs tend to be un-armed, when they do have weapons, they are as violent as their male counterparts.

"Males will just fire enough rounds; females will empty the gun into you," he adds.

Once again, the fatherless girl, engaged in this type of violence, is hoping to ensure that she is in control. If the person doesn't die or isn't significantly injured, then that person will return to hurt her. Further, the fatherless daughter sees in her mind's eye the people who have hurt her. She is looking to get even, to settle the score. It doesn't matter if her targets are male or female. Both—mother and father—in some way have caused her agony. They should pay.

Sometimes the fatherless woman in the throes of the RAD Factor turns the dagger on herself, and the rage and anger become a depression. She is unable to act; this inability to advance the course of her life may seem to some to be bland and without hostility. But while it is a passive song, the screeching wail has reached such a fever pitch only the soul hears it; the fatherless woman suffering depression deliberately wounds herself over and over each day.

When Sandra's relationship went bad with her telemarketer, she thought of suicide. When Misty's play daddy died, she tried committing suicide. At least twice in my life, I harbored the same anger, believing that I didn't deserve to live. That summer of 1988—that Summer of My Discontent—I was trying to steady myself after being fired, when the guy I had just begun dating decided to break up with me. I don't know why I re-acted so strongly, but it seemed the entire world was crumbling beneath my feet. There wasn't anything or anyone I could grasp to help me anchor myself. Twice in less than a month, I had been rejected—first by my em-ployer, then by this man. These were indications, I convinced myself, that I was useless and worthless. And while I pretended to be someone—an editor of a major black newspaper, featured on radio and television shows—in the back of my mind I knew it was all pretense, a masquerade.

The firing and the breakup had proved it. In a little while the entire city would know, I told myself, and if they looked deeper, beneath the surface, they would find me out. They would know that for all these years, no one ever wanted me. My family had ridiculed me and my fathers had abandoned me.

This thinking fully consumed me for days and weeks. Then one measure of that overcompensation the fatherless girl suffers took hold. It saved me. Had I not been so determined to be the one to say, "That'll learn ya," I am certain I would have taken my own life. As I pondered the thought, I realized that if I did so, then my fathers would have won; I wouldn't be alive to rub their noses in my success. I called a psychologist friend who referred me to a therapist. After two or three sessions, however, I left, only to return to behavior that exhibited various symptoms of the Fatherless Woman Syndrome.

The National Women's Health Information Center reports that studies of "women of color" found that "black adolescent females tend to report depressive symptoms at higher rates than white adolescent females. Rates for completed suicide among black adolescent females remain lower than rates for white adolescent females, although rates among these young black women have increased in recent years."

The Stories RAD Tells

If it is true, as Maxine Harris tells us, that the child who loses a parent early in life carries a "destructive metaphor in which they are cast as dangerous and deadly perpetrators, metaphors of toxicity in which the individual believes herself evil," then it is easy to comprehend the assertion that the external expression of violence is really nothing more than our screams to ourselves. The first step for dealing with anger is listening to yourself. Often we suppress the voice that tells us we are unhappy, the voice that wants to affix blame beyond ourselves. Instead, we internalize it. If we listened to that voice, we might find that anger, when properly channeled, can be healing. It can allow us to recognize that things really aren't right in our world. It can help us focus on what or who is causing us to get out of whack and it can direct us to the path of peace. But none of this can happen if we ignore the message our soul is screaming.

There are many faces of anger—not all of them bad. Carol Tavris, author of *Anger: The Misunderstood Emotion*, says that "anger, like love, is a moral emotion."

Tavris adds, "I watch with admiration those who use anger to probe for the truth, who challenge and change the complacent injustices of life—who take an unpopular position center stage while others say shhh from the wings."

Consider my first reaction to Joe Black. I believed my anger was rooted in righteous indignation; the haves in society were not treating the have-nots well. I wanted something done about it. Properly channeled, that anger could have propelled me to seek solutions, to force the government or others in the community to act. But my anger wasn't simply about injustices. Had it been, it would have more perfectly sculpted my consciousness and spirit, leaving me a more caring, loving human.

Moral rage emboldens. Think of it as a kind of heightened and heated compassion. "It is essential to the first phase of a social movement. [Rage] unifies disparate members of the group against a common enemy; the group becomes defined by its anger," asserts Tavris. The women who first launched the women's movement were angry—even enraged. Theirs was a moral anger. But as Anne Roiphe notes in *Fruitful*, that anger went off track. Their rage became misdirected and eventually caused them injury.

Similarly, the rage, anger, and depression that are evidenced by the RAD Factor are destructive—to the fatherless girls and anything or anyone sprayed with those emotions. The voice of that anger is not the mature, wise voice of moral anger, but rather a child's voice—the one who remembers vividly the last day she spent with her father; the one who remembers the exact number of father-daughter dances she missed or, like Helen, the number of Father's Day cards she had to make for her grandfather when everyone else in her elementary class made cards to celebrate their dads. She didn't know hers, and when she found out who he was, she didn't like him at all.

But in order to heal herself, the fatherless daughter must put away childish thoughts and behavior. After all, anger, rage, and depression do not alter the historical equation. Our fathers left and in many instances they are still gone. We cannot repair that tear. I can't go back to that day in 1956 when I sat resplendent on the Buick with Noel, regardless of how long I hold that photograph in my hand, regardless of how many Our Fathers and Hail Marys I recite as penitence. It's all water under the bridge. We really must get over it.

Marching past the pain requires unflinching determination to grow and take responsibility for our own lives. It wasn't until I was able to answer Joe Black's question, and my daughter's question, that I began to see change in my life—positive change. I came to understand that the entire world wasn't against me, that, if anything, I had been my own worst enemy. The anger I held, like a treasured possession, was keeping me from reaching and relating to people in my life.

Even more important, my anger was blocking my own access to myself. I couldn't even begin to appreciate myself, the quirks in my personality, the principles for which I stood, the way I wanted to love and be loved, if I permitted this weapon to be drawn every time I got close or someone else came too close for comfort.

The most difficult thing, and one with which I continue to struggle, is my still insufficient ability to release the need to control. Each time I find myself in a friendship or romantic relationship, I work hard to accept the person the way she or he is. I try not to demand immediate answers to questions that I have just now placed on the table. I remember that everyone is entitled to her or his own views and that if those views are in opposition to mine, that difference of opinion does not imply that my view is worthless or that my new friend is rejecting me. Most of all, I remember something that people in twelve-step programs learn, and repeat often, commonly called the Serenity Prayer: "God, grant me the serenity to accept the things I cannot change; courage to change the things I can; and wisdom to know the difference." This prayer gets to the core of freeing oneself from anger, rage, and depression.

There really are things we can't change.

11. PURPLE DRESSES, LAVENDER BEDROOMS, AND NO ONE LOVING ME

I vory remembers that Easter as if it were yesterday instead of over twenty-five years ago. She, her mother, sister, and brother lived in public housing at 317 East Ranor Street in Syracuse; their telephone number was 475-4780; she can't recall the area code. Her grandmother and grandfather also lived in Syracuse. Her mother worked as a domestic to supplement the welfare check she received. On a specific day of the month, Ivory and her siblings took the shopping cart to pick up the food commodities that the government regularly distributed: peanut butter, cheese, and canned meat.

To Ivory, the public housing complex felt like a middle-class neighborhood. Their town house shared a front porch with one neighbor and a back walkway with another. The sounds of Motown escaped from their record player. Her mother was a fanatic about cleanliness. On Saturdays the children dusted the furniture and cleaned the house with the kind of thoroughness most people reserved for the annual spring overhauling. The linoleum floors were kept bright and slippery with wax. Imagining themselves at an ice rink, Ivory and her sister often slid down the long hall that separated their room from their mother's.

For a time she thought Harvey was her father. He and her mother had married and had a daughter of their own—Donna. Although he was only her stepfather, she held on to Harvey; he offered her security and consistency. There had been pleasant occasions with Harvey: Early one morning, she got out of bed before any of her other siblings. Harvey was already awake and getting dressed to leave. "You wanna come?" Ivory nodded her head yes, eager for an adventure with Daddy. The two spent hours together. It was almost noon before Harvey finally called his wife to say that Ivory was with him. This memory brings smiles.

But then Harvey and Ivory's mother divorced; Ivory was six. Three years later, her mother brought Ivory into her bedroom. Ivory doesn't remember the season, or the weather, or even the date that her fatherlessness was brought into sharper focus, slaying her with double abandonment.

"Do you know who this is?" her mother asked, handing her the two photographs.

"No."

"It's your father."

"I thought Harvey was my father."

"No, he's not."

"Is he Nate's father?"

"No, he's not."

"Is he Donna's father?"

"Yes."

"Well, if he's Donna's father, why can't he be me and Nate's father, too?"

Ivory stared at the pictures: In one, a slender man dressed in a white shirt, string tie, and dark jacket looks into the camera; a trace of a smile rests on his face. His hands cup his crossed legs. A small television sits on a huge black trunk—the kind college students used to take with them when they went away to school. On the other side is a table with a long, white candle, unlit.

The other photograph is slightly faded. The man in it isn't smiling anymore, although he still looks directly into the camera. He looks a bit worn and lonely. Instead of the television, there is a record player on a dresser. Next to it is a black doll, still in her box. Maybe the doll is for his daughter. Maybe he intends to keep it no matter how long it takes for him to get to her. Maybe he is leaving soon, on his way to Syracuse. He never arrives.

Perhaps Ivory's mother called her into the bedroom that day to prepare her for the distinctions that were sure to be made between her oldest and youngest daughters. Perhaps she had already seen the hurt in Ivory's eyes and wanted to soothe it by making clear that Harvey wasn't her father. But the sudden appearance of another father sent Ivory's world into further chaos. Suddenly she felt more alone, depressed. She felt ugly and unworthy. As a young girl, she couldn't articulate those feelings. The words refused to take shape in her mouth. There was just a heavy weight she dragged around with her, like wearing an overcoat in the heat of summer. She began to wonder about the father who left her. Where was he? Why hadn't he stayed?

She consoled herself with the fact that she had Harvey; he was still like a daddy to her. But the divorce began to change their relationship. His attention turned more toward his biological daughter, Donna. The first unforgettable shift came the Saturday before Easter:

"He came by the house with a real pretty dress. It had flowers and a purple sash for you to tie at the waist. But he only had one dress. My mother always told people that anyone who did something for one of us had to do it for all the others. She didn't want them making a difference between me and my sister.

"Donna was lighter than me, but we had the same grade of hair and it was the same length. My mother often dressed us alike; sometimes we had on different colors but similar outfits—almost like we were twins. I think that's how we felt about our relationship.

"But this Easter, Harvey brought a dress just for Donna. He said he had enough money only for one dress, and that he'd get me a dress on his next payday. I never got that dress from him."

I'm Not Good Enough, Ever

Rejection is indelible. It imprints a child's mind with a scorching pain. The fatherless daughter replays the image over and over throughout her life, unconsciously. Each experience is consumed by the ever-present questions: Am I worthy? Am I lovable?

Neil Kalter, a professor at the University of Michigan, sharing with readers of the October 1987 edition of the *American Journal of Ortho-psychiatry*, the results of his study, "Long-Term Effects of Divorce on Children: A Developmental Vulnerability Model," offers that girls often experience "the emotional loss of their father egocentrically as a rejection of them."

Kalter continues, "While more common among preschool and early elementary school girls, we have observed this phenomenon clinically in later elementary school and young adolescent children. Here the continued lack of involvement is experienced as an ongoing rejection by him. Many girls attribute this rejection to their not being pretty enough, affectionate enough, athletic enough, or smart enough to please father and engage him in regular, frequent contacts."

Harvey's failure to bring that Easter dress created, in Ivory's mind, the feeling of unworthiness. Each time I revisited the Charity Hospital story, remembering the words "black sheep" and my desperate search for a face like mine, I reminded myself of my unlovability; my self-esteem sunk lower. When Helen's father abruptly discontinued their twice-monthly visits, it cut her deeply, leaving a scar that shouted, Can anyone love this girl? Afrika states emphatically that in her case no one does: "No one loves me." The statement is born of the rejection and abandonment that my daughter, too, felt by her father's departure.

"When the heart of a child is broken something inexpressible—and up to the moment whole and unquestioned—snaps. And nothing is ever the same," explains Geneen Roth. "We spend the rest of our lives trying to minimize the hurt, to pretend that it didn't happen, trying to protect ourselves from its happening again, trying to get someone to love us the way we, as that child, needed to be loved."

At the root of all the symptoms in the Fatherless Woman Syndrome— sex for love or anti-intimate behaviors, the Triple Fears, the "Over" Factor, the RAD Factor—is the simple but oft unspoken question: Do I matter? Am I worthy of love and respect?

"Once you realize the crux of the psychological issue is, *Am I any good, am I love worthy?* only then are you able to take steps needed to overcome it, to grab hold of your own life," explains clinical psychologist Wade Horn.

It wasn't by accident that I spent those quiet evenings in front of my grandparents' house on Mexico Street, plucking rose petals and saying, "He loves me; he loves me not," and that I didn't stop until the final phrase uttered was, "He loves me not." Who could love me? All my fathers—the man my mother married, my biological father, and then Noel, the man I wanted as Daddy—had left. Who would leave a child unless something was wrong with her?

Once a boyfriend asked me to change my hairstyle. Then, as now, I wore my hair in a natural. Until then, I had not put any straightening comb in my hair since graduating from high school more than twenty years ago. Although I was sure I did not love this man, I did not want to meet his disapproval, nor did I want to be alone. For the first time since leaving my mother's home, I put chemicals in my hair for a perm; my hair started to fall out. He insisted that I try something else, so I had a weave—a very crudely done weave. Finally, after a few days of being totally uncomfortable, I had it taken out. Needless to say, the relationship was on the track of failure. Several months later, he went his way and I went mine. I persecuted myself for being too weak to change my looks until I began to understand that there was nothing wrong with them in the first place.

No issue remains untouched by the question of worthiness and by the fatherless daughter's unspoken perception that she is not good enough. When she finds a great relationship, she sabotages it (the way I did with Willie), believing she is undeserving and fearful that it will slip away. She bends over backward to please everyone, not just men, harboring concerns that she will not be liked, that she will be alone and then lonely. She tosses her anger around like an explosive because she is too afraid that if anyone gets close, they will discover who she is; they will conclude as she has that she is unworthy of their time, their attention, their investment; she is unlovable.

"Girls whose parents divorce may grow up without the day-to-day experience of interacting with a man who is attentive, caring, and loving. The continuous sense of being valued and loved as a female seems an especially key element in the development of the conviction that one is indeed femininely lovable," says Neil Kalter. "Without this regular source of nourishment, a girl's sense of being valued as a female does not seem to thrive."

When Society Whispers "You're Not Quite Good Enough"

Arriving at a place of comfort is made more difficult for African American women, who each day meet a mainstream culture that absent segregation does not fully embrace the black aesthetic and personality. Even today, when more and more young people are singing black music, can recite the names of African American athletes, and don urban, Afrocentric attire, the whole of society still whispers to the black woman, "You're not quite good enough." Your hair is too nappy, your butt too wide, your nose not pointed enough, and your lips too full. This kind of subliminal rejection by America's patriarchal society forces African American women into the syndrome even when they are reared in two-parent households. That rejection accounts for the aggressive drive in some women—the desire to succeed, and the increased expressions of the RAD Factor through the burgeoning numbers of black women suffering depression.

The response to societal pressures is compounded for women and girls who grew up without their fathers. And so many black women are walking around today with complexes: We find it difficult to love and appreciate ourselves unless we have received external validation. The certification that we are all that and a bag of chips, too, can't come just from a girlfriend. Most often, we need a man to say it, to show it, to restore the confidence we permitted our father's departure to steal from us.

"Every day, a woman makes a choice between state of the queen and state of the slave girl," notes Marianne Williamson, author of *A Woman's Worth*, a book that explores the role of women in the world and the mistakes we make that minimize that role. "In our natural state, we are glorious beings. In the world of illusion we are lost and imprisoned, slaves to our appetites and our will to false power.

"Our jailer is a three-headed monster; one head our past, one our insecurity, and one our popular culture," she adds. "Love should never ask you to relinquish your own feelings."

There isn't a blueprint that a woman follows to learn to love herself, to forget the sins of the father, to soothe the pain and the scars of fatherlessness. Each girl or woman must find her way. But there are some common, generic keys that can help open a few doors. We must learn to celebrate ourselves and sing our own songs.

Sometimes when I'm blue, when something has taken me aback and my self-esteem is at its nadir, I climb into the bathtub or shower and sing about how beautiful I am, how much God loves me, how fortunate I am in being his daughter. There may be no man on Earth who appreciates me, but God does, I tell myself. The song is an affirmation of my worthiness that helps me to rebound. Creative visualization is another technique that I frequently employ. There are no men in the scenes I paint in my mind's eye, just me, walking in a meadow, talking with myself, stopping for a drink at a nearby lake, feeling the sun beaming on my face. It is a warm moment brought to me by me. Each day I find something to celebrate about myself that requires no external validation.

My ex-husband used to tell me that for every one of me there are twenty-five of the others. It was his way of forcing me to look at the unique traits and characteristics I bring to the table each time I come to sit. Once acknowledging the difference in me, I could acknowledge and accept the difference in others. It was, for me, the first step toward learning the meaning of unconditional love.

Too often, because of the trauma of our fatherlessness, we place conditions and limitations on the terms of engagement, if there is to be any involvement with others and ourselves. Sometimes, because no one can meet the superficial standards we set—not even ourselves—we go it alone. It is either everything we want or nothing. Sometimes what we want isn't good for us, but we think we deserve the worst, and so we reach for it.

"One of the most serious consequences of feeling you have to earn love is that you don't believe you deserve it if you haven't earned it. The moment your performance slips—whether at work, in your earning capacity, as a lover, in your physical appearance, or in some other external way—you feel that your partner will leave you. It's hard to believe that you can be loved just for yourself, because in the past that was never enough," says psychologist Masa Aiba Goetz, author of *My Father, My Self: Understanding Dad's Influence on Your Life.*

Balance is the goal to which the fatherless daughter aspires. In many situations, the dichotomy of "everything or nothing" does not need to dictate her choices, her course in life. She can have both worlds, even if not in equal proportion. She can permit herself to feel, to have an emotional response, and not to block out everything that might possibly cause her pain. To discover her worth, she need not look to the past, and any other person's response. What is inside her—the internal locus—is much more important. There she finds herself and the true meaning of her character.

By coming to a wholesome definition of who we are, what we want out of life, a definition void of others' interpretations, dissected from past failures, we may be able to arrive at a place where we finally come to love ourselves. Then the door has been opened to loving others and to understanding the impact of our fatherlessness.

As we assess ourselves, we should not reach for pathology, although clearly the Fatherless Woman Syndrome focuses on that. The effect of fatherlessness should not be a review of the gross behavioral or pathological activities, concluding that if they aren't present, then the father's absence had no impact.

"We have to ask about the psychological and emotional health of those kids," says Wade Horn. "We don't want to say to kids growing up, or to adults, 'You're doomed.' We do want to say, 'There may be some effects.' These effects are not isolated, however. They are universal." And, with attention and hard work, they can be assuaged.

12. HOME REMEDIES

When I realized I had to change my life—my approach to myself, my approach to other people, and my relationship with my past—I didn't go to a therapist or a psychologist; I didn't have the money. What I resolved to do was study everything I could about fatherlessness and its impact. As a result I developed some helpful insights, words of caution, and action steps. They are not all-inclusive, and each person must craft her own remedy. These are the lifelines that have helped me. They are offered in capsule format for your review; use them as you wish, and, as they say in AA-based programs, "Take what you need and leave the rest."

1. Achieving true sexual healing sometimes means abstaining from sex. Love and sex are not synonymous. Determine which you are seeking. If it's love, hold off a little while on the sex. Try to imagine what would happen if you or your partner suddenly became physically incapacitated. Could your relationship survive? Would you know he loved you, even if he didn't make love with you physically? Abstinence doesn't always mean physical abstinence; it could mean emotional abstinence, which protects the heart from seeking love for the wrong reasons.

2. Substitution is a wonderful solution for fatherless daughters who find themselves obsessed with the notion of having a baby. Take that drive to the nearest Hale House or hospital where infants have been abandoned and need human touch; try mentoring a young girl; volunteer at a local recreation center; enjoy the children in your neighborhood. Once upon a time in African American communities, it didn't matter whose child you were, you belonged to the community, and everyone watched out for you and treated you as their own. There is nothing to stop us from reviving that tradition.

3. Develop platonic friendships. Such associations offer the fatherless girl or woman an opportunity to better understand the male species, to feel comfortable in his world, and to distinguish a male friend from the father we unconsciously long for. I go to brunch with platonic male friends, to the movies, to dinner, to professional events. Some women may not believe this, but I have learned that men also like having platonic relationships. They can relax, free of the need to perform. And they can talk about other women: what to do about this one who is ready to get married after knowing him for only three months; or that one who is afraid to be close. (Sometimes we know the real reason for her behavior, even when she isn't telling him.)

4. Take the time to reflect. If we took the time to reflect between intimate relationships, the time to chart the patterns in our sexual encounters and failed relationships—why we entered them, when we entered them, and how we entered them—we would come to understand the flaw in our behavior. The point of reflection is not to assess blame, or ensure you have the latest HIV test before moving on, but to have a wholesome dialogue with yourself about what and who you are actually seeking. After a while, you come to know yourself.

5. Trusting others can come only when you trust yourself. Knowing yourself helps you develop confidence in your relationships with others. The constant need to please and convince others that they shouldn't reject you or abandon you is diminished. You also stop believing that every person is poised to reject you; therefore, you are willing to move in a little closer. You are willing to make a commitment. You trust that you can handle the situation because, yes, you have what it takes. And when you don't have what it takes, you know that, too, and you walk away not out of fear that the other person will leave you first but because he or the situation is something you don't want.

6. *Unlink Love and Loss.* See them as separate dancers in a room. Reach for love; hold his hand, move across the ballroom floor, fluidly, without any stumbling, as sure of his rhythm as you are of your own name.

7. *Face the difficulties. Life is one big, exciting challenge. We grow from the tough times.* So he has to go to work, and it's Saturday; find something to do with yourself. Don't cling. He will come back. You can't agree on whether to go to dinner or stay home; he wants to watch the game, you want to have a nice meal with candlelight and wine. Talk it through; be willing not to get your way all the time, without thinking he has disconnected emotionally or escalating difference into dispute. That he doesn't want to be with you every minute of the day doesn't mean he's looking for another woman. Relax. Even if he is looking, the world won't end.

8. *Sometimes it's better to fight than flee.* It can get downright tiresome, running every time something goes wrong in a relationship. Ask Judith Scott—for years that's what she did. Most fatherless daughters will flee, instead of staying and fighting for a relationship. Their flight is a testimonial to their own sense of self-worth and their confidence in their abilities. It is also a clear indication of their deep-seated fears. What if she stays and then he goes. Then once again she is rejected. So she goes first. Sometimes we should run from a situation or a relationship as fast as we can. Other times, we need to give ourselves an opportunity to know other people, time to work through difficulties, time to reconstruct our perceptions. We need to give ourselves time to see that we can make a commitment, that someone can make a commitment to us and the world won't end.

9. Take a lesson from soap operas like As the World Turns, *but forget the drama.* Each day there is some traumatic episode to report: Some woman has run off with another woman's husband; someone has lost a job; a cousin in the family has lost a baby. Each day the same cast of characters appears, affected but not destroyed by the tragedy of the moment. The next day it all begins again. Some of yesterday's problems have been solved; there are new challenges to surpass. The world still turns.

10. "It is better to be alone than to be living at half throttle," Marianne Williamson wrote. Gwendolyn Brooks, taking the same perspective in her book *Aloneness*, reminds us that aloneness and loneliness are not the same. "Loneliness," Brooks says, "is the absence of something or someone." Aloneness can be delicious; you are with yourself, enjoying every minute of it. Loneliness can be turned into a pleasurable aloneness.

11. When you find the right mate, be honest. Tell your partner—the one who hung in there with you even though you waited months before making love; the one who has become a real friend; the one about whom you've reflected; the one you see as love, unlinked from thoughts of loss—that sometimes you are a basket case; you experience a certain syndrome. Explain to him what it means and what he can expect.

12. Don't use food, drugs, or work to fill the lonely spaces. Abusing any of them can only cause greater problems. If you overeat, redefine the role of food in your life. If you've become addicted to food, drugs, alcohol, sex, or work, seek out any of the various AA programs, which are based on the wonderful twelve-step model.

13. End your relationship with overcontrol; control is central to compulsion. Geneen Roth notes, "Love and compulsion cannot coexist. Compulsion is the act of wrapping ourselves around an activity, a substance, or a person to survive, to tolerate, to numb our experience of the moment. Love is a state of connectedness, one that includes vulnerability, surrender, self-valuing, steadiness, and a willingness to face, rather than run from, the worst of ourselves. Compulsion is a state of isolation," she continues, "one that includes self-absorption, invulnerability, low self-esteem, unpredictability, and fear that if we face our pain, it would destroy us."

14. Learn the difference between the things you can change and those you simply can't, regardless of how much huffing and puffing you do. Many years ago when I lived in San Francisco, I was sitting in a car at a service station while a girlfriend pumped gas. An old African American man had been sitting in a chair; he came up to my side of the car and said, "Honey, what you worrying about? It's just a waste of time. If it ain't happened, it might not happen. If it has already happened, there's nothing you can do to undo it." And then, I kid you not, he walked away. I had been worrying about my job and events that had occurred two days earlier. It took me many more years before I could put that advice into practice, even partially, because I always believed I could control every detail and experience of my life. That was so foolish. Now when I catch myself trying to manipulate and maneuver for the purposes of controlling an outcome, I simply ask, What would happen if . . . if the worst thing I could think of did come true: if he left; if he never came back. Would I die? In 1988, I may have thought that breakup with my boyfriend would end my world; today, I have come to appreciate my resilience. I can't always handle every situation, but many I can, and when I can't, I'm smart enough now to reach out to friends. I don't have to do it all alone.

15. Amazon women are an endangered species; don't join that tribe. There is a reason these tough, hardworking, superwomen end up either alone or dead. It's simply too much for them—absolutely exhausting. Such behavior won't get the fatherless woman the relationship she wants with a man; why would any male mate with such a woman? What role could he play in the partnership, if she commandeers the masculine? And while isolation built the wall of protection around her, keeping others outside, she will discover that a lonely splendor is not what she wanted, after all.

16. Reclaim your femininity. Being a woman doesn't mean being helpless, but it also doesn't mean being a cold, steel beam. Rather, there is great strength in the feminine—ask any man.

17. Beating up on the world won't bring him back. Anger is as much a natural response to loss as sadness and grief. When you so much as break a glass at home, you are angry, especially if it's one of your best glasses. So why shouldn't you be angry if your relationship with your father has been broken, especially if that rupture was not a result of anything you did. But just as beating your neighbor who wasn't even in your home when the glass was broken isn't rational, whipping the hell out of the world won't bring your daddy back.

Check out the reason for your anger. Is it rational or irrational? Beth Erickson notes that "when loss is chronic and unresolved, all emotions have long since gone underground. Usually they leak out as displaced anger that smolders just under the surface." Like a fireman searching for hidden heat and potential danger, you may want to locate the smoldering emotions that Erickson talks about. If it's old "Daddy stuff"— douse it.

18. Don't turn the dagger on yourself. Now that you've quenched the fires of the unfounded anger you felt for others around you, don't turn it against yourself. The loss of your father, or of subsequent relationships in which you hoped to recapture the paternal love, is not reason enough to destroy yourself.

If causing injury to others doesn't bring your father back, neither will causing injury to yourself. If you feel suicidal or entertain thoughts of doing bodily harm to yourself, including actions associated with bulimia, anorexia, and substance abuse, seek help immediately. If you don't know where to go, simply call the nearest hospital; experts there can refer you to the right person or organization.

19. Listen to the voice within. If you are angry, acknowledge that anger. Try to discern the reason for it. Try to direct the anger properly. If you lost your father through death, then you did not play a role in that; you can't be angry with yourself. If he did not take care of himself and died from poor health, then you can't bring him back; forgive him and move on. Try to find a way, other than anger, to channel your grief. (I'll give you a few suggestions in later chapters.) If you lost your father through divorce, and he didn't maintain a relationship with you, reach out to him. Don't try to hide your anger; present it in a healthy dialogue about the pain you experienced. (See later chapters for more on this.) Try to understand that as a child, we saw the world differently. Our parents couldn't always articulate the challenges they faced; they made mistakes, too. Forgive them and move on.

20. When you ask, "Who is the fairest one of all?", make sure your mirror says, "You!" Building self-esteem is critical to the fatherless daughter. And yet, it may be the most difficult task she faces as she attempts to heal her loss. The first thing to remember is that your father's absence has nothing to do with you. Our egos may want us to think we were a factor, but we weren't. Although my mother said she didn't want John, my biological father, to see me because he threatened to take me away, the real reason is connected more to their dysfunctional relationship. I dismiss her logic and with it eliminate myself as the cause. I have learned, through the years, that controlling my ego gives me the opportunity to appreciate myself as I am. I think of myself as yet another of nature's wondrous snowflakes—each still unique among the millions of unique others. Growing to know yourself leads to growing to love yourself—flaws and all. It took almost twenty years after I wrote the poem "Peace" before I really found peace and truly learned to love my wide ass and spaghetti-thin legs. Now that I have, I have found a light no one can extinguish—self-love. Without it, I can never know real love.

21. Develop an internal locus. Several years ago I took a gender communication class at Trinity College in Washington, D.C. There I learned that men have an internal locus, while women have an external locus. That is, women often need external validation. Ever see the Special K cereal commercial, on which the men are all spouting lines that we have heard women say, including "Does my butt look too big in these pants?" It is a classic example of how we women, even those of us from two-parent households, often think. What matters to us is what our girlfriends say; the compliments, we get from our boyfriends. Fathers individuate their children; that is, they help them develop that all-important internal locus. Improving self-esteem means balancing that equation, so that our opinions of ourselves become more important. Did you fight to get to the top because you wanted to hear the praise of your peers, or to rub your father's nose into it, or because you wanted to achieve a personal, private goal that would make you happy? If it's the former and not the latter, then you've got problems: You don't think pleasing yourself is important enough. Change that.

22. Everyone is worthy of love and worth loving. The greatest gift we can give to anyone, especially ourselves, is unconditional love. That doesn't mean we don't work to improve ourselves—take off those few extra pounds that threaten our health, take that Spanish course, etc. What it does mean is that we don't beat ourselves up, and we don't allow others to abuse or humiliate us because we aren't perfect. I developed a reminder for myself after reading the book *Jonathan Livingston Seagull*, which describes the plight and determination of a young seagull who was not willing to spend his life in merely scavenging for food; he wanted to fly high and fast in the sky. When the elders of his village learned what he was up to, they banished him from their group. Jonathan continued with his mission. Finally, when he reached what appeared to be perfection, two other seagulls guided him to another land—essentially, Jonathan died. From that book, I learned that perfection comes with death. All of us struggling here on earth are still imperfect beings. We are all in more or less the same incomplete and, perhaps, misshapen vessels. So when I or anyone else whips me over my imperfections, I smile and love myself— warts and all—even more fiercely. And because I want unconditional love, I am learning every day how to give it to others. Can't have one-way streets where love is concerned.

23. *March past the pain.* Display an unflinching determination to grow. Take responsibility for your own life. You had no control over your father's leaving, but you do have some control over what your response will be to the tragedy. Don't go crazy, trying to overcompensate; don't become angry with the world; don't chase every man, trying to get him to love you the way you wanted your father to. Do allow yourself to feel the loss and grieve the loss. Then refashion your world.

24. *There is a big, wonderful world awaiting your full, undivided attention.* Too many people live their lives at less than half blast. Researchers have long said we use less than 10 percent of our brain power. Most of us don't even use that much. We are too timid about exploration and frequently permit circumstances to dampen our general curiosity about life. We are caught in the clutches of fear. The fatherless woman knows fear far too intimately. We fear we are unworthy; we fear we are unlovable; we fear we have no future without Daddy or some man to love us. Certainly Daddy was and is important. And both receiving and giving love are crucial to the total illumination of the soul. But you can't know any of this unless you release your historical relationship with fear. Resolve that fatherlessness

won't stop your world from turning. Things won't be sunshine, lollipops, and rainbows, but life isn't a ninja warrior waiting to ambush you and wreak havoc, either.

25. *Sing your own song—not "Strange Fruit," and not the blues.* Sing a sexy, energetic jazz song, filled with riffs and other surprises. Celebrate yourself, even if the world doesn't know your name.

BOOK THREE

. . . you fed me

red beans and rice
changed my diapers, afraid
all the time of being
tied to land
a woman who could possess you
the sea called you

—Excerpted from "Father,"
   The Corner Is No Place for Hiding

13. FATHERS AMONG US

I t is the kind of summerlike day that has earned Hawaii the moniker "paradise." Two young girls are on a small inflatable rubber dinghy, headed to a rock formation in the Pacific Ocean. When they arrive at their destination, they will hunt for seashells and catch fish trapped in the small pools of water. Their mother, who is on the shoreline, is worried that perhaps they are too far out. But their father isn't bothered. He swims alongside, pushing their dinghy to this location; it is one of many excursions he has organized—part of an unofficial course to sculpt his daughters into well-developed, independent women.

Already he has enrolled them in swimming, gymnastics, and music classes. He has taken them with him to his rugby games. He says that competitive sports are "character-building" and that they provide the opportunity to "work as a team; to learn to win well and to lose well."

"I wanted to get them interested in activities that, I thought, were important for their physical and emotional makeup," explains Russell, reflecting on that summer trip and his role in rearing his two daughters, who are now twenty-something. "I controlled almost everything with my girls. I have always wanted my daughters to become young women who were financially independent, living comfortably in their own homes, in professions that have to do with justice or service to humanity, linked with a man who shares the same values, and having hobbies and interests that uplift the spirit."

Back when Russell and his wife were in their twenties, they made a conscious decision to start a family; they stopped using contraceptives. They had had what he calls a sort of extended honeymoon for a few years.

However, unlike some modern couples, they had never imagined a marriage that didn't include children. Still Russell harbored some initial concerns. He wondered about how children might affect the lifestyle he had created, one that saw him forever involved in sports, work, or some social activity with his friends. How would a child change his life? he wondered. What would he have to give up? Was he prepared?

"I wanted a family. When I would have it was a different matter. It was postponed for practical reasons. We were busy doing things toward our careers."

Russell's own mother and father had separated when he was quite young. His mother returned to her parents' home in an Asian village, providing him and his two siblings with the comforts of a large extended family of aunts, uncles, and cousins. His brother and sister went away to boarding school, leaving him as "the surrogate kid," he says.

He wanted a similar environment for his own children. Consequently, he and his wife went to Asia. When they learned they were going to have a child, she left the task of finding a name to him. He came up with only female names. He seemed determined that they would have a daughter. "Probably it had to do with my personality. Also, I had been surrounded by women most of my life. I'm not one to play the traditional father role of playing ball with the boy. I don't have that macho image one associates with having sons. I wanted to mold my daughters in a nontraditional way," he says.

The couple's first daughter was born in 1975; two years later they had their second. He had wanted the two children, regardless of their gender, to be companions as they grew older. "I have seen families with one child, and I don't think it was the best thing for the child or the parent.

"I always thought of, definitely, a second child, and the second child should be close to the first so they could grow up together and do things together. I've always thought of my daughters as close friends, dating together and in general doing things together.

"I was quite happy to have daughters," Russell adds with a smile.

His children spent their first few years in the environment that had been Russell's during his childhood, covered by a warm blanket of loving great-grandparents, grandparents, uncles, aunts, and cousins. When Russell and his wife returned to the United States, his relationship with his daughters was not affected. Despite the switch to a "nuclear family," Russell remained a continuing influence on his daughters' development.

"I was always there with them," he says. "My wife always took a backseat. She trusted and respected my decisions. I am the one who picked the schools they went to. I was the one who picked the colleges," he continues. "Every major decision was made by me."

Russell was exact about the path he wanted his daughters to travel. Many fathers are the same. "I want [my daughter] to flourish in life, to find, if not answers, then good questions; to live at peace and even find serenity in her life; to be a good person to herself and to others; to understand that collaboration is a high art; one that involves deep understanding of human nature, people's foibles, their insecurities, and their fears, but also their dreams, wishes, aspirations, and deepest beliefs," says Michael Gregory Stephens, who is a contributor to *Fathering Daughters*, a collection of essays, which was edited by DeWitt Henry and James Alan McPherson, written by men about their relationships with their daughters.

"I want her to have true humility, which is not being too small or too large, but just the right size. I want her to express gratitude for her gifts," explains Stephens. "Yet I am articulating fatherly values, here, not daughterly ones."

Imagining Father

When I hear the stories Russell tells and read the aspirations Michael Gregory Stephens has for his daughter, I wonder what my life would have become if I had had a father who took such an active role. I realize that I have no solid definition of "father." What should he do? I ask myself. How should he talk to his children? What are these "fatherly values" that Stephens talks about?

I circle around these questions for months. I wonder: If I had known the answers to them, would I have reacted any differently in my relationships with men? Would I have dated different men, married different men?

"My mother never married," says Judith Scott, "so she didn't know enough about men. She didn't know the male perspective of the world. So when I decided I was going to get married to this guy that I met in the unemployment line, she didn't say, 'Wait a minute.' "

She explains, "If I had had a father, I know I wouldn't have dated half the men I did. Sometimes a man is able to see stuff guys do for what it is—bullshit."

A girl or woman who loses her father through death, divorce, or abandonment doesn't lose simply because he is not there with her, as Russell has been for his daughter; she loses, too, because she is left without models, definitions, benchmarks, and barometers. Like a person who once could see and suddenly becomes blind, she gropes in the dark, lacking other fully developed skills and senses that would have helped her compensate. Therefore, she is more apt to stumble, to fall, to injure herself.

"My wife grew up in a household headed by her mother. In fact, nearly all her aunts, female cousins, and sisters raised their kids without their fathers being around. Therefore, she didn't witness firsthand the partnership, compromise, and teamwork needed to make a marriage and a two-parent household successful," explains Steven Brown, a Maryland resident who read an earlier article I wrote about being a fatherless daughter.

"Not knowing exactly what the role of a father and husband should be means that my wife has expectations that are sometimes unreal, since they are based more in imagination than experience. She realizes the burden is not all on her shoulders as it was on her mother's, but doesn't always understand the sharing of responsibility that makes a group of people a family. It's a learning process, like everything else in life."

When I watch Russell help his eldest daughter search for her first apartment; when I hear him tell of their running around, locating furniture for it; and when I hear about the first time she invited him for dinner, I wince. I can hardly bear the agony of knowing what I have missed.

There wasn't a father there to take me swimming in the ocean. Hell, I still don't know how to swim. There wasn't a father to offer me a ride when it was snowing. No father picked me up from the supermarket when I purchased more than my small hands could carry. No father hung out with me at the movies, shared a joke with me, or offered manly advice. Certainly none helped me with furniture. When I got my first apartment, no one helped me to move in. I was well into my thirties before my mother ever came to my home for a visit, to say nothing of dinner.

I try to push aside the memory of this reality and embrace the opportunity for enlightenment. I watch and listen to men like Russell; along the way I come to understand what constitutes a good father.

Divining Father

"A father should be able to command respect of his daughters, by his profession, his activities, his behavior in public and in the home. He should be able to command respect of them and the people around him. It gives the kids confidence in themselves and gives them a sense of self-esteem if their father is engaged in activities that are respected," says Russell.

"He should be loving to the whole family and always there for them—to protect them, to support them. His children should be able to trust him," adds Russell who, on a rating scale of one to ten, gives his own fathering skills "about a seven."

"A father should battle for the right to spend as much time as the mother with his daughters," he continues. "In his daughters' growing stages, he should do as much with his daughters as he would do with sons, if he has any.

"Later in life, it's important for a father to be open to his daughters so that they are able to discuss things, like the men in their lives, and get advice. He should instill in his daughters the value of men—what men value in women; it's important they retain their femininity. In their quest for independence they should have sight of the value men place on femininity; one can be independent and self-reliant but at the same time be vulnerable and feminine," Russell says.

"I was always my daughters' great protector. I wouldn't let anybody take advantage of them, and was always fighting on their behalf. I felt my role was to provide security, as head of the household—making sure the environment was secure, which includes relations with my wife and finances of the home. I tried to protect them from various trials and tribulations; to support them, to advise them; and to love them."

Interestingly, Russell's perception of a father's role and what constitutes a "good father" is not far removed from those of the acknowledged experts.

Psychologist Masa Aiba Goetz suggests that a father always makes a priority of being there for his children. He expresses his affection freely and gives his children unconditional love and acceptance. He instills values and self-discipline, not by words but by his actions.

A good father also shows love and respect for his wife—such demonstration is critical for both male and female children. It is nearly impossible to develop expectations for a relationship if you have no model; a father's relationship with his wife serves as that model. Further, says Goetz, children should be included in family discussions, especially important ones. This kind of group interaction helps children develop negotiating and compromising skills, critical to any successful relationship.

Yet, we cannot share what we do not have. Many African American males are without the self-esteem that would anchor them in the confidence that Russell exudes. It is not untrue that they have been blasted and badgered in American society—stripped, in many instances, of their masculinity. And much attention is being focused on their plight. More frequently than are African American women, they are the subject of national conferences, forums, or seminars.

Lafayette Barnes, former president of the Washington, D.C., chapter of Concerned Black Men, says three traits make up a positive African American male: Respect for God and elders comes first. "*Spirituality* has got to be very important." Honesty comes next: "If a man is honest with himself, then there's a good chance he will be honest with his family and others around him.

"Then I think the other part of that is a love of life. You also have to enjoy yourself and not be so serious about everything. Enjoy playing with your children, enjoy loving and learning," he adds.

Jerome Meadows, an award-winning sculptor who lives in Savannah, was for many years a single father. Only because he was anchored was he able to rear his female child when his ex-wife determined that it was time for father and daughter to come together.

"Since my daughter and my son were young, I had taken on myself to become a person of the world. I needed to have a sense of globalness. I had a lot of opportunities to travel and made it a point to always involve them. My ex-wife was not in support of this; it became clear her values were not focused on the world," Meadows explains, echoing experts' conclusions that fathers frequently are the ones who introduce their children to their external environment.

When his daughter arrived to live with him in Washington, D.C., she was in her teens. And while society may say a daughter belongs with her mother, Meadows says that a daughter needs both parents.

"I found, dealing with my daughter, that she's got her own mind. That mind reached a point where it said 'I am.' It may have reached that point long before her mother and I or even society thought it should exert that kind of independence," he adds.

"She is comfortable with being a female. So some doors, regarding her femininity, are closed. The difficulties come not in her relationship with herself and other women, but in the relationships with men. I'd see her doing a lot of searching in terms of her identity with herself, issues of insecurity, love, self-confidence in her relationship with these young men. When I looked at these at the end of the relationship, the issue wasn't about discovering herself but how [she could] assess a male and his worthiness.

"There is a daily deluge of negative imagery about black men. Every time I'm in the paper for completing a successful piece of art, for me that erases the negative effects of weeks of photographs of black men raping people, killing," Meadows continues.

"To the extent she is able to come to me as her father or at least think of me as a male presence in her life, loving and giving and positive, that will help her, I would hope, to keep some bearing and not get so caught up in the confusion that she gets lost."

Drifting Apart

Clearly, being a father isn't any easier than being a mother. And as much as I have seen Russell's, Jerome's, and other men's successes, I have also seen and heard their frustrations. Sometimes father and daughter drift apart.

The rift between Russell and his daughters came when they entered their midteens. They were enrolled in boarding school in England and came home to Nigeria only for holidays. Sometimes he was home when they arrived. Other times, however, he was away, working in some remote African village, teaching farmers about irrigation systems or some other slightly modern function that had not earlier come to their homelands. "I started losing that connection; they were much closer to their mother."

Still, he involved them in his life. "I would swim with them; try to get them to ride horses; try to get them into playing golf with me, or tennis. But they were now having their own friends and not wanting to do things with me anymore.

"When they went away from us and I was concerned that they had a full life, I made sure that they pursued these things even though they were not with us and that they joined the right people. I was always very particular about who their friends were. I wanted them to move around with the right kind of people—warm, simple people, who were not pretentious. I wanted them to have friends who had the right sense of values.

"As they got older and I came to the [United States] with them, they became women. I was alone with them; their mother remained in Africa. I was probably too controlling—not giving them their space; trying to determine their every move, even the subjects they took in college.

"That created the conflict between us," Russell adds. "When they became women, I was not willing to let go."

Not long after graduating from college, his oldest daughter moved into her own apartment. The younger one still lives at home, but she, too, may move out soon. The last few years have been difficult for Russell, as such change is for most fathers who watch their little girls grow into women, ready to spread their wings and fly.

"Fathers have to learn to let go at a certain stage," he says. "They have to realize they are not going to be the only man in their daughters' lives."

I smile when I hear him say this. Fatherless daughters don't have anyone to let go of them. We wish desperately to have someone to cling to us the way Russell clung to the very last moments with his daughters. We want the security, the protection, the love he offered them. And although we are not absolutely sure how to define *father*, we still spend much of our lives searching for one—everywhere we go. Sometimes our search is internal—inside our own families; sometimes we must look elsewhere.

14. SURROGATES

My siblings and I called my grandfather "Daddy." For some reason, the rest of the children in the neighborhood took to calling him "Daddy," too, although most of them had fathers. They called my grandmother "Honey," which was the name my grandfather gave her. Her real name was Rose; I don't remember anyone ever calling her that. Sometimes, late in the evenings, to our delight, my grandfather loaded us into his blue Mustang so we could collect Honey from Buck's Famous Fried Chicken Restaurant in the French Quarter, where she worked as the head cook. As a special treat, Daddy stopped at Central Grocers and picked up a muffaletta. The Italian sandwich, loaded high with cold cuts, cheese, olives, and dressing, was a delicacy. It was big enough to feed at least four people. My grandfather divided a half into twos or threes, depending on how many of us had stayed up past ten o'clock to take the ride with him. In the backseat, our mouths smothered the sandwich, making it impossible for any crumbs to sneak past. Even today, when I want to recall those cherished nights, I stop in the French Quarter at Central, pick up a muffaletta, walk to a park or sit curbside, and devour my sandwich as I did in the back of that blue Mustang.

By calling my grandfather "Daddy," we fashioned a more intimate role for him. He tried as best he could to meet our expectations, taking us to school on some mornings, greeting us in the evenings after work with trinkets and tales, which we later came to know were lies, in the tradition of African American storytelling. Sometimes he acted as a brutal disciplinarian: Once my older sister and I had gotten into an argument and decided to see who could use profanity the best. We didn't know the next-door neighbor, Mrs. Bell, had heard us. That night as my sister and I washed dishes, my grandfather took a handful of soapy water and put it in our mouths; it felt more like a slap in the mouth than a simple cleansing of empty, dirty gourds.

"Next time watch what you're saying and who is listening," he admonished. I, of course, was indignant about the episode, challenging him that he certainly could not be any friend of mine and hit me. Eventually I forgave him his actions.

When my grandfather was too busy with work or his music, I would reach into a barrel of relatives, hoping to find comfort. Then, my extended family was filled with men of music and women of dance and spiritual magic.

My uncle Amos and aunt Loweska lived a short ride from our home. Although he eked out a meager living, working in the Zanco grocery store during the week and hauling trash on the weekends or in the evenings, to me Uncle Amos was king. He sported a muscular body and dark skin that shone like a jewel; my aunt's mulatto hue contrasted so starkly with it that on several occasions during the height of southern segregation, he received beatings at the hands of angry white men who, seeing the two of them together, believed him to have slept with one of their women. Despite the subsistence wage he earned, he provided my aunt with a wonderful home and lavished her with great affection and respect. He also extended himself to helping meet the needs of others in our family.

Before my aunt Loweska and uncle Amos moved to Louisa Street, we all lived near one another on St. Ferdinand Street; when we moved to 4712, they moved into 4712½. Sometimes when my mother had to work late, my siblings and I found ourselves around their table, eating dinner and listening to his jokes. My mother's absences and the absence of a father were made bearable by my aunt and uncle.

I recall the threat of a hurricane swooping down on tiny New Orleans. The city rests below sea level; any strong storm threatened to send the water rising up to drown us all. Knowing we were alone, Uncle Amos gathered us together in their tiny house. The wind whipped through the trees and pounded against the windows and doors, seemingly determined to destroy the little shack we called home. Uncle Amos passed out small shot glasses of beer to us three girls, saying that if something happened, no one should die without having a drink of Dixie. My aunt objected, but we held on to our glasses with my uncle's insistence. We sipped our beer and listened to his stories, ignoring the night and the storm. I can't remember when we all drifted off to sleep on the sofa, but late in the night we were awakened by my mother's gentle touch. The hurricane spent, none of us thought further about it, but for years we talked about that night we first drank beer.

My uncle Cephas was tall and lean—but not skinny. I watched him wrap his huge hands around his saxophone, the same way my grandfather's shorter fingers embraced his instrument. Uncle Cephas and Aunt Laurita took my brother in for a summer or two, allowing him to live with them in Dallas; we all hoped the hiatus from New Orleans might rid him of his demons. We sisters were lathered in Uncle Cephas's warmth and love. We could count on him to tell us stories of his travels, teaching us geography and business in the process.

I also could elect to spend time with Uncle Walter and Aunt Alberta, or Uncle Henry and Aunt Sarah; and then there were the neighbors, who also were like family, opening their homes, kitchens, and hearts. They were my extended family, which as a concept can be defined as a multigenerational, interdependent kinship system. It was once as common to African American culture as colds in winter (but a whole lot more benevolent).

"If a person has a healthy relationship with a man, pastor of a church or older brother or next-door neighbor, that connection can have a curative effect," says Audrey Chapman.

A Network of Relatives and Friends

The African American extended family is a carryover from the tribal and communal lives of Africans who were transported to America against their will as slaves. Because they were forced into quarters that partly replicated a village, a refashioned tribalism emerged. "This happened mainly because slaves were responsible for raising most of their own food, had to care for their own sick, house their own homeless children, and bury their own dead. They had to develop and enforce a code of conduct among themselves because the behavior of one slave could jeopardize the welfare of all.

"They had to share with one another techniques of survival on the plantation. Furthermore, much of their recreational, religious, and social life required group participation," say sociologists Elmer Martin and Joanne Mitchell Martin in their book *The Black Extended Family*. It explores the rise and decline of the cultural practice that found relatives, cousins, and even neighbors gathered communally to care for one another.

All through World War I and the Depression, this sort of community survival system continued to cooperate, and was strongest in the South. The extended family focused on child rearing, religious beliefs, strict discipline, respect for parental authority, and reliance on the experience of the aged, and was nourished on the philosophy of hope, perseverance, and faith in God.

Most baby boomers, including me, can recall those times when the entire community seemed responsible for caring for a child. Once, my second-grade teacher came to our home and spanked me as my mother and grandparents sat watching. I had disobeyed her instruction, leaving school without permission. That act of mine caused problems for a girl-friend who, with me, rode the bus to my home in Pontchartrain Park; we got lost on our return trip, arriving home well after eight P.M., wet and sneezing from the rain. No one thought anything of the experience; certainly no one considered suing my teacher for corporal punishment. The concept expressed itself in every relationship within African American communities.

Children, even where mothers and fathers weren't married, seemed to be the real beneficiaries of the extended family structure. In her book *All Our Kin: Strategies for Survival in a Black Community*, Carol B. Stack notes that a man's willingness to claim a child, even when he and the mother do not marry, opens up an intricate network of kin from which the child may draw both resources and role models.

"By validating his claim as a parent, the father offers the child his blood relatives and their fathers and wives as the child's kin—inheritances, so to speak," Stack says.

When my sister had her first child, although she did not marry his father, her son was not denied access to his paternal relatives. In fact, for much of his young life he lived with his father's mother—his paternal grandmother.

"As long as the father acknowledges his parental entitlement, his relatives consider themselves kin to the child and therefore responsible for him. Even when the mother 'takes up with another man,' her child retains the original set of kin gained through the father who sponsored him," adds Stack.

Although my sister later married and she and her new husband had their own children, the relationship her first son had with his paternal relatives was not altered. They continued to care for the boy, notwithstanding that his mother had married someone other than his father.

Often relatives of the father activate his claim to rights to the child. "Kinship through males," says Stack, "is reckoned through a chain of social recognition. If the father fails to do anything beyond merely acknowledging the child, he surrenders most of his rights. This claim can be shared or transferred to the father's kin, whose claim becomes strengthened if they actively participate as essential kin."

It wasn't just because the father of my sister's first son had said, "Yes, I impregnated her" that he could claim the boy. Rather, it was the bevy of resources he brought to that claim—his involvement and his parents' involvement in the boy's life—that permitted them certain rights to the child, a say about what did or didn't happen to him.

The extended family didn't always emanate from the paternal, however. Ruthie Bolton, in her memoir *Gal: A True Life*, tells the story of being given away by her thirteen-year-old mother to her grandmother and step-grandfather. Bolton never learned who her father was and therefore did not tap into the paternal network of kinship. Rather, maternal relatives for a time became her salvation. She found a surrogate father in her mother's stepfather, whom Ruthie called "Daddy."

When Meri Danquah's mother and father divorced, her uncle Paul became a surrogate father; Paul is her mother's brother. When he was out of the country, she often pulled out postcards he'd sent her, telling friends they were from her father. "He was what I imagined a perfect father would be." Meri, her mother, and Meri's younger sister spent Christmas each year with uncle Paul. And each year he gave Meri the same present—a huge jar filled with money.

"When he was in town, Uncle Paul made time to be with me. We had regular weekend dates for trips to the opera, the ballet, the theater, or to Gifford's Ice Cream Shop, where we ordered thick, rich vanilla milkshakes," Meri recalls.

Tonya Butler describes her stepfather: "I was Daddy's little girl. There were no beatings. I could do no wrong. What I wanted, I got. For some reason he wanted and needed a child in his life. Maybe because he knew my mother did not love him, he decided to love me. He basically, on a very emotional level, took me from her. While I loved and envied my mother, the down-to-earth, day-to-day relationship was with him; he did everything."

"I always knew [he] was not my father. But I don't remember being angry. My stepfather was the best father at the time. I also had a step-grandfather. I had two strong males who lavished me with attention," she continues.

Six feet, two inches tall, with dark shining skin, Tonya's stepgrandfather appeared godlike to her. He wore his hair closely cropped and had a booming, yet smooth voice. Her stepfather was equally striking, but pale. He looked Asian. His friends called him "Chang." When he smiled, his straight, white teeth sparkled. And when he sang, you had to stop and listen. Tonya loved him.

Misty tells similar stories about the man she called her "play daddy." He was her mother's best male friend. They worked together at the train station in New Orleans. Often he visited the family, bringing with him gifts for Misty and her brother. By then, the family lived in the Magnolia public housing project, a sprawling complex of two- and three-story apartment buildings. Misty, her brother, and her mother lived on the third floor in a two-bedroom unit. While it didn't have the outdoor balcony that the second-floor apartments boasted, it was nonetheless gorgeous in Misty's eyes. She had her own bedroom, filled with traditional mahogany furniture. Dolls covered her bed and tons of books could be found in corners and on shelves. She eased the meteoric speed of her father's reappearance and disappearance with her "play daddy."

Edward was tall, deep brown, with a voice that made women swoon. Also, he was a master chef and often used his skills in preparing elaborate meals for Misty, her brother, and her mother. The relationship he had with Misty's mother was platonic; Misty wished it were more.

"He filled everything a daddy could do; he was tender, loving, and kind. He listened to me. He gave me a lot of money. He brought me everything I wanted."

She often asked her mother and him why they couldn't get married. "He said, '*I am* your daddy. I am more your daddy than your real daddy. What do you want?' "

Sandra remembers there were other men in her mother's life, including Mr. James, whom Sandra "loved," although he was an alcoholic and sometimes got on her nerves. He never came to their house empty-handed, often bringing her favorite Kentucky Fried Chicken for their dinner. But few of her mother's male friends wanted to be a surrogate father to Sandra and her brother. Her maternal grandfather tried to provide the balance. Some days he picked up the children from school. He read books to them, prepared their meals, and distributed love and nurturing, which they needed. But there were other times when all the adults worked and Sandra and her brother were latchkey children, left to their own devices. He found refuge with a gaggle of friends; she remained a hostage to their project apartment, wrapped within the fantasies of books.

Holes in the Network

While some fatherless daughters were the recipients of the extended-family system, partly filling the holes of father loss with uncles, aunts, and goodwill neighbors, by the late 1970s obvious changes had descended, all but demolishing that benevolent, caring, unofficial system, much the way the government did the neighborhood of my birth.

The shift seemed gradual: For years the country had been mostly agrarian—farm-based communities—where everyone assisted everyone. People worked the land and traded with neighbors. Then factories and assembly lines punctuated the country, sending people racing to fill those factories and to increase their earnings and their "standard of living." There was little time to talk and visit with neighbors. The dollar became the commodity, and people did almost anything to get it. Cities and towns shot up around these factories, creating along the way urban centers, reducing incrementally and permanently the interdependence on one's cultural group and family.

After a while, whole segments of the country, facing failed factories or disruptions in assembly lines, began to rely almost exclusively on government subsidies; the extended family was severely disrupted.

"Members found themselves dealing with impersonal bureaucratic institutions instead of a loving family," say Elmer Martin and Joanne Mitchell Martin, authors of *The Black Extended Family*. The shift meant the adoption of values foreign to black tradition and culture and an unprecedented narcissism.

Urban social ills, along with the everyday burdens of living with too little money, ravaged the informal network of mutual assistance—people helping relatives and friends. Too many black men found themselves on the wrong side of the law, using unacceptable survival techniques to provide for themselves and their families. David Warnick, writing in the July 1995 issue of *Destiny: The New Black American Mainstream*, noted that in June 1994, an estimated 778,761 dads who had children under eighteen were behind bars. An additional 105,500 incarcerated dads had children over eighteen.

"When a close link such as that of the father is broken, it has a profound effect on the shape of the personal kindred," says Stack in *All Our Kin*.

"Given the economic deprivation of urban black families, the impersonality of the urban environment, the cultural push toward individualism, and the difficulty of maintaining strong kinship ties in the urban environment, the reciprocal exchange system is not as effective [as it was before]," Elmer and Joanne Martin explain.

But not all fathers or surrogate fathers landed in jail or were the victims of a vicious economy; and the extended family didn't take a beating solely because of alterations in the country's industries. Perhaps equally dramatic were the shifts in roles being experienced by men and women— some the result of the gender wars.

American men became less involved with their children. Too often they did not lay claim to their children, preventing the mother from effectively tapping into the extended-family network and thus improving the child's chances of survival and normalcy. Many contemporary African American fathers, in particular, slept with women, impregnated them, and moved on to the next fertile territory they could claim.

And where once the maternal families like Ruthie Bolton's didn't hesitate to assume the parental role, contemporary African American grandparents became even more disinclined to carry such enormous burdens of caretaking. The abandonment of the extended-family philosophy is directly related to the swell of pregnant teens and the wholesale disintegration of the family; it is a sort of catch-22.

Mothers, not quite finished with their own child-rearing responsibilities, saw their daughters giving birth to children. If the daughters were too young for motherhood, then certainly their mothers were too young to be grandparents.

"The new black mother is [very close in age to] her own mother, and her mother is not playing the grandmother role that my grandmother played for my mother," explains therapist Audrey Chapman. "She wants to be out there.

"So then they shuttle [the children] out to different places where they can be kept," continues Chapman. "Every now and then you find good old-fashioned grandmothers. But a lot of these grandmothers are forty-five; they are still dating."

Perhaps the greatest damage came out of society's emphasis on the nuclear family, and not the village from which it sprang. The focus was in keeping with the narcissism that during the final three decades of the twentieth century overtook America, creating more than one "me-generation" and trashing previous interests in community.

"Not only wasn't my father there, but society made it so that the family wasn't there," laments Judith Scott. "The extended family ended."

Sometimes Substitutes Aren't Enough

Meri's Sunday outings with her uncle Paul stopped long before she became a woman. The demands of his life increased. Later, he moved out of the country. Misty's "play daddy" died; she tried to kill herself just after a heart attack claimed him.

Tonya's stepfather and stepgrandfather eventually came under siege: Her grandmother and mother never had smooth relations with men. Although she didn't know it, Tonya witnessed very early in her life what happens when a father is absent or emotionally unavailable. She saw, in the women in her house, the distrust that develops; the belief that men are superfluous, important only for having sex, or moving things around as do handymen. The reaction of Tonya's mother and grandmother to their husbands was stereotypical of the Fatherless Woman Syndrome overcompensation symptom—one that infected Tonya later in life.

Although Tonya's grandmother had grown up with a father, he was remote, distant. He drank a lot; his habit bordered on alcoholism. When he was at home, it was as if he weren't. Still she had no words of criticism for him. "My own mother didn't meet her father until she was fifteen; my grandmother was determined not to let her have a relationship with her father. By the time she did, he was really broken. She looked up and he was old, and she didn't really have a father figure," Tonya confesses.

Sitting in the kitchen one morning, Tonya overheard her mother and grandmother comparing notes. Each complained about her spouse. Their conclusion: They could do better without them. In no time at all, the stepgrandfather and stepfather were gone.

"They left when I needed them most," Tonya says. "Even though I knew the things my stepfather and stepgrandfather did, looking back, they weren't doing anything that you'd really [think would] break up a marriage today. But these two women, being so strong, and really having married them for peculiar reasons, made it even more difficult to stay tied to these men."

The two men, having laid claim to Tonya and hoping to maintain some connection, found houses in the neighborhood. Still, a chasm developed in their relationship with Tonya. Her grandmother forbade her to see her stepgrandfather. Tonya was conflicted. If she kept up the relationship, she risked losing her grandmother's love. It was the same feeling I had that day when I discovered Noel wasn't coming back. I couldn't bring myself to blame my mother because I was afraid to be without anyone who loved me.

Tonya hadn't realized she had made her choice until one day on a public bus. Coming home from school, she spotted her stepgrandfather right away. He may have noticed her, too. But she didn't utter a word: Not, "Good evening. How have you been? I miss you." She walked right past him, as she did the strangers on the bus. He didn't force the acknowledgment, either. That was the last time she saw him alive.

One day, while reading the daily newspaper, she came across an obituary notice. Her stepgrandfather had been killed in his apartment—

the one three blocks from where her family still lived. The one to which he moved after Tonya's grandmother put him out. The one he hoped was close enough that he and his granddaughter might continue their relationship.

Tonya remained in touch with her stepfather, who was an illegal numbers runner. During those days in African American communities, such a position wasn't necessarily frowned upon. His bankroll allowed him to provide many luxuries for the family. When lottery became legal, Tonya's stepfather wasn't sure how he might make his living. What's worse, he believed himself incapable of providing for the family as he once had. He was lost. Yet it wasn't the dip in his cash flow that knocked him off Tonya's pedestal.

"I found out he had children. That was very difficult for me. The reason he was my saint and knight in shining armor was that I felt he was different from my father; he was responsible.

"So when I found out he had these children and that he did not have contact with them, I was crushed, just crushed," says Tonya. "My whole house of cards came tumbling down."

Not My Father, Just Granddaddy

I can't remember when reality hit me. Perhaps it was that night when in the second grade I came home from school alone. Maybe reality met me that day at the Bynum Bakery when the owner announced he had my trumpet and no one came to my rescue. I cannot say for certain what triggered the realization that regardless of what my grandfather did, he was not my father.

Oh, sure, I can point to valuable lessons I learned from him about being a woman, lessons that chaperoned my relationship with myself and rooted me in a southern woman's tradition. But throughout my life, there were things he could not do.

Certainly, he couldn't quite erase my longing for my own father. He couldn't quite make up for the fact that I didn't have one to attend Brownie and Girl Scout programs or the father-daughter dances. There wasn't a father at the door telling my prom date to bring me home early and not to make any detours to any secluded parks. My grandfather couldn't get out on the pitcher's mound and toss balls for me to practice my batting. He never pushed me in the swings or helped me practice riding my bike without hands. In the final analysis, he was just a grandfather, a good one, but still a grandfather—limited by age and an arduous work schedule. I needed a father.

15. MISSING DAUGHTERS

A s much as we fatherless daughters long for our fathers, many fathers also long for us. Just ask Milton. The day he and his daughter separated is forever imprinted in his mind: "April 22, 1987.

"My daughter was in our gray four-door Volvo. She was in the back, in her car seat. She had on her blue velvet Laura Ashley coat and matching pageboy hat. It was almost like she was going to church, instead of going on a trip.

"My daughter was three years old. I think she knew. It's a cruel thing when one parent talks to a child and tells her to keep a secret from the other parent. The child doesn't understand, but does understand that the parent is serious.

"The moving van was in front of my car; my father-in-law was there. He had come to assist. I watched them drive away. Then I turned around and walked into the house. We had renovated this huge brownstone. We had Victorian furnishings. It was elegant. There I was, alone in this empty house. It was kind of like, 'What do you do now?' I had this tremendous sense of loss."

It wasn't supposed to end that way. Milton had been ecstatic to learn he was going to be the father of a daughter. Until his wife had the amniocentesis, they had been calling the child inside her "peanut." Then they began the ritual hunt for names. The day of the delivery, he was there. In the room. He saw his daughter as she emerged from her mother's womb to enter the world; watched his daughter as the nurse held her up, giving her her first view of the world. He had smiled, looking at the expression on her face. He knew then she was going to be a character. "It was like she was making a face at me," Milton adds.

And then, there were all the things they had done together. He had prepared her food, cleaned her. At night when she couldn't sleep, he walked the floor with her, talking to her about sundry things. From the beginning he took her everywhere; he carried her in a small pouch on his chest, whispering to her as they walked the streets of New York City.

"I loved being with her. I loved getting her out to explore, opening her eyes to the big, vast world," he says. "There is such a special feeling that little girls give their dads."

On a scale of one to ten, with ten being the highest, Milton gave himself an eight. "The only way you could be a ten is to be there all day, every day, doing everything. I did have a job, and I traveled a lot."

The separation arrived like a tornado, without much warning. He and his wife had been having marital problems for slightly over a year—not because he didn't love her or because he had been unfaithful. The marriage had suffered mostly because of family circumstances. Not long after the wedding, his wife learned she was pregnant. Then Milton had to move his elderly parents into the new house, while he and his wife were still renovating it. His mother and father were sick. Not long after his parents moved in, his mother died. The events of that first year were sometimes overwhelming—especially, he says, for his wife, who was ten years younger than he and who had been an adopted child, doted on by her parents and unfamiliar with such pressures.

Milton and his wife started seeing a family counselor, hoping to mend the tear. She had begun to hunt for a more senior-level post at Xerox, where she worked. When she announced she had been offered another assignment with the company, he was excited—until she said the job was in another city. She said she and their daughter would be leaving—in two weeks. Milton was aghast.

He could not believe the tragedy being visited upon him. His father had died only six weeks earlier. And while he had just been hired for a new job with New York City mayor David Dinkins, he knew the road wasn't going to be easy—politics never is. And now his wife was telling him she was leaving.

"I just remember feeling like I had been hit with a ton of bricks," he said, adding that he tried reasoning with himself. It was okay that his wife wanted a separation, "But she wants to move and take my daughter?! And she's only giving me two weeks to adjust to this idea. It was a heart-wrenching period.

"[My wife] was packing stuff up. I paid for the moving van to come get her stuff. At first I had said I wasn't going to offer any assistance. I considered taking all sorts of actions to stop her. Then I thought maybe a separation would be good for a while. I thought she would just be gone for a short while," Milton added. But a little while turned into weeks and years.

Milton threw himself into his work, but not before removing all substances from his home: "I stopped drinking cold. I stopped smoking my pipe. I refused to allow myself to sink into any kind of dependence. I don't have a dependent personality, but as a measure of self-control I stopped everything cold," he says.

Milton overcompensated for the loss with work. He wanted to demonstrate to the world that it wasn't his fault his family disintegrated.

"I've always been a workaholic. So I threw myself into the job I had in a way unlike ever before. I worked through the issues by applying my energy to being good at my job. Before my marriage, I defined myself by my work. My family had allowed me to refocus that.

"[Now] with no family present, every day I became more of a workaholic then I ever was."

Milton sacrificed everything in his life. Work was used to compensate for the void left by his daughter's absence. He had to work; it was a compulsion. He needed to work to wash away the pain, or at the very least keep his mind focused on something other than the wound left by his daughter's being snatched away. Milton also wanted to convince himself that he was lovable and worthy, that he was still a good person. His self-esteem had been devastated by the episode. So he used the accolades and achievements he made on the job to set the measure of his self-worth.

Rather than the internal locus of validation often employed by men, he resorted to external validation, as fatherless women do all too frequently.

"I was emotionally devastated. I loved my wife and I really loved my daughter, and I wanted us to be together. In many ways I felt that I should have had the capacity to prevent the family's breakup. I should have been able to prevent my daughter from going through this. I was sad for her and sad for myself.

"There was an issue of a loss of self-esteem: If you are a father and you can't be with your child, you beat yourself up. It may not be your fault, but you think you should have been able to control it. I worked through those self-esteem issues by working to prove to myself that I was, in fact, a good person. I had to remind myself of that."

A few months later, he began traveling to Washington, D.C., where his wife and daughter had moved. He stayed at their home. All three did things together. The proximity allowed him at times to pretend they were still a family. But painful scenes at the train station, when it was time to return to New York, reminded him that the separation was real.

"My little girl would cling to me; she would plead for me not to go," recalls Milton. "It was such a heart-wrenching scene that it would rattle me. I would just get on the train, and I'd be drained."

Both Milton and his daughter eventually adjusted to their circumstances. He took her on out-of-town trips to Disney World and New York City. He took her shopping. Sometimes his ex-wife joined their excursions. Sometimes he just simply spent the day at home with his daughter. Still, maintaining their relationship was difficult, since most of the time he was living in another state. Then there were the occasions when his former wife tried to program their activities, asking questions about where the duo intended to go and who would be with them.

"Our time was affected because her mother did not want her to be around my new friend. If she thought that was the plan, she would create a scenario to defeat that. Although she said she was not keeping me from my daughter, I saw her behavior during that period as constructive denial;

she created an environment where I didn't want to go through all that. It became a real hassle [to get my daughter]."

Milton says he agreed to making his wife the custodial parent because she had been adopted and their daughter was her only blood relative. Even this concession failed to ease tensions between him and his ex-wife.

Although Milton initially was permitted to stay in the same house as his daughter during visits, he soon lost that right. "It later became clear she was trying to establish that legal time period sufficient for separation; I couldn't stay [with her and my daughter] anymore, which made coming to Washington, D.C., a challenge.

"I had to stay in a hotel or a friend's house. If I stayed at a friend's house, that meant the time I had with my daughter was always out, never in a relaxed environment."

Milton decided to move permanently to the Washington, D.C., area, buying a house that was a ten-minute ride away from his former wife and daughter. "I wanted to get over there as often as possible. But given that her mother had her own life, everything had to be prearranged."

The Other Side of Fatherlessness

It wasn't until Mother's Day, 1998, that Sandra fully realized there was another side to her fatherlessness—her father's side. She was driving; her mother and her brother and his girlfriend were in the car. "I was commenting about how blessed we were and how we turned out all right and my brother said something like, 'Yeah, because we could have been stuck in Nebraska somewhere.' "

The comment seemed odd. Sandra's father had left Pennsylvania in 1965 with a buddy and his buddy's girlfriend. They all were looking for work. They landed in Nebraska and then moved on to Rockford, Illinois. Somewhere along the way, the buddy married and divorced his girlfriend. After that divorce, Sandra's father married his buddy's ex-wife, claiming their four children as his own.

He visited Sandra and her brother once or twice a year. As with Bebe Moore Campbell, his arrival in Philadelphia was an occasion for celebration. "I would tell a lot of people that my daddy was coming or if I talked to him on the phone, I would say I talked to my daddy."

Sometimes Sandra and her brother went to visit their father for a week or two in the summer. After he remarried, those visits offered their own trauma. She watched with envy as the other children interacted with her father. He sometimes took everyone fishing. And, while Sandra enjoyed the outings, she couldn't help feeling envious, jealous, and sometimes angry that when the visit ended, and she and her brother went back to Pennsylvania, the other children would still be with *her* daddy.

Matters were made worse when she was twelve years old and learned her stepmother had given birth to yet another child—a daughter— bringing the total number of children the couple had to five.

"It wasn't enough that he had these four kids; he had this daughter and she would be growing up with her mother and her father.

"I grew up thinking my father left us to go and be with some other kids. That made me feel bad, like we had done something."

Sandra had tried bridging the gap between them when she reached her twenties. She wanted him to know that bad things happened to her because he walked away. She wanted him to know how much she hurt all those years without him, how much she still hurt. She wanted to hear him say he was sorry for the chaos he threw into her life—a baseball sailing through a glass window, shattering everything in its way. But instead of the recognition and penitence she sought, her father admonished her, questioning whether she was the "good Christian" she claimed to be; the door between them slammed closed, remaining so for almost a decade.

But death has a way of making all of us reflect. It makes us acknowledge our blessings and forces us to reach for the living, including those from whom we may have been estranged. And who can resist a hand given in kindness during a wake or a funeral? There is something deemed evil and stingy about refusing the gesture.

When Sandra's father and stepsister reached out, sending flowers in 1994 following the death of her grandfather, she could hardly refuse their warmth. She realized she needed to preserve the relationship she had with the living. After the funeral, her father and stepsister telephoned her. A long conversation ensued, boring a hole in the wall that had separated them.

"I started to call him and we started communicating pretty regularly. He felt that my brother wouldn't accept him."

The test came in 1995 at the Million Man March, held that October in Washington, D.C. Sandra's grandmother had died a few months earlier, adding a further sense of urgency to the need for family reconciliation. Although her father and brother each planned to attend the march, they had not discussed going together.

The week before the march, Sandra was in Pennsylvania. Her father also was in town. He was preparing to come to Washington, D.C. She offered to drive him and his friends. She lived with her brother; when she arrived with the carload of people, they landed at her brother's house. The next day, father and son attended the march together.

"They were experiencing a relationship; it felt like a dream come true. It was almost like a miracle." Sandra's father urged her also to attend, noting the historical importance of the event, although women had been asked to stay at home. She went with girlfriends. That evening, she arrived home from the march before her father and brother and climbed into bed. Her father and friends dropped off her brother, then left to go back to Illinois. She was a little disheartened that he didn't wake her to say good-bye. "He called me a couple of days later and he said, 'I left without saying good-bye to you. I will never do that again.' That made me feel so good."

In 1996, she had gone to visit her father, hoping to unload on him all the turmoil she felt growing up but had muzzled. Instead she discovered her father's pain. Like Milton, he agonized over the separation from his children. "He was hurt behind what had happened, too. I just thought it was a thing he couldn't deal with, in terms of the family. But he was really, really hurt behind that whole situation just as my mother was hurt.

"He was even hurt the marriage didn't work out. I was surprised about that information. His desire was to have a family and when that didn't work that caused him a lot of pain." Still, Sandra harbored the feeling that at one point in her life, her father had rejected her.

But on that Mother's Day in 1998, her brother had said something that was confusing; she wanted to know what he meant; she prodded. Her mother finally told her that their father, in an attempt to present his best case for reconciliation, had persuaded a literate woman friend to write a letter urging Sandra's mother to come to Nebraska with the children. Sandra's mother refused.

Sandra couldn't believe what she was hearing. Why hadn't her mother told her this before? Why had she let her suffer all these years, believing that her father hadn't wanted her, believing she hadn't been loved by the one man whose love she needed the most? At that moment, Sandra felt much as I had that summer of 1988 when my mother called asking if I wanted to meet my real father.

"I was angry that nobody had ever told me this when I was little—when it really mattered," Sandra recalls.

Suffering in Silence

"How could a man suffer through the loss of a child every day?" asks Ben, the father in Alexs Pate's novel *Finding Makeba*. "He was embarrassed that his relationship with Helen had destroyed his ability to have a relationship with his daughter. That was what was wrong. The way men relate to children. The way men are taught to make their connection to their children through women. That was what had separated them. When love dies between mother and father, it is the father who catapults away. . . . What else had history demanded?

"Many men suffer through this dance of life. They promise. They leave. They try to act like they don't hurt. But they do. If you are a child of a missing father, you already know this. Then again, maybe you don't."

Yes, fathers who experience involuntary separation from their daughters, usually through divorce or cohabitation disintegration, come to suffer loss as we do. Many experience the same symptoms as their daughters—although for shorter periods of time. As Milton, Sandra's father, and Pate's fictional Ben indicate, they worry that they are unlovable and unworthy; they suffer bouts of depression; they express anger and rage; and they even fight problems of substance abuse and food addictions. They also suffer under/overinvolvement. Overinvolvement is an attempt to make things go a certain way, to provide predictability and a sense of stability. Underinvolvement is a way of gaining control of emotions. "By saying to themselves, 'I don't care,' men try to minimize the pain and resentment within," says William C. Klatte, author of *Live-Away Dads: Staying a Part of Your Children's Lives When They Aren't a Part of Your Home.*

"It would be surprising if they didn't have feelings of rage or experience depression," says clinical psychologist Wade Horn. "There's the old saying that just because you're paranoid, it doesn't mean someone is not out to get you. . . . The same could be true of fathers who have lost custody of their children. They are depressed for a good reason."

"Our powerful responses grow out of loneliness, loss of control over our lives, separation from our kids, feared loss of our father roles, and material losses. For men, our response often comes in the form of anger," says Klatte.

The rage men feel sometimes can become suicidal or homicidal. How many times have we read in the newspaper that some man methodically stalked his ex-wife or mate and, when the opportunity presented itself, killed her. Sometimes men even kill their children and themselves. The breakup and the thought of living without their family are too traumatic. These are the rare cases, however.

Other times their response may be obsessive, as in the case of men who suspend their own lives as they battle their wives for custody of their children. "There is this low capacity to accept things in their lives that they can't do anything about," says Horn. "It's not good to obsess, nor is it good to deny."

For African American men like Milton and Sandra's father, the rage is intensified. They are not only confronted with the internal pressures associated with their families, but, like their women, they must address external conditions that often make it difficult for them to take care of their families in the style and manner they desire.

Black men often define themselves by their work and the status of their families. When the latter is destroyed through no fault of their own, the rage then teams with that generated by the sometimes immovable barriers to success placed before them by corporate America. Thus, they walk away with a greater sense of failure. The spiral is downward, and the pit into which they descend seemingly bottomless. The result is increased violence, apathy, and general destruction, or nihilism. Author Cornel West defines nihilism as "the lived experience of coping with a life of horrifying meaninglessness, hopelessness, and lovelessness. [It] is a disease of the soul."

The pain seethes inside of fathers like it does within their daughters. And for years they are unable to express it with words. Their actions tell the story of the unbearable wounds hidden beneath the surface.

"The frightening result [of nihilism] is a numbing detachment from others and a self-destructive disposition toward the world. Life without meaning, hope, and love breeds a coldhearted, mean-spirited outlook that destroys both the individual and others," West explains.

Fathers who lose their relationships with their children often enter into a sort of self-destructive behavior that, if left unattended, extends into society and their communities. But the answer, for fatherless daughters or the fathers themselves, is not some government-funded program. Rather, it is love and care.

"Any disease of the soul must be conquered by a turning of one's soul," continues West. "This turning is done through one's own affirmation of one's worth."

Managing Hurt, Discovering Hope

Milton's daughter is twelve years old now; she knows her father loves her. "When she's with me, I sometimes just look at her and smile to myself. She's really a beautiful child."

Still, the ache of separation remains fresh. "There was a part of my daughter's life I missed. Every day you're not there you miss something. There's an experience you can't have."

He continues, "Someone recently asked me what was my daughter's favorite color; her likes and dislikes. I had to confess to myself that some of that I didn't know. I didn't know because when we do have time together, it is spent doing a lot of other things. When you're there every day and engaged, you know things naturally. When you're not there, you're robbed of that knowledge."

Maybe Milton is even more frustrated because as a young boy living at home, he saw the importance of a father-daughter relationship and the havoc it can wreak when it goes awry. "I'm reminded of my father's relationship with my sister: She looked just like him; she had his big gray eyes. And they had battles because she often disappointed him. . . . She once said that when she was a little girl he never held her or told her that he loved her, and that was all she wanted him to do. I think early on, because she got pregnant at twelve or thirteen and he prevented her from getting married, there was always a hurt and distance he had—always a longing that she would do better. Whenever she needed to come home, he always opened the door for her. There was that brief period in her life when she returned to the church; he was very, very happy. She was, too; she had his approval.

"Girls look for their father's love and affection. And fathers hope that their little girls grow up to be darling women and not disappoint them," Milton says.

"It's a very complex relationship."

16. HIS PRESCRIPTION

It seems so obvious that fathers, like their daughters, also would suffer from their separation. Yet how many of us have even attempted to view pain from their perspectives. We think, as Sandra did, that their departures in the case of abandonment and divorce were of their own volition. Milton and Sandra's father give us reason to pause—to offer a conciliatory hand, or to pass the salve and offer a little advice.

1. Permit yourself the opportunity to grieve. Losing the care of a child, especially one you have lived with and guided, is no small thing. Like any other relationship, you have developed a bond that has offered you love and opportunities for growth. These things—time for sharing, learning, and loving—will be challenged by the separation, or perhaps completely destroyed. They are reason enough for your sorrow.

2. Don't be afraid to cry, and to cry in front your child. Let her know that leaving her is also very difficult for you. At the very least tell her the truth. Let her know you don't like being away from her any more than she likes being away from you.

3. Don't be afraid to accept blame, but don't persecute yourself, either, for the marital difficulties that led to the family's disintegration. Everyone makes mistakes, mishandles a circumstance, or simply doesn't rise to every occasion. Step back, acknowledge your role, analyze how you might respond in the next situation, and then embrace life again. Michael Farris, author of *How a Man Prepares His Daughters for Life*, identifies

several stages of emotional growth: Acknowledge your pain; accept responsibility for your actions and commit to change; stop negative behavior; and replace negative thoughts and behavior with positive thoughts
and behavior.

4. *It's okay to be angry,* especially if the separation from your daughter is
not of your choosing, as was the case with Milton. Some experts suggest
keeping a diary as a way of releasing the anger you may feel over the separation from your child. Talk with your friends or consult a therapist to help
you handle your feelings. Don't permit your feelings to drive you to injure
yourself or others.

5. *Don't turn your anger on yourself, becoming depressed.* If you have lost
your appetite, aren't sleeping well, find more and more that you aren't interested in being with other people, or have thought about killing yourself
or someone else, then chances are you are suffering from depression. You
should seek the help of a licensed therapist or other medical expert immediately. Then, alter your pattern of behavior. Create situations where you
can have friends over to your house and enjoy a meal. Get into an exercise
program; if you haven't tried it, you can't imagine the wonders a regular
physical fitness program does for the mind and the spirit. Often when I am
lethargic or sad about something, my spirits perk right up after a sixty-
minute workout. One thing's certain, if I work out in the evening I'm
bound to sleep better; and sleep in itself can serve to improve attitudes
and outlooks.

6. *Don't oversaturate or overcompensate.* Not drugs nor alcohol nor food
nor work is appropriate balm for what ails you. Each serves only to camou-
flage your real problems, and in the long run those false remedies can only
complicate your life. Addiction of any kind requires real, hard work and
effort to overcome. The best defense against it is preventing any dependency in the first place. Follow Milton's lead, and remove addictive

chemicals—drugs and alcohol—from your house. Try as best you can to keep a regular meal regimen. Most single men find themselves eating very poorly. Invest in a cookbook or find a decent, inexpensive restaurant and make yourself a regular there.

7. Don't close down; continue communicating with your daughter. Wade Horn and Jeff Rosenberg, authors of *New Father Book: What Every Man Needs to Know to Be a Good Dad*, say continued communication is critical. They urge fathers to telephone their daughters frequently and write a lot. "Instead of writing to an attorney, spending thousands of dollars fighting in a custody fight, fathers should write to their child once a week," says Horn. "They could spend their energy creating a website or setting up a computer system so they and their child can communicate." When Milton's daughter began having academic problems because she wasn't completing homework assignments, he set up a computer system and fax at his ex-wife's home that enabled his daughter to talk with him every night about her homework. He could tap into her system and see exactly what she had done and where the problems were in her assignments. The result was a stronger relationship for them and better grades for her.

8. Don't wait for your child to say she wants to see you, wants to be with you, or wants simply to talk with you. Especially when something is wrong, take the initiative, say Ross D. Parke and Armin A. Brott, authors of *Throwaway Dads: The Myths and Barriers That Keep Men from Being the Fathers They Want to Be.*

9. Do battle for the right to spend time with your daughter. None of this "boys for him, girls for her" stuff. A father should battle for his right to have his daughter spend as much time with him as she does with her mother. And during those moments when they are together, he must instill in her the value system of men—what they hold to be important, in friendships and in romantic relationships; how they communicate; and, most important, exactly what a man is.

10. Develop shared interests with your child. It isn't enough to take her roller-skating with her friends; join in the fun. As Milton rightly worried, developing a relationship with your child that focuses primarily on entertainment sends a false signal about the elemental foundation of the father-daughter bond. Don't become locked in the "overinvolvement" response to your separation from your child. Never let her think you have to perform to win her attention; never buy things to win her affection. At the very least, she will start to believe the same about her relationship with you, and will not feel she must strain in any way to "buy" your affection or the affection of other men. Say Horn and Rosenberg: "Your child needs a father, not a special-events coordinator." Milton says he made a point of simply spending days at home with his daughter. No shopping trips, no movie theaters. Just downtime, where they talked and became reacquainted with each other.

11. Keep your commitments. You have a choice: attend the office party or your daughter's recital. Every time, absolutely every time, your daughter's recital should win—hands down. *She must always be your priority.* As Naomi Wolf mentions, too many children have too many stories about why their fathers couldn't keep their commitments and none of the reasons is valid. Certainly Helen's father's failure to keep his promise destroyed what little ground he may have gained with his daughter and her mother. Further, it left her self-worth severely compromised. A child lives or dies by promises.

12. Money doesn't buy happiness, nor can it take the place of real time with your child. Too many parents separated from their children think it's enough to send a few dollars and everything will be all right. While experts have charted the impact that divorce and domestic disintegration wreak on the economics of a family, using money as the bricks and mortar of a relationship can only cause trouble, creating in the daughter's mind a picture of the father as sugar daddy, rather than as guide, protector, friend, and concerned parent.

13. Be emotionally available. It's absolutely dreadful to visit your father only to have him maintain a distance. He won't hug, won't say nice things, and never utters the words *I love you.* How absolutely awful. A father may as well not bother, if he intends to remain emotionally aloof. The ills of a father's absence are acquired even when Dad is at home, if he is watching television, talking to the boys, sleeping in the chair, or eating at the table and not speaking with anyone.

14. Be physically available. Even if the court order says you are responsible only for weekends, holidays, and summer vacation, please understand that child rearing is a full-time job. Milton says there have been dozens of times outside of their arranged schedule when his ex-wife has called asking him to keep their daughter. He has always made sure he can respond favorably to those requests. And when work began causing him to reduce the number of visits he had with his daughter, he quickly altered his schedule.

15. Be careful about what you say. Your behavior, both within the home and without, determines the level of respect your daughter develops for you, other men, and herself. Hold the profanity, don't demonize her mother, and, above all, don't criticize her by calling her uncomplimentary names—even in jest.

16. It's no good just loving some of the people some of the time. A father has to love all the people in his family, all the time. Most important, he can't be afraid to demonstrate that love—through words and actions.

17. Be her protector. He doesn't have to be ADT or some other high-security system, preventing his daughter from meeting people and spreading her wings, as Russell once did with his children, but *a father must be seen as protector.* He has to step in when his daughter has been wronged, even if the injury is self-inflicted.

18. Help her build self-confidence. In deeds and words, he must present her with a self-confidence that invites her to take risks, to explore the world, to be self-reliant but not overly independent, to believe that the possibilities the world offers are not the sole possession of men, to assert her right to make her claim, and always to celebrate herself and her contribution to that world.

19. Be gentle with yourself and with her. Sometimes, regardless of how hard you try, things are going to be difficult. You may say the wrong thing; she may think the wrong thing. Her mother may intrude, as Milton's ex-wife did on occasion, forcing compromises or needless delays in repair of the father-daughter relationship. Don't become disillusioned by such detours; they offer further lessons for all. Simply remain positive and move forward.

20. Don't stop your life. Some children find difficulty in adjusting to their fathers' new lives. While it is important to make your child a priority, you can't stop living. Part of maintaining a relationship with your daughter will require that you demonstrate by your actions that she is a part of your life—invite her in. If she has trouble, communicate.

21. Above all, remember this: Only forgiveness and love can ease the pain and heal the wound. Give the mother of your child, your child, and yourself plenty of both. You won't regret it. Forgiveness and love really are magical elixirs.

BOOK FOUR

i wanna

lay hands on you
make you rise
from the pain
erase the bruises
make you believe
in miracles
tell the world
you will live
always.

—Excerpted from "Big Jesus' Double,"
   The Corner Is No Place for Hiding

17. LOCATING THE MISSING

No war ends without casualties and fatalities. Even the victors are injured, bruised, or crippled by the lives they have damaged, the landscape they have plundered, and the spirits they have fractured. If it is true that in America for the last thirty years unprecedented gender conflict and a major assault on families has prevailed, then who can dispute that fatherless children in general, and fatherless girls and women in particular, are the victims, the prisoners; their absent fathers, the missing in action. Sometimes as in cases like Milton's, the fathers also are victims.

When the Vietnam war ended, the American government, joined by veterans organizations and associations involved in foreign aid and relief, launched massive campaigns to locate all unaccounted-for military personnel. Spouses, parents, sons, and daughters seated in living rooms or on front porches had the right to know what had happened to their loved ones sent to fight in America's brutal, protracted war in Southeast Asia. No one questioned this logic. A family had only to send a letter, requesting information about their relative, and one of the world's most powerful institutions shifted into gear. Even private citizens and wealthy businessmen entered the effort, spending millions of dollars to rescue persons they had been told were being held as prisoners of war. As recently as 1998, when questions arose about the identity of the person in the Tomb of the Unknown Soldier, the federal government spared no expense or resource to determine just who was buried there representing the veterans of the Vietnam war.

But who aids in the search for missing fathers when, despite their best efforts, uncles, stepfathers, grandfathers, or neighbors prove unable to fill the gaping hole in the fatherless daughter's heart? What organizations exist to aid these girls and women in their pursuit? How do they find fathers they have never seen? Do they print posters and distribute them around the nation? Do they print pictures on milk cartons? What if there aren't any photographs? What if even the mind can't recall the color of a father's eyes or the way the lines formed around his mouth when he smiled? What if she can't even remember if he smiled?

These are hard questions. Myriad answers arrive, depending on how a girl became fatherless. Death seems a final thing, but there are ways a fatherless daughter still can come to closure. If her father and mother divorced, and he remained even remotely a part her life, then the fatherless daughter's task of reconciling and relocating her relationship with her father may be relatively easy. If, on the other hand, a father, after a divorce, completely abandoned his daughter or never laid real claim to her in the first place, then building a bridge between the two may be difficult. Either way, the fatherless daughter, hoping to come to grips with her past and to establish some sanity in her life, is obliged to begin the process at the beginning—with her father.

Ofttimes, running away from one's history seems a much easier prospect than standing to face it and coming to terms with the destruction it wrought. As I discovered, unfinished business forces us to return to the landscape in which the original injury occurred—no matter how long ago. We circle back to those beginnings, knowing that we must lay our ghosts to rest or permit them to rise and tell us the truth.

Losing our fathers through death, divorce, or abandonment stunted our growth. Consequently, we are still little girls. We can never become mature adult women until we honor that little girl in us; telling her, in language she understands, that she is without blame for the course her life took. "We are not responsible if we grew like a twisted plant reaching for a shaft of light in a darkened room. We didn't know better. But then, neither did our parents," Geneen Roth reminds us. "We are not responsible for what happened to us as children, but we are responsible for what we do with our pain as adults."

The search for our fathers is a real and necessary part of becoming accountable for our lives and what happens to us. It is a critical first step in bandaging, and later healing, that wound. While there are no organizations such as those that search for missing children, and no standard procedure for locating these lost men, there are methods that have been successful. Some women have used a simple telephone book approach: Look him up; dial the number. Others have relied on corporations with expertise in finding missing people. Still others have put to use the new technology now available to citizens throughout the world.

Whatever system a fatherless daughter employs, clinical psychologist Wade Horn cautions against the fantasy trap that many fall into: searching for their fathers and expecting to find demigods—this great guy who is going to come along and will turn out to be warm and loving. "What's the evidence that this guy is going to be like that? It's not strong. Odds are the fantasy is not going to come true," says Horn.

"What I say to people, when they go on these searches, is that they have to be prepared," says psychologist Maxine Harris. "They may have one of these happy endings: A great big family opens its arms, hugs you. Or they may be people you wouldn't cross the street to say hello to; these may not be the relatives of your dreams."

Still, "two people made you and you need to know the second person," says Sandra. "You shouldn't be concerned with the outcome; the person could be alive or dead. The person may not welcome you. But you have to try."

Where to Begin

Tonya didn't know what she might find when at thirteen she decided to try to locate her father. "I knew someone was missing," she says, admitting to years of traipsing through the attic in her family's home looking for remnants of her father among scraps of history—the litter from lives lived. She tracked him through mounds of pictures, believing she might discover something tangible that linked them. "It was so ridiculous." The chase was made despite the fact that her stepfather worshiped her and she him.

Insistent inquiry from one of her mother's girlfriends may have been the fuel behind her decision. The woman repeatedly asked: "Have you seen Ben lately?"

Tonya remembered once meeting her biological father, Ben Knight, back in the mid-1960s: She was three or four; her mother was twenty-six. They had just moved into their own apartment. Tonya's mental picture of her father becomes opaque; she can't see or hold on to anything else. It all disappears. But, late at night, alone in her room, she can hear the question, "Have you seen Ben lately?" replaying, the refrain from a song she imagined her father performing in his nightclub act. Sometimes, staring in a mirror, she puzzled over the matter of whom she resembled. "I did not look like my mother; I wanted to. People kept coming up saying, 'Oh she looks just like him.' 'Him' who? I guess I was haunted," says Tonya.

After years of exploring the family's attic, she found two or three letters from Ben to her mother. She welcomed the discovery, thinking she would get a glimpse of their romance; she might feel the intimacy they shared. He might ask about his baby girl. Like a teenager surreptitiously reading *True Confessions*, she made herself comfortable for the experience. But there were no sweet nothings; nor was there any admission of deep, unabiding love.

"The letters were requests for money where he would be stuck on the road somewhere. I don't remember the dialogue, exactly. Something like, We're here, can you send twenty-five dollars," confides Tonya.

Attractive, with auburn hair and tan skin, Tonya has eyes that are too old for their thirty-four years. Spiritualists say the eyes are the windows to the soul; Tonya has an old soul. Fatherlessness makes adults of us before our time.

At first glance, she appears to be a woman who lets no one do anything for her; she presents a fiercely independent facade. She is the Amazon woman of the Fatherless Daughter Syndrome. But her strength is all

Hollywood. Humor and 1990s girlfriend slang mask her distress and her bouts of self-doubt. Beneath the steely veneer is a gentle, vulnerable woman who spends many evenings alone in her huge Victorian house in Washington, D.C.'s Columbia Heights neighborhood, surrounded by her three cats, sharing secrets with them that no one else will be told. She whispers her worries about relationships with men; she thinks her male boarder is trying to take advantage of her—she will have none of that. She agonizes about the effect that fatherlessness has even on her relationships with women. Then she quickly dismisses her fears.

There is a tentative truce between Tonya and the past. She wants to build an emotionally secure future, replete with a husband and children. Once she read a magazine article—she was in her early teens—in which some celebrity, whose name she has since forgotten but whom she admired, said he always looked for women who came from intact homes—two-parent homes. She made a vow, then, to do everything in her power not to pass along fatherlessness.

One day, after becoming weary of wondering if she looked like Ben, tired of her mother's girlfriend's persistent inquiry, Tonya, at thirteen, took the public bus to downtown Washington, D.C., and entered the newly opened Martin Luther King Jr. Memorial Library at Ninth and G Streets NW. Remembering she had heard someone say that the last sighting of Ben Knight was in Detroit, she found the Detroit telephone book and scribbled down the telephone number and the address of a Ben Knight. She wrote him several times, saying please call or write. "I said I needed to find him and if he were the one to let me know." She never received a response to those letters.

After a couple of years of waiting patiently, Tonya called the Ben Knight to whom she had written. "The wife answered, and I knew right away it wasn't the right Ben Knight. By her voice, I assumed they were white.

"She did let me talk with him. He said yes he had gotten the letter. Years had passed; how much would it have taken for him to say, 'I'm not your father'?" Tonya was a junior in high school when she had that con-versation. She was brokenhearted but undaunted. Still, she didn't know what step to take next.

Her mother discovered she was attempting to reach out to her father and called a local television station for assistance. WJLA-TV, Channel 7 in Washington, D.C., had a program called 7 on Your Side, which placed investigative reporters and anchors at the disposal of residents who had been wronged by some company or faced a major dilemma. Perhaps her mother was remembering that the delay in her own search for her father had meant they never had the opportunity to enjoy a father-daughter relationship; perhaps she was motivated by her own desires to see Ben Knight again. Whatever the reason, Tonya was disturbed by the intrusion. She feared the public disclosure might disrupt her relationship with her stepfather.

"I didn't want Robert [my stepfather] to know—although he didn't know his father, either; we discussed several times how he had found his. I did not want him to know that he wasn't enough. I felt he had done so much; all my girlfriends who had their natural fathers loved my stepfa-ther. So I was afraid of losing him. And here she was writing to 7 on Your Side. Thank God they weren't able to do anything."

In the early 1980s, while still a student in high school, Tonya decided to write to all the black radio stations in and around Detroit. Her father was an entertainer; surely some disc jockey had heard the name Ben Knight.

"Talk about some pain. I called them and most just said, 'Yeah. All right.' There was this one guy who made me cry. It wasn't that he was mean. It was that he said, 'Poor child,' and that made me depressed. I re-signed myself to the fact that I wasn't going to find him. Then I got an atti-tude: I hadn't gone anywhere. I'm right in the same house. My mother had the same name. If he wanted to find me, he could. Why am I going through this? He's the parent. Fuck it!"

There it was, the RAD Factor setting in. She had begun, as many fa-therless girls do, to direct her anger toward her father. The man who had abandoned her. Later, she would, in a rather passive-aggressive manner, aim that anger, as she might a weapon, at all men.

"The fear I had was unreal. There had been nothing but abandonment—emotional and physical abandonment." But rather than confront these emotions, Tonya ran away. She enrolled in a Virginia boarding school. By the time she was seventeen and had finished high school, she had made three unsuccessful attempts to locate her father.

Then one day, sitting in church, she experienced a sort of epiphany.

"I was in Metropolitan Baptist Church, sitting in the seat I always sit in. Before service started I heard this voice say, 'You think you're so holy and righteous, but you haven't even forgiven your father.'

"I just froze. I asked myself, Why am I hearing this? I don't understand. Why this thought? Why here? I do remember thinking, not long before that, that I couldn't really have a relationship with a romantic partner until I resolved those issues."

In 1993, Tonya had already graduated from college and was a second-year law student, working part-time for a legal software company. She decided to put the new technology to use on an old project.

"I put a search together; I put a whole bunch of terms in—his name and the name of one of the groups he sang with that my mother gave me, the Falcons. I put all that in, and of course everything came up.

"I had to go through two or three hundred references; somewhere near the end was a reference to this singing group. I said that must be an error because I had never heard of them; certainly no one else had.

"I was so excited because I was like, This is impossible."

Tonya raced home, hoping that the miracle would not fade before she had an opportunity to grasp it. Both eager and anxious, she called the *Detroit Free Press*, which had published an article about the group. The reporter whose name appeared in the byline couldn't remember Ben Knight. He suggested that another of his colleagues might recall her father, since he had just written about the group. He offered to pass Tonya's telephone number to the other reporter.

Unwilling to leave the search for her father to strangers and chance, she called Tower Records in Washington, D.C. Her computerized search had revealed the group once recorded a collection of its music under the generic title *Best Of*. Many music companies had begun rereleasing classics in CD format. Fate became a willing partner.

"Sure enough, they had this CD. I asked the clerk to tell me who the distributor and producer were. I talked to this guy the same day and he said send my picture because he wanted to see if I was telling the truth."

Tonya lambasted the guy, telling him she wasn't a groupie, and that her father owed her. Despite the hostility she displayed, the producer remained supportive. Tonya sent the picture. The producer called back, telling her he would do everything he could to assist her.

"He said 'I have such a dysfunctional relationship with my daughter. I'm going through a divorce, and my daughter sided with my wife. I wish my daughter were looking for me.' "

During their third telephone conversation, he brought the news Tonya wanted to hear. He told her her father knew she was looking for him and that he was going to call her. But he didn't—not immediately, anyway.

She waited for two weeks, slowly becoming a wreck. The first week, she retraced her steps, calling again the contacts who had promised to come to her aid, annoying everyone with her persistence and impatience. She agonized over the change in tone of those conversations. Where once people seemed to want to be helpful, they now were slightly hostile. She grew frightened, believing that their change in attitude meant her father had expressed disinterest.

"I thought once again he was rejecting me. There were a lot of tears. I didn't want to communicate with my mother, although at some point she conned me out of the telephone number for the guy and she, too, had talked to him.

"But I didn't want her to intervene; I didn't want the pressure, and I didn't want my father calling back to talk to her. I wanted him calling back to talk to me."

In the meantime, Tonya confided in her grandmother, telling her that she had been searching for her father. Her grandmother was genuinely shocked and disturbed that her granddaughter had looked for a man the grandmother considered "no damn good."

By Sunday of that second week, Tonya made it to church, but when service was over, she couldn't exit the pew. She was frozen in place. "I saw someone I knew from school, and I didn't want that person to see me in such a state. I was so bad off, I couldn't pass it off as anything minor. Finally, I decided to go see one of the female ministers." Tonya hoped the woman might say something that could inspire her, help her to get home, or at least to get to the bus stop. She made it home that day, but her spirits remained low. The telephone call she'd been waiting for finally came; all the despair vanished with his voice.

"It was like, Daddy won't forget your birthday again, that kind of thing." Later, Tonya was angry with herself for the way she allowed herself to be manipulated, although she was sure he hadn't done it deliberately. He had given her a telephone number at which she could leave messages; he was living with another woman, whom he didn't want to upset. Months later, Tonya ignored her father's warning and called him at home anyway.

"I got this woman's daughter." The revelation that Ben Knight had a daughter whom he wanted to keep secret baffled the stepdaughter, who also didn't know *her* biological father. The two women shared a common bond of fatherlessness; they became friends. "She came to visit me in 1995; we are still in contact with each other." But that was after Tonya went to Detroit to meet her father and his family.

As psychologists Wade Horn and Maxine Harris would have warned her, the reunion between Tonya and her father in 1992 was not exactly the typical version of *Unsolved Mysteries* with Robert Stack, wherein the long-lost relatives smile, embrace, and live happily ever after. "It took him two or three hours to find me at the airport. He was not in the right terminal. He had his best friend with him, and I couldn't tell which one he was, but I remember wishing it was the other one because he looked healthier."

Tonya had insisted on staying in a hotel, since she wasn't sure what conditions she might find at her father's home in Detroit. One thing she discovered when she arrived there was that her father lived with a white woman. Intellectually, she took their interracial relationship in stride.

"It didn't hurt because I recalled that one of my most vivid conversations with my mother about my father was when we were on the bus; she was crying. It was close to the date they were supposed to be married. I remember her telling me that my father had left her for a white woman with whom he had twin daughters. I remember her telling me he also had three older sons.

"I was very upset that she was upset. I had a hard time with interracial relationships for a long time because of that. Not so much with black females and white men but with black men and white women."

Before the trip and reunion ended, Tonya learned her father had sired as many as ten children—most with white women; many of the children lived in Detroit. Some he'd never met, nor had he been actively involved in the lives of any of his children. Tonya dedicated her time to finding some of them and forcing him to at least acknowledge their existence. With that mission accomplished, and almost out of money, she gathered herself to return to Washington, D.C.

There were subsequent trips, each connecting her more firmly with the half brothers and sisters who had been fathered by Ben Knight. Still, she believed the matter resolved as much as it could be resolved, after living nearly thirty years of her life without her father. "Everything was cool and dandy. They were there, and I was here."

Yet instead of the peace that she had hoped reconciliation might bring, Tonya found herself swirling in acrimony. Not long after she had her first reunion with her father, her mother began communicating again with him. Tonya doesn't know how it happened, but in 1994 the two decided to marry—for the first time. Tonya wondered, why now? Why hadn't they done the right thing when she was young, when she desperately needed two parents?

She was angry about the planned nuptials. She had promised her father when she first visited him in Detroit that she would not disturb anything in his life. That she would not try to change any equations she found, regardless of how imbalanced they appeared. Now, after she'd sorted things out and become comfortable with her self-image and with her relationship with him, he was jeopardizing all that.

"I thought that was very disrespectful and that the relationship was much too new for that; that is just not something you do, unless you're a predator. But I was realizing that he didn't have a lot of choices. He was desperate or whatever. So, of course, anything that looks like a solid footing, he was going to take it.

"I felt that I had sacrificed enough in not having him, and then for him to turn around and jeopardize my homestead was really very traumatic for me. Probably the most traumatic thing I've ever been through, and hopefully the most traumatic I'll ever go through."

Tonya didn't hesitate to tell her parents she disapproved of their actions. Perhaps because of her stated dissatisfaction or some other reason, she isn't sure which, her mother and father, ignoring the potential impact their wedding might have on her emotional stability, did not invite her to the ceremony.

Ben Knight stayed a little over a year. Perhaps he and Tonya's mother had grown too different from those early days when young love tapped their shoulders and whispered in their ears. Perhaps the pressure of fatherhood and husbandhood was now, as in the past, too much for him to handle; for some people commitment is a foreign language they are unwilling to learn or to translate. Who knows why he left. No one offered any reason to Tonya. She doesn't even know whether her parents divorced or merely separated.

These days, Tonya says she can take or leave Ben Knight—most often she leaves him. Sometimes, a stray blond-colored cat comes to the door of her Victorian. She and her mother have taken to calling it Ben.

Timing Is Everything

The fatherless daughter often seeks healing when she approaches thirty, say most experts. The hunt could begin sooner, depending on the press of the Fatherless Woman Syndrome. Tonya made her final search for her father when she was in her twenties. I met my biological father when I was in my thirties, which, experts say, is around the time the fatherless daughter begins to take note of the patterns in her life: the promiscuity, the bad choices, the misdirected rage.

"Initially you believe it's happening to you because there are no good guys; they are all dogs; you're not good at selecting the good ones," explains Audrey Chapman.

"[Fatherless daughters] find themselves going through a cycle of abandonment issues, a whole series of them—just continual pain, continual heartache. Then, finally, maybe because of something they've read in a book, or heard on some television talk show, or [because of] some kind of crisis, they find themselves in such severe pain that they seek answers to why," adds Chapman.

Meri Danquah had had one crisis after another when she resolved to take matters into her own hands; to change the quality of her life and to try ending her agony. She was living in Washington, D.C., in the early 1990s when she determined she would reach out to her father, maybe she could wrap their relationship in a different, brighter-colored paper. She called her father three times, inviting him to visit her new apartment. Three times he said no, citing work or other obligations. Each rejection picked at the scab of a wound not completely healed.

Then one Sunday morning, when she had almost given up on building some bridge to her father, Meri's telephone rang; her father was on the other end. He wanted to know if he could come by. "I went to the window so I could look at his car pulling in; when I saw it, I started crying. I was so happy. It was a major milestone. He took the time and went through every room. It was really wonderful for me."

Still, this wasn't the reconciliation Meri sought. After all, she and her father had maintained some contact, albeit tension filled. It was more an internal reckoning that needed to happen for her. Instead of taking out on society the rage she developed over her fatherlessness, she had turned the dagger on herself. She had a string of failed relationships, mostly with older men; oddly, older white men. She gave birth to a daughter but didn't marry the father, and that relationship disintegrated. She was in a constant state of depression. Before she could fully heal her relationship with her father she had to mend her own self-inflicted hurt.

She decided to write her memoir, recalling her struggle with depression. She wanted to put on paper what she had lived through. The book also could serve as a vehicle for her to reflect deeply on how fatherlessness impacted her life. How had her parents' separation and subsequent divorce rippled in her life? What was that cardinal nexus between herself and her parents?

As she wrote the book and anticipated its appearance in stores throughout the country, she realized that she had exposed so much of her and her family's private lives that she was creating the opportunity for a permanent and irreparable breach in her relationship with her parents. "I didn't want it to happen, but I was prepared. When one makes a decision to speak up, one must be prepared for the consequences. The preparation for that loss was interesting . . . fascinating."

What do I want from my father? What do I need from my father? These were the questions Meri repeatedly asked herself as she anticipated the familial controversy from the book's publication.

"I wanted him to acknowledge that he walked out on me, and that was not something he was trying to do. I wanted him to acknowledge that his absence had a profound impact on how I ended up. . . . It informed who I ended up being and what I ended up doing in my life. I wasn't looking for an apology." She wanted him to understand her pain; an apology merely minimized it. "I never felt there was a true understanding of the domino effect that pain has had. I don't think he truly understood it. I don't think my father is the kind of man who would have, if given a choice, not been present. Things happened."

Although she prepared herself for the worst, thinking everyone would shun her, much as the Africans once did villagers who had broken some sacred communal law, instead of separation, the book brought reconciliation. Meri doesn't remember his exact words—the ones whose memory still makes her smile when she recalls the reunion. But it was enough to smooth the way, to wrap her in that brighter-colored paper, to make her imagine a new relationship with her father.

As she enters the third decade of her life, Meri has arrived at a comfortable place with her father. The desire to have him make amends for the past has dissipated. "I'm not twelve and I'll never [again] be twelve. He can't be what he could have been to me when I was twelve, and really needed him. And, there's nothing he can do to change that.

"I'm not mad at him and that's the difference. What I was feeling as a lot of pain was really rage. There was this twelve-year-old child who was lost in the shuffle, and nobody looked back and said, 'I see you.' That was all I wanted."

It is all Sandra ever wanted, too, in 1995 when she and her father began their journey to reconciliation. "I don't feel that I need him now the way I needed him then. I'm an adult now. When I was growing up he told me he loved me, but there was nothing to back that up. Just the fact that [now] he calls me and I can talk with him openly. . . . Now I know he loves me."

Seeing with Adult Eyes

Both Meri and Sandra admitted to seeing their parental relationship for many years with the eyes of children. When they were ready to view things as adults, they were prepared to face the reality of what happened with their parents and with themselves. They were ready for the truth, which is the first natural step in the healing process.

I take the truth and slather it over my daughter one evening in the fall of 1998—a full ten years after I faced my own truth. Afrika and I are seated on the couch in our living room, watching television. Neither of us is terribly interested in the series of reruns that bombard the airwaves. Television, like meals, serves as a vehicle for us to come together—to visit, if you will.

I pull our attention away from the screen to some seemingly remote aspect of our lives. I ask about the boyfriend with whom she recently broke up. Although I understand her reasons for discontinuing the relationship, I do not agree that they are significant issues—especially if she really liked the person as much as she had claimed. I try to offer advice about how the tension of her relationship with him could have been resolved. She listens but is vehement about not reopening the door between them.

I shift gears slightly, discussing, in general terms, women's relationships with men. I repeat what psychologist Wade Horn once said: "A lot of women say the problem is men are no damn good. What the real problem is, is that that guy was no damn good."

He says the fatherless daughter takes a leap in logic and concludes that "*she* is no damn good." What's worse is when these women get married, if they have not recognized their own problems and "still believe men are no damn good. They are constantly weary about this husband of theirs—the father of their child.

"You're sending off all sorts of signals to the guy and the kid that that's what you think the problem is—men are no damn good. [Fatherless mothers] transmit this false issue intergenerationally to their own daughters."

I do not want my daughter transmitting such messages. I do not want her to carry the disease of fatherlessness into another generation. In capsule format, I tell her things about my life that, unquestionably, were shaped by father loss. This is a good segue to her relationship with her father.

I ask when she last called him. She dismisses my inquiry. "He needs to call me sometime. I'm always calling him, leaving messages, and he doesn't call me back. I get tired of always being the one to call. I'm not calling him."

The anger in her voice is lethal, suffocating. I can hardly breathe. It takes me a minute to recover. I tell her about the demands of raising two small children; the mastectomy his wife underwent and the trauma that must have caused him and the entire family. These possible reasons for his reticence do not satisfy her. She demands a place in the circle. "I'm part of his family. He can make time for me, too."

Who can argue with her statement?

Since I have opened this door, I must enter the room and lead her to a comfortable place—a place where she can find a measure of peace, although there isn't a place in our lives that can offer complete and unending calm and solitude. We merely travel the path toward it, never really reaching nirvana.

Once upon a time, I tell her, there was a man who believed his daughter to be as precious, if not more precious, than the air he breathed; as precious as the sun and the rain. This man took his daughter almost everywhere he went, introducing her to the world, so that when he could not be at her side, she would know and understand its language. He spent his weekends riding a bike with her, teaching her the geography of the city in which they lived, helping her to understand in simple terms its demographics, and informing her that, contrary to what people may say, because her skin is black, she is not a minority; she is a majority, not only in her hometown but throughout the world. People of color are the mainstream, he often told her.

He took her on picnics; sitting side by side, they dined on sandwiches and they drank juice he had made with his juicer. He wanted to show her the treatment she should expect from boys who come knocking at her door, confessing love and affection but unwilling to do even the smallest things for her pleasure.

This man also introduced his daughter to organizations in which he was a member, nonverbally imparting the standards and values to which he hoped she would adhere; the kind of "fatherly values" Michael Gregory Stephens wanted to bequeath to his daughter.

This man, I tell her, was her father.

That evening, as the television droned, I reached for the only balm I believed could heal my daughter: the truth. With few embellishments, I told her the story of Afrika and Tommy as I knew it. As in the children's song game, I said, Rise, daughter, rise, "and wipe your weeping eyes." If she looked around, I told her, she would see love. And while she couldn't have her father in the home with her, she could still have him.

Afrika asked me, as Sandra had asked her mother that day, why it had taken me so long to explain the story behind her mother and father's separation. Maybe I had finally stopped licking my own wounds long enough to notice that my daughter was hemorrhaging. Maybe, as Audrey Chapman said, I had grown weary of seeing and experiencing the habitual pain.

Today, there is a calm between my daughter and her father. Weeks after our talk, Tommy arrived from New York to celebrate Kwanza in the city. He brought along his oldest son, who adores his half sister and who expresses a fondness for me. The trio went to candle-lighting ceremonies, had dinner together, and generally spent a few days enjoying one another's company. In the spring, Afrika went to visit her father in New York. They returned on the train together. I met them at Union Station, ostensibly to take her luggage home while the two of them ventured off. Tommy smiled. "You wanted a daughter," he said as I reached for her suitcases. Indeed I did.

Afrika has finally decided she no longer wants to be twelve. She is happy, at least for the moment, with being twenty-one. The rage she once used like a Molotov cocktail has been drained, the bottle turned over, emptied of all combustible materials. She no longer talks of the possibility of her father and mother getting together again. Instead, she seems to have reached the conclusion that even if they don't, she will be all right.

"I decided I just needed to move on," she says of her change in attitude. "I needed to leave the past in the past."

Wishing for a Miracle

But for Ivory Nevada Sanders the past is still too undefined to be left behind. Without a miracle, she may have to satiate her father hunger with grainy images that she has held for years, calling them "Daddy" and wondering about Eddie Calhoun. Like other fatherless women, she has raced through a bevy of dysfunctional, failed relationships, producing her own fatherless son. While she knew of this missing father, she had given little attention to his significance or the role he had played in charting the course she had navigated for more than thirty years. Then a series of events took her to the door of reality, forced her to knock, forced her to enter.

It began while she was still in the military, stationed in Arizona. She stood in line at the checkout of a convenience store. A woman who could have been her twin sister walked in; Ivory did a double take. Minutes later, as Ivory entered her own car, the woman she had seen came out of the store—and opened the door to a car exactly like Ivory's, except for its color.

It was eerie—Ivory felt as if she had stepped into Rod Serling's *Twilight Zone*, where the familiar world suddenly turned atilt and almost anything might happen. Ivory shook it off but stored the occurrence away in her mind, as we do most things that affect us. And maybe that woman would have remained there, gathering cobwebs, were it not for what happened on Ivory's trip to West Africa in 1996.

She was in Senegal, seated in a restaurant teeming with tourists, mostly African Americans from the United States, when a similar unsettling moment occurred. Like other travelers returning to their mother country, they were on a spiritual journey, one as meaningful as any devout Muslim's pilgrimage to Mecca. They had come to discover their roots, to connect with a past that was not all slaves, whips, chains, cotton, and tobacco; a past not totally dominated by the sins of the "white man," but one regulated by the powerful stories of blacks as kings, scholars, and visionaries—before that word was ever captured in any dictionary.

These sojourns began before Ivory was born. But they became more popular during the civil rights movement of the 1960s and the Black Power and Black Arts movements of the 1970s. There was something purifying, cathartic even, about standing on Goree Island, looking onto the massive expanse of the Atlantic Ocean, wondering what it must have been like for those men, women, and children snatched from their homeland centuries ago, stuck like sardines in the holds of ships, smelling sickness, death, and fear. Reportedly, some people have cried while standing there.

Ivory had traveled to Senegal with more than a thousand black Americans. She was eating breakfast when suddenly, across the room, she saw a woman who could have been her twin sister. Fate had tapped her only lightly in Arizona; now, in Senegal, it was hitting her over the head with a two-by-four. "My thought was, How could I be coming to breakfast again. I'm sitting right here. It was scary."

As with the experience in Arizona, Ivory resisted the urge to race to the woman and ask, like a protagonist in an American Express commercial, "Do you know me?" Later though, on another day, after she had finished a bus sight-seeing tour and people had gathered at tables in an outdoor courtyard, she couldn't restrain herself any longer.

"I asked her if I could take a picture. It didn't matter whether she talked to me or not. I knew nobody would believe my story if I didn't take this picture back. After I took the picture, I got my courage up and went around to the other side of the table and spoke to her. I asked her if she thought we looked alike. She said there was some resemblance, but that I actually looked more like her sister, whom she pointed out to me there in the courtyard.

"When I finished talking with her, I went to find a seat near this stone stairway and one of the vendors saw the picture and asked, 'Is that your sister?' I said no, but her sister looks more like me than she does."

The experience with the sisters she met in Senegal pushed Ivory to confront realities she had dodged for years. "I thought, Suppose I do have a sister out there, who looks just like me. Suppose?"

Back at home in Baltimore, Maryland, Ivory became obsessed with the question. She looked at the photograph of Harriet and Vicky. She looked at herself. Then, she looked at the two pictures of her father. She resolved to reignite a project she'd placed aside two years earlier: the search for Eddie Calhoun.

In 1992, while listening to a local radio station, she heard a company advertise that it could help locate missing people. Thinking that perhaps this company could help her locate her father, she wrote to it. She paid about forty dollars and received a list of persons with the last name of Calhoun. While she received the list almost immediately, she waited another two years before deciding to write to anyone. She was a little anxious, about the potential results and about the reality that she was now announcing to the world that she was a fatherless African American woman.

She sent out two hundred letters; most came back undeliverable. Failing to receive a favorable response convinced her she had wasted her time, the mission to find Eddie Calhoun was doomed. But after the trip to West Africa, she was reinvigorated. She gained additional courage and sent out this letter:

> My name is Ivory Nevada Sanders. I am 37 years of age, and [I am] searching for my biological father, whom I have never met and [about whom I] have very limited information. I was born on October 30, 1960, in Syracuse, New York. I don't want anything from you, except to know you and a brief family history and the opportunity to meet any siblings, grandparents, and other paternal relatives. Please do not ignore my request.
>
> If you are the individual I am seeking or if you know of Eddie Calhoun's whereabouts because you are his (mother, father, sister, brother, son, daughter, or other relative, or friend), please contact me at the address stated below. Please include your current address and telephone number.

The salutation for the letter was simply "Searching."

She sent a copy to Harriet and Vicky, telling them that if they'd rather not get involved, she would understand. The two women never responded.

She wondered if perhaps a chord was struck. She had never asked about their father. Maybe they were as fatherless as she. Maybe they were engaged in their own search.

Ivory has not heard anything from Eddie Calhoun. She waits patiently by the phone, the computer, and the mailbox. Recently she received a letter from an Eddie Calhoun who is serving time in prison. She had written to this individual at another address and the letter had been forwarded to him. He is not her Eddie Calhoun. Too young. But he knows a guy who knows a guy who might be the one. Ivory remains optimistic, but anxious.

"I feel like I'm running out of time. I'm thirty-seven, my mother's almost sixty. She said my father was about ten years older than she. Another reason is, I have lupus. If you don't take care of yourself, it can become fatal. Having lupus makes me think about my own mortality more than other people my age do. It's also hereditary, and I have a son."

I smile at these pragmatic reasons Ivory lays out, the way a carpenter might dispose his tools before building a bookcase. But these are diversions, a buffer that protects her, keeps the listener carefully away from the open sore that still aches. Who can question health as a motivation for seeking family history, seeking a father who keeps stories of doctor's visits under wraps?

I do not probe further. I know this brand of denial; it is a version of invincibility proffered frequently by far too many of us fatherless women. But Ivory's words do not cooperate with this conspiracy; instead they expose her despair. There is someone out there she is related to, doesn't know, but desperately wants to know.

"If I find out he's alive, I just want to be able to look in his face, one time."

Without Hope

There are times when life strips us of the possibility for miracles, when our fathers have been taken away through death and we are faced with a terrible suffering that cannot be healed by any search. Years after Misty Brown reached out for her father and was told he was dead, she discovered he wasn't—not at that moment.

What would have happened if Misty Brown's mother had given her Samuel Brown's telephone number instead of lying to her daughter? What issues of inadequacy and love might she have been able to resolve? What explanation would he have given her for that night in her mother's bedroom? What would he have said about the seven-year-old girl and her pedophilic tale? What might he have said to Misty about her relationships with men, and whom among them would he have told her to marry?

Mothers who engage in fierce battles with their husbands during divorce or domestic disintegration do not realize the damage done to a child. These women become embroiled in bitter custody, child support, and alimony disputes that often make the child the rope in a tug-of-war. And even after the mother has secured what she believes necessary for her and the child's economic welfare, the emotional scar lasts forever. There isn't enough money in the world to erase the hurt.

I think of this as I sit across the table from Misty, listening to the closing chapters of her story, watching as the energy drains from her face. She is exhausted by the series of interviews that have occurred over several days in New Orleans, where she lives. This first-time compilation of her story has thrust her into the reflection that Chapman mentions.

She sees the patterns. Perhaps she saw them early but was too afraid to acknowledge them; what do you do after you realize you're lost and you've been circling yourself? Before our interview, Misty saw her life as I saw mine: pieces of torn photographs scattered across a barren landscape. Now she is startled by the connections, the cycles, the bruising. For years she did what most of us do: She pretended. She adjusted to the limitations life has dealt, much in the same way children in poor neighborhoods hang old rubber tires from trees and call them swings or learn to use the street as their ball field, deftly avoiding the cars while concentrating on the game.

"God, all of that happened to me?" Misty asks at the end of our last interview. She is befuddled by the fact that she managed not to go crazy. A well of sadness rests in her eyes. She holds back the tears, but I can hear her heart humming the fatherless song, achingly, the way Billie Holiday sings "Strange Fruit."

I do not say anything. I leave her in the silence of her awakening, alone—alone to lick her wounds. The unanswered questions that rest in the hearts and minds of fatherless girls and women are the most lethal. I watch Misty reach deeper and deeper into the wound hoping to discover its bottom. I tell her what clinical psychologist Wade Horn says—that "acceptance" is the closest we may come to a cure. But even that "won't take away the pain, or close the hole in someone's heart where a father ought to be."

"I am really damaged," Misty says, softly, calmly. Her voice betrays the fear that overtakes her. She is a doe caught in the headlights.

"All wounds heal," I say assuredly.

18. FINDING PEACE WITH OR WITHOUT A FATHER

T elling the truth is the first major step toward healing. What would have happened if my mother had told me early in life, as Ivory's mother did, that my father was not Bill—the man she called her husband; and that he wasn't Noel—the man she lived with for several years and "the daddy" with whom I was in love? Rather, that he was John—a man who, until 1988, only my subconscious remembered, a man with whom she had a brief relationship and with whom she had fought about me.

We cannot perpetuate lies told to us by others. Without theatrics, embellishments, and scene-scaping, we must assert this truth: The absence of our fathers wounded us, is wounding us. The first man we loved was taken away from us, through death, divorce, or abandonment. We suffered all or various symptoms of the Fatherless Woman Syndrome. We ran from bed to bed, desperately seeking physical warmth—the feeling we had when our fathers hugged us, tucked us in bed, or like Qubilah Shabazz, used our fingers to sweeten their coffee.

We—like Afrika, Sandra, and me—obsessed about a baby, hoping to secure unconditional love. We overate, abused substances, and worked ourselves damn near to death trying to anesthetize the pain or simply prove our worth. We screamed out in anger, when all the time it was the pain of the loss that prompted our uncontrollable rage. And, not unlike Meri Danquah, when shouting and lashing out at others didn't soothe us, didn't offer protection from our anguish, we turned the dagger onto ourselves, falling into deep depression or committing suicide.

We did these things because in the end, the loss, the abandonment, told us we were unlovable and unworthy. Who could love a girl or woman whose father didn't want her?

"We lost something that is irretrievable. We lost the choice of going through life with the absolute knowledge that we are lovable. That was our birthright, and we never received it," says Geneen Roth. Or, if we did receive it, it was snatched from us before we were ready to relinquish it. We are forever changed by this single act.

I stand before the full-length mirror in my bedroom, examining my right breast; this is the one a surgeon's scalpel reached inside, cutting out the mass of tissue, as I lay on the cold table praying that tissue was benign. A scar remains from the procedure. Foolishly, I wonder, aloud, if it will ever disappear. Then I turn around and catch a quick glimpse of the one on my back; I received it when my husband pushed me forcefully, sending me backward into the closet onto a hanger. It ripped open my skin. Like the blemish on my back and the one on my breast, the scar of fatherlessness is permanent.

"The scar she carried was just that: a scar. It would not go away with a telephone call—not even a hundred telephone calls. It was a scar," Ben, the father in Alexs Pate's novel *Finding Makeba*, realized about his daughter and the effect of all those years she lived without him. This is the truth a fatherless daughter bears all her life.

Acknowledging our loss permits the opportunity for us to grieve. If I had been able to say at nearly eight years old that my heart was broken over Noel's departure; if I could have just put the words together, with my limited vocabulary, to let someone know the deep pain I was experiencing, perhaps I would have been guided to a proper grieving process. The same is true with Meri, Misty, Helen, Tonya, my own daughter, and so many other fatherless women. Psychologist Maxine Harris is so correct when she says children have no organizing text.

"Sometimes you go through stuff, and parents don't realize how the situation is affecting you," says Ivory Nevada Sanders. Because we are without words, we do what I did: We blame ourselves. At whom else can we point the all-accusing finger—our mothers? Along the way, we come to minimize the importance of our fathers, implicitly authenticating the myth of the superfluous father—until there is an epiphany that forces us to face ourselves, the lives we have lived, the late-night weeping, the fear that has gripped us in every relationship, and the absolute aching of our hearts. Then we are ready for change.

After truth comes grieving. "You have to grieve the loss, however the loss occurred. Whatever fantasy you had with that parent, you are not going to have that parent," says psychologist Gayle Porter about the missing father.

"Grieving for the lost years is a courageous act because it takes time and we are used to moving fast. Grieving can seem like a full-time job, and with a family to care for, work to report to, and a life that demands our presence, it's hard to believe that we can make room for something as big as grief. Grieving is courageous because it looks like wallowing; in a culture that values success and achievement, we believe we have more important things to do than cry over something that happened thirty years ago. Grieving is courageous because while we are in the middle of it, it seems as if it will never end. Most of all, grieving takes courage because we have no idea what comes after grief," explains Geneen Roth.

"In the final stage of successful mourning, children come to see loss and their ability to survive as part of the same tapestry. Rather than feeling overwhelmed by grief and despair, they are aware of their own strength to manage adversity," says Maxine Harris.

"When you grieve you let go of defining yourself by how much and how badly you've been abused. You begin living in the present instead of living in reaction to the past," says Roth.

After Tonya Butler located her father and experienced yet another life crisis because of him, she realized that she might never fully heal herself, but was not debilitated by that reality. "Yes, I have an imbalance, a sickness," she confessed. "My main goal is to make sure that the imbalance has the least effect that it can, so that I can survive, if I have to, by myself. I just want to manage it."

She had come to a place in her life, as Afrika and Meri did, where she found that she could assert control; that while she carried this pain, she did not have to let it regulate her life. Perhaps it was the combination of acknowledging the loss and submitting herself to honest grieving that helped empower her.

Those of us who can, go looking for our fathers. We want to fully reconcile, to learn our fathers' truths: Why did he leave? Why didn't he spend more time? What can he do now? Simultaneously, we want to know what we still need from these men.

As women who, by and large, have led dysfunctional lives, we need some of the same things we needed as little girls—unconditional love and guidance. We may not need those essentials in the same proportion or in the same expression as they would have been bestowed when we were children, but we need them nonetheless. We need them because we are still attempting to define ourselves as women, still caught in understanding the terrain of men, still trying to develop meaningful relationships— with men; most important, however, we are attempting to clarify our relationship with ourselves.

There are dozens of ways to find our fathers. We can ask our mothers where they are. We can approach the search like Tonya and Ivory by making phone calls or writing letters to locate them. Or we can do like Meri, Afrika, and Sandra; we can reconnect with our fathers and engage them in adult dialogue. And when the overtures are not welcomed, or they cannot be made because our fathers are dead, then we can try to consciously father ourselves or find solace in surrogates.

"There are attributes that go with being a parent that you can give to yourself or you can find appropriately in other people. You can find people who really do care about you, who are going to be there for you, and who will make decisions that take you into account. But, they are not going to take you into account the way they would if you were three years old," warns Gayle K. Porter.

Fatherless women must also learn specific skills that will help them assert themselves. We must know how to ask for what we want. We must know how to take no when it's appropriate and even if it isn't appropriate. How to be neither passive nor aggressive.

The most important lesson for the fatherless daughter is learning how to love herself. If all symptoms of the Fatherless Woman Syndrome are ignited by one infectious germ—believing ourselves unlovable and unworthy of love—then eliminating that destructive element in our thinking begins to guarantee a more wholesome and healthy life.

But how do you learn to love yourself? That has been one of the hardest struggles for me—the girl who heard she was the black sheep, with nappy hair and a wide nose. The girl who later added to her physical misfortunes by having a wide ass and spaghetti-thin legs, in a society that fawns over less voluptuous hips and more ample calves. I have changed my locus from external to internal. I have set my own goals, my own standards, and my own ethics, which strangely enough reflect those of the broader society and not those marketed by television, magazines, and the general media and entertainment industries. Unlike in the past, I have refused to alter myself for others—alterations are mine to declare and mine to make. I have sought and found friends—male and female—who know the value of a book is more than its cover; they have helped me nurture my femininity, and other parts of me that fatherlessness almost completely destroyed. And when life's events sometimes prove overwhelming, thrusting me back into bad patterns of behavior, I have adopted a daily spiritual cleansing ritual that keeps the pollutions of the world at a minimum. "We're all in some doctor-patient relationship with God. I don't think there are many things I can do to direct that course of treatment; believe me I've tried," declares Tonya. "I'll leave it up to God and his plan to resolve it, if it's to be resolved."

To be sure, for fatherless women this process of learning to love yourself requires diligence and unwavering dedication—not to the point of narcissism, however. We know we have arrived at the healing well when we not only celebrate each day, but we celebrate our own unique contribution to it; when we sing, without hesitation or timidity, our own anthem.

19. THE HEALING BALM

There are other specific steps the fatherless daughter can take to heal herself that I have discovered through my own life or that have been shared with me by experts. They are summarized here to inspire your healing journey.

1. Speak the truth, unabashedly. Father loss is painful. It is affecting and has affected your life. You should not be ashamed of this.

2. View life through your adult eyes. For most of our lives, we fatherless daughters have seen the world with a child's eyes. Like Meri, we sit at the window looking onto the world, waiting for our fathers to return. We are angry with the world for taking him away. Angry with our mothers for sending him away. Angry with ourselves for not being special enough to keep him at home. It is hard to know what drove your mother and father to divorce, or never to marry, or for your father simply to walk away. We cannot fathom or manage the complexities of adult interpersonal relationships because emotionally we are still children, believing that if we don't behave as our mothers did, then our husbands, lovers, and mates won't reject us; they won't abandon us. We do somersaults, leap tall buildings; we try to effect our own miracles, all because we are living neck-deep in fear and seeing the world as children.

3. Let go of the fantasy. Your father, even before he and your mother got a divorce, wasn't perfect. He wasn't perfect before he abandoned you. He wasn't perfect when he died. Therefore, he comes with his own set of human flaws that may have affected his relationship with your mother, or caused his death. The reality is, he was just a man—someone you loved, and maybe someone you still love.

4. *Identify the ways you believe you were affected by father loss.* Start with the symptoms listed under the Fatherless Woman Syndrome. Were there others? Knowing specifically how you were affected helps with beginning to change your behavioral patterns. You want to be your best self. You have been hurt; you are in pain, but sleeping with "two hundred partners" won't make it better. Nor will running away from love guarantee a life without further anguish. In fact, anti-intimate behaviors increase the likelihood that the opposite will occur.

5. *Come out of the closet.* "Once you are out of the closet yourself, you will discover that there are many, many others like you, others who can understand exactly how you feel because they have been there themselves," says Harris. "It feels wonderful to find another survivor who knows first-hand what you are going through. Pain is miraculously halved when it is shared."

6. *Refuse to see yourself as a victim.* "A victim is someone who has no choices, someone who is dependent on those around her to protect her. A victim looks outside herself, not inside, for clues about her feelings, her next move," asserts Roth.

7. *Enough with the mea culpas.* You are worthy! You have not committed a mortal sin. There isn't a need, as I believed as a child, for the fatherless daughter to beat her chest and cry mea culpa, mea culpa, mea maxima culpa. God did not single you out for punishment. You are not Job. You are not personally responsible for your father's absence. You do not have to make penance. You were not responsible for your fatherlessness. But you are responsible for what happens from this point on in your life. You can

choose whether you will be forever handicapped by your experience, or whether you will use adversity to your advantage, allowing yourself to be empowered by it.

Consider this: Two people experience near fatal accidents; both are left paralyzed from the neck down. One gives up and demands, repeatedly, to be allowed to die. Another does what Christopher Reeve did: She attempts to enjoy life, investing herself in some cause, keeping her mind occupied, her body healthy, and her heart giving and receiving love. Who would you rather be?

8. *Go ahead, cry. Grieve.* Cry all day and all night, if you want. "Tears belong to the wounded woman. The tears can be congealed in icy form with the daggerlike points and edges of icicles. Or they can rush out in a torrential storm that can flood the ground upon which a woman stands," says Linda Schierse Leonard, author of *The Wounded Woman: Healing the Father-Daughter Relationship*, which explores the father-daughter relationship from a feminist and psychospiritual perspective. "But the tears may also fall like the fructifying rain which enables growth and spring's rebirth." For years you have lived a pain-filled life. You masked it with dysfunctional behavior. You slept with every Joe, Curtis, and Michael. You took your anger out on anyone who ventured into your environment—even your children. You were too afraid to love anyone, so you made them keep their distance, and when they didn't you made a beeline for the nearest door. You used drugs, you overate, and maybe you tried to prove you were queen of the mountain. You must be worn out. Your spirit must be screaming to be comforted, to just realize all of that frustration, all of that sadness. "Healing is about opening our hearts, not closing them. It is about softening the places in us that won't let love in. Healing is a process. It is about rocking back and forth between the abuse of the past and the fullness of the present and being in the present more and more of the time," says Roth. Go ahead, let it out. Then get ready for the rest of your life.

9. *Learn to trust, again.* The fatherless woman is riddled with fear. She is ruled by fear. She is a slave to her fears. Fear, as Audrey Chapman says, is the absence of trust. Because we lost our fathers, either through death, divorce, or abandonment, we develop an enormous fear about rejection and being alone. Those fatherless women, like me, whose fathers just walked out on them, have even greater trust issues, not just with the external world but with themselves. If we can't trust our fathers to hang around, whom can we trust? If we can't trust ourselves to select the right men, whom can we trust? The issue is always there, plaguing us, unresolved. Before the fatherless girl can heal fully, she must learn to trust again.

One step at a time is the method I used and continue to use. I don't test people or even myself: If he does this, then I know he can be trusted. That's game playing, and no one has time for that. But I do pay attention to the little things. Are promises kept? If they aren't, what reasons are given? Is my date on time? If he isn't, what reason is given? If I'm in trouble and call for a favor, how does my friend respond? And then I ask myself how much any of this really matters to my friendships, and to my survival. Will I just die because someone is fifteen minutes late? Have I permitted my sense of self-worth to become attached to someone's response?

Once I was blaming someone for something terrible that had happened to me. My ex-husband stopped me cold. He said, "You allowed that person to do that to you." I didn't understand then what he meant. But it was about trusting myself, more than trusting others; having a confidence that my intuitive responses were valid and should be honored. We all know instinctively when we're headed up the wrong tree. But we don't trust ourselves to bail out in time. Once we trust ourselves, trusting others is much easier.

10. *Gain mastery over your life.* Some people use their careers as a way of gaining control over their lives. But the fatherless daughter has to be careful about how important she allows her career to become in her life.

Instead, she should seek balance while developing a plan to reconcile herself with herself.

Spend a few days listening to your inner voice: This is where meditation might be useful. There are hundreds of books on proper meditation techniques. Ask yourself what you are saying about you. What do you like about you? What don't you like about yourself? Are you happy with your current cast of friends? Are you tired of being the aggressor? One day I simply resolved to evict my masculine self; she had gained control over every room in my internal house. And, while she was getting things done, Lord, she was creating a bunch of other issues and wearing me out. Reconnecting to yourself offers an opportunity to discover what you have done to separate you from the parts of yourself as a woman. The realization that the masculine had taken control over my internal house was the beginning of reclaiming myself. Every now and again the masculine me escapes, but I quickly find her, by whispering to myself a line a platonic male friend once said to me: "You've been eating too many gorilla biscuits." Reconciling myself, returning to my feminine energy, gaining a sense of confidence about it and its enormous powers, permits fatherless women like me to view their male counterparts in a different light. The definition of the masculine comes into clearer, shaper focus. It creates for the fatherless daughter an occasion to reduce the tension between herself and her male partner. And while she may not be fully capable of reading the legend on the map of the male terrain, she will be less fearful of the exploration and much more open to having a guide.

11. Feel free to re-create yourself. Each year political candidates try to repackage their successes and their failures. Some people call that process spinning. The spinner characterization may be not quite accurate, but not fully fraudulent, either. The fatherless daughter unable to locate her true self may want to start at the present. She may want simply to remake herself. She can't forget her past, but she can reduce its importance. Just as she tried to remake herself for others, she may want to do it for herself. It took me nearly twenty years finally to arrive at a place where I am happy with myself, although, to be sure, there are things that need further improvement. Considering my starting line, I haven't done too badly—but the greatest improvement came after I met my biological father.

12. Find that father. Each of the women in this book found their father, literally or figuratively. They returned to where the problem all began. They reached out to their fathers, telling them about their pain, telling them what they thought they had missed, asking them why they left. And while there were mixed results, none was dissatisfied for having made the journey. As Sandra says, two people made you; in order to have a complete picture of yourself, you need to know the other side—the father. Find him.

13. Choose a good surrogate. If you can't find your father or you are not interested in reconnecting with him, because he was abusive or simply "no good," then create a father for yourself. Find a male relative, family friend, or older friend who will serve in that role. Let him in on what role you want him to play and why. Don't use him as a sugar daddy, someone on whom you would grow dependent. Do use your surrogate as a confidant, a guide, someone with whom you can share parts of your life and can trust to handle them with care.

14. Hold a funeral and say good-bye. When a father has died or there simply is no chance reconciliation can occur, and a surrogate isn't enough to sufficiently heal the wound, do a dance, write a poem, write a letter, hold a funeral, do whatever you need to do, but say good-bye. Harris tells of one woman who took her résumé to the cemetery and buried it beneath a rock near her father's headstone. You can also *write your own affirmation* that asserts your right, even without a father, to a wonderful life, one filled with loving, caring people; and then read it every day until it becomes a part of your conscious thinking, until it becomes a part of your belief system; *visualize the father you want and then say to him what you've always wanted to say; wait for him to answer.* The Creator and the spiritual energy in the universe always answer us and guide us, if we allow them; *write a letter to your father,* even if you don't know where to send it. Ivory wrote letters trying to locate Eddie Calhoun; maybe, in time, she'll write a letter telling her father about the young girl he missed seeing growing up and about the woman she has become. The main thing is to do something tangible, albeit symbolic. Take an action that can separate you from him; can reestablish your self-esteem, your sense of self-worth, and your right to be loved. I told a young fatherless woman at American University in Washington, D.C., to take a trip to the beach, pack a picnic basket, and, if she wanted, take a friend or two. Consider it a celebration of spring. Once at the beach, I told her to situate herself nicely—lay out her towel, arrange her snacks and drinks, turn on the music, etc. Then make a paper boat and write her father's name on it. Take the boat to the ocean and place it in the water. And as it sails away from her, say her good-bye aloud. Let the sadness she feels be expressed; let the anger she feels be expressed. And when all that needs to be said to her father is said, release him.

15. Forgive and forget. These are the greatest gifts the fatherless daughter can give to herself. If there is no forgiving of her parents, especially her father, then there can be no moving on to her future. But even before she forgives her father, she must forgive herself the mistakes she has made in her life. Every misstep she took was designed in some way to ameliorate the pain of father loss. My daughter has helped me to understand and appreciate more deeply this notion of forgiveness. If I ask her these days about her troubles with her father, about those days when she saw a baby as mythic rescuer, she says only, "That was in my past. I was in pain then. I am not now." We can all pronounce—proclaim—those words when we give up the anguish to the universe, forgive our fathers and ourselves, and then resolve to salute our present and become infectiously excited about the glorious future that awaits us.

EPILOGUE

When I met my biological father, John Asemore, all I could think about was that at last someone would nurture me and love me, and proudly claim me in the way I had always dreamed of. I hoped our reunion would finally connect me with a "daddy." I was blind to the obvious limitations caused by his physical condition and the fact that we lived hundreds of miles apart.

I had spent far too many years being the well at which a thirsty soul could always find a cool drink, the primary caregiver, the sturdy brick wall. Fatherlessness unwittingly caused me to cast myself as the invincible superwoman. I was the Amazon starring in the Fatherless Woman Syndrome. Naturally, when I was in the throes of being all things to all people, I never linked it to father loss. I simply accepted the applause for my overcompensation and touted my ability to cope with anything and everything. Sometimes I felt as if I had taken on the armor of a man, and I desperately wanted to discard my indestructible facade and return to my natural feminine attire. But that wasn't a possibility.

With the discovery of my father, I believed that such a transformation might be possible. I believed the work of everyday living might become easier. I believed I had found a compatriot, a person with whom I could share my dreams and musings. What fatherless woman has not imagined at least once in her life, late at night and in the privacy of her own bedroom, the universe presenting at her door the perfect daddy? The all-powerful, all-wise hero, who would sacrifice his kingdom if necessary to save his little princess.

Women like me, who have lived lives without the daily or continuous presence of our fathers, frequently embrace such fantasies. The absence of a father—and the concomitant arrested development or vandalization of our childhoods—promotes such custom-made mythologies. Somewhere in Tonya's mind was a romantic image of her nightclub-singing father. Ivory has not yet found her father, but already she sees his face, his smile, his protective embrace. Fatherless daughters picture our daddys as tall and handsome, able to slay dragons, find and deposit pots of gold at our feet, while showering us with love unfathomable—except we do fathom it; we can feel their kisses on our cheeks, their arms wrapped around our shoulders, their "I love yous" constantly sounding in our ears. They smile protectively as they defend us against life's harms, silencing all threats with a possessive "That's my little girl, that's my daughter. . . ."

Charles Ballard, founder and executive director of the Institute for Responsible Fatherhood and Family Revitalization, often suggests that women father themselves. Even before I met him and heard his theories about the effects of father absence, I had already created the perfect father in my mind. But I had not measured the potential danger of this strategy.

In my first meeting with my biological father, even faced with the reality of his aging body, I had invested him with all the positive traits of Noel and none of the callous disregard I witnessed in Bill. John was my knight in shining armor—made visible. When I told him that I had lost my job and didn't know how I would pay for the rent or anything else, I thought he would gallop to my rescue. His promise was enough. "I'll send you a couple of dollars." I knew he didn't have much, but I waited for weeks and weeks. Help never arrived. His failure to come to my aid and fulfill my rescue fantasies rekindled old feelings of rejection. I felt I had been abandoned all over again. Unconsciously, I reverted to the wounded child. Although I didn't realize it at the time, I began to unleash the anti-intimate arsenal of the Fatherless Woman Syndrome. I refused to let John get close ever again. My biological father would never have the opportunity to reject me again. Once was too much.

I didn't breathe a word about my disappointment or anger or hurt in any of the three letters we exchanged. Our correspondence was filled with great caution. He wanted to know if he could he call me "daughter" and if he could sign his notes "your father." My letters were equally tentative: "Of course you can call me daughter. After all, I am your daughter."

In two years, without ever daring to challenge our fears, my father was gone. Dead. We had never managed to form a true father-daughter bond.

Not Ready to Say "Amen"

It happened in 1990. It was a typically cold, wet day in Washington, D.C. I had spent the morning writing. The telephone interrupted my concentration. It was my mother; John had been taken to the hospital. I wasn't sure how to respond to this news. How should a daughter who has had only brief encounters with her father act when that father lay dying? My mother suggested I send flowers; maybe call the nurse's station at the hospital, just to leave a message. Just say "his daughter called."

I was terribly conflicted. One part of me was furious about his disregard for my needs, evidenced, I thought, by his refusal to provide financial assistance or any response at all. "Daddy, you promised!" the wounded child inside me railed. Another part of me wanted to display some compassion. The man was dying. It was clear that the state of his health had prompted his final plea to my grandfather for help in locating me. He wanted to repent. Who was I to deny my father this? Besides, I didn't know the life he had lived. Who was I to judge? After listening to Milton's and Russell's stories, I know, now, that fathers live with their own frustrations and guilt, too.

What had driven me to my biological father was in part curiosity. But mostly I needed to see a face that looked like me and to proudly look at myself in the mirror, no longer feeling inferior to my sisters or anyone in my family. More than anything, I wanted to slay the demons that had worked as co-conspirators in my own destruction.

Later in the week, another telephone call came; this one from a woman I did not know. She was my father's sister. I listened to her faceless voice and tried to imagine how she looked. Was she tall like my father?

Was she dark-skinned? Did she know me, or had she only recently learned of my existence? What did she want from me?

"Your father is dying," she said. How could I tell her that he came alive for me only two years before? There was no denying that the bond between us was flimsy. How could I tell her that he's still a mirage, one that moves away every time I get closer? I'm terrified to get close, afraid he will do exactly what he is about to do—leave. Then, my mind and emotions translated any departure—even dying—as abandonment. For days after my aunt's call, I was afraid to answer the telephone. Afraid she would be on the other end, whispering my father's name as if it were some prayer, waiting for me to say "Amen." Or I was afraid the ringing phone would be my mother, telling me that if I didn't want to, if I didn't have the money, then I shouldn't come—but your father is asking to see you.

After much agonizing, I called Delta Airlines to determine the cost of a ticket to New Orleans; it was out of my reach. Too much for me to spend on a man I'd only recently met—even if he is my father. Too much for me to spend on a man who hadn't come to my rescue when I needed him. I had needed him all my life. And though I tried to deny it, a part of me still needed him. I finally decided to make the trip. It wasn't for me, I rationalized. It was for him. The next morning as I readied to pack my bag, my mother called. John had died during the night. He kept asking for you, she said. I was devastated.

"Are you coming to the funeral?" my mother asked.

"You know I hate funerals. Is it raining there?"

"Yes."

"Ma. Let me talk to you later."

I held the phone for a long time before I finally placed it back on the hook. Then, I sat on the edge of my chair unconsciously beating my chest with my balled fist as if I were back in St. Anthony's Catholic Church, my bony knees on the wooden floor rests, whispering "mea culpa, mea culpa, mea maxima culpa."

Looking for an End to the Story

It is eight years later: 1998. I am in the Plaza Hotel on St. Charles Avenue. There is a great view of the green-and-brown streetcars clanking their way along the track up St. Charles Avenue and back again. I like the quaint sight of them. When I was in my early teens, I'd ride the streetcar, sitting on the hard wooden seats watching from the huge window the unobstructed view of people on the sidewalks. We clanked our way through the Garden District to the place where the river hides just behind a man-made levee. I never dreamed that one day I might have a room in one of the old hotels; it was too rich a vision for my status. If I wasn't on the streetcar, I was on the ferry, leaning on the rail watching as the boat crawled across the muddy Mississippi River to Algiers and back again. Or I walked the streets of the French Quarter peering inside antique shops, imagining myself wearing some of the exquisite old jewelry. I scanned the galleries for art I might buy for my own home on Elysian Fields or Esplanade, if I ever got one. Those were, of course, the dreams of a silly girl.

Today I cannot retrace those steps. It is raining. I hate the rain. It reminds me of death. In 1965, just after I started McDonogh #35 Senior High School, Hurricane Betsy came, thrashing homes and businesses, bringing tons of water with her. We had to evacuate the house on Mexico Street, finding refuge in a nearby Catholic convent. Rows of single cots, covered with military-issued green blankets, filled the auditorium. We ate bologna sandwiches on white bread and drank chocolate milk. For a day it seemed fun. But I grew weary of the crowd, the lack of privacy. I wanted to sleep in my own bed. Taste my grandmother's thick French fries.

When we finally made it out of there, I learned the hurricane had destroyed the front side of old McDonogh #35. I lamented the loss. But my most vivid memory of those rains had little to do with buildings. The storm swallowed my aunt Claudia, my grandmother's sister.

Aunt Claudia lived with her mother—my great-grandmother—who had been visiting us when the storm hit. We thought Aunt Claudia would have been evacuated with the others. When my grandfather and my great-grandmother went to the house in the Ninth Ward below the Industrial Canal, they found her in bed, where she had gone to sleep. Her body was swollen with water. At her funeral the casket was closed. Regardless of how much I tried to bring it into clearer focus, that closed casket denied me the opportunity to say a proper good-bye—face-to-face. The same kind of proper good-bye that I denied myself with John Asemore.

So whenever it rains in New Orleans, no matter the season, I think of dying. Maybe it's because I'm still trying to resurrect the dead. I have come here ostensibly to locate my father's relatives. I want the closure I denied myself in 1990. Then, I permitted my anger to construct a wall between us. I want to resolve these years of guilt, although this thought will only become clearer to me months later. The combination of anger and guilt, stirred by the tendency to place blame—mostly on myself—had been a Molotov cocktail in my life. Fatherless women frequently dance with this fiery triumvirate of blame, anger, and guilt.

Like the little girl in the movie *Eve's Bayou*, I half blamed myself for John Asemore's death. I had wished him ill because he had disappointed me. I secretly hoped he could feel what I felt. In a year, my imaginings became reality. The wounded child hurts deeply. Her emotional response is not always grown up. She sits in the corner plotting her revenge, counting each offense, sticking pins in the voodoo doll of the father who didn't want her or love her. I was the reason my father died.

Even before arriving here in New Orleans, I sought absolution. I telephoned the Veterans Hospital where John died, hoping to receive more specific information about the cause of his death and the telephone number of his next of kin—the whispering woman who called herself his sister. The hospital staff could not assist in my exoneration. I tapped my sister's memory: She knew a man who attended my church, a cousin, she said. I went to the Bishop and received Roscoe's telephone number in Arkansas. He hadn't kept up with "that side of the family." His sister Peggy may know, he told me. She and another woman, Irene, who had introduced my mother to my father, agreed to meet with me. I felt as if I were a subject on *Unsolved Mysteries* and Robert Stack was about to reunite me with my long-lost family, whose members would encircle me with huge soft arms and equal amounts of love.

Hours after arriving in the city, I called them. I left messages for them. They have yet to return my telephone calls. Finally, today, the day before I am to leave, my persistence paid off. I reached Peggy at home. She said she was going to New York and didn't have time to see me. I offered to rendezvous in New York; she fumbled for yet another excuse. Finally I squeezed out the words: "Don't you want to meet me?"

"It's not that. My daughter called and asked me to come to New York," she said.

I stopped listening, just the way I did when my mother began telling her side of my fatherless story.

Finding My Way Home

Sometimes being without options is a blessing. We are forced to confront our circumstance whether we like it or not. Without the benefit of paternal relatives to ease my anguish, I was forced to look inside myself for answers. For years, like so many other fatherless women, I had successfully raced away from myself, smothered myself in work, and sought solace in the arms of dozens of men, with my fathers' faces. I dared them to relieve the gnawing sense of unworthiness and unlovableness that held me prisoner.

Self-exploration or self-analysis is a bitch. What self-respecting Amazon queen wants to admit there are chinks in her armor? Who wants to commit to the work required to alter decades of bad choices and bad behavior? Frequently our egos play at self-repair and self-restoration. All the while our souls scream for genuine help.

Looking back now, I know my entire being was begging for relief. I could continue to race away from the issues that haunted me or I could turn around and look at myself squarely. I knew, even if I never articulated it, that I wanted to find peace of mind—a place of comfort. All my efforts to find this place outside of myself had proved futile.

Reading volumes of materials and interviewing dozens of experts, I knew what ailed me. Hadn't I confessed it in my essay in the *Washington City Paper*, albeit a partial admission of the damage father loss inflicted upon me? I knew the symptoms even if, at that time, I hadn't given them a name. Late at night, when the rest of the world slept, I agonized over the symptoms I displayed, cautioned myself against repeating patterns, and invariably found myself walking in my own footsteps. Admitting the problem was one thing, doing something about it consistently was another, and believing that I alone had the power to change the course of my life was absolutely in a different ball field.

Often the answer to a problem comes from seeing the situation differently. You know, like those inkblots: You think it's one thing, and then you flip it around, and voilà! For nearly ten years I had called the summer of 1988 the Summer of My Discontent, strapping it forever in negative impressions. But in truth, that summer had launched my journey from chaos to self-discovery and self-love. Peggy had closed the final door to my father and his history. The sound of its shutting instigated my resolve to be my own healer.

Like everything, the path to self-actualization and healing the wounds of fatherlessness has been a process. Though I couldn't articulate it then, it began in earnest when I realized that I was no longer a child. I had to put away childish things. I could not wallow in the tears of father loss. I had to force myself to see the world as a woman, not as that little girl badly wounded by the untimely and traumatic departure of her father. I also counseled myself to make no judgments, no comparisons, and to release the need to understand every minute detail of life, and always, always to forgive.

When we enter the "no judgment zone," we embrace the reality that we are all human. Everyone suffers similar frailties and shortcomings. I finally understood that my fathers—John, Bill, and Noel—were ordinary men. What man, knowing his wife had had an affair, however brief, and had become pregnant with this man's child, would not react to the child the way Bill had to me? Each time he saw me, I was a reminder of his wife's infidelity. I could argue that if he had taken the time to know me, his response would have been different. I still do not know the reason Noel left. I know my biological father had been rejected—more than once. My mother had made it clear she didn't want him around her or their child. I could argue that he should have fought for me. Then I would be passing judgment, as I did during the months between our meeting and his death.

None of this is to let any of my fathers off the hook. Believe me, I feel more strongly now that fathers and mothers, after giving birth to children, must make the sacrifices to rear them, with love, together. Even joint custody or weekend parenting often denies the child the valuable lessons and important moments of sharing and receiving love that often come only once in a lifetime. If men and women must separate or divorce, they must still dedicate themselves to honoring and respecting their children. It has taken me years to understand that regardless of how I might like to rewrite my history, I cannot. It is what it is. My fathers left. I was wounded by their leaving. That is the reality of my life.

The dream of being rescued by them was only a dream. I had focused so much on the absence of these men that, as a substitute, I sculpted the perfect father from magical clay. This one was always there for me. He knew just the right things to say and absolutely smothered me in love. There was never an unpleasant moment with him. How could there be? My perfect father didn't have a job at which he had to work every day, didn't have to struggle to pay the mortgage or rent. There weren't any mood swings. How could there be? My father didn't interact with the rest of the world—he was there just for me.

The world has changed profoundly since our parents' generation. The social and economic circumstances they lived through were vastly different. They simply did not have the opportunity for the kind of self-reflection that we take for granted today. My idealized *Father Knows Best* father wouldn't have survived the challenges of the twenty-first century.

I remember one day, when I was piecing together all the issues of fatherlessness, I tried to draw on my mother's memory. Each time I asked her to think about some part of her past, she resisted. Toward the end of writing this book, I finally understood this wasn't a deliberate evasion on her part. Life had been hard for a single woman with four children. She couldn't afford the luxury of deliberating on any single event, probing it for its deeper message or lesson. She simply stored away her dark moments in an even darker closet and willed herself to forget they were there. Remembering them, at any time, might have made it difficult or even impossible for her to proceed. I am sure my father had similar trunks in which he stored his deepest secrets and failed dreams. Any life must be measured in context. Eastern philosophers call this living in the moment. And in this moment, I understand that no matter how much insight I possess, I cannot change the lives my parents lived.

I would like to tell you that when I made the decision to leave history to its own destiny, my problems vanished. They didn't. There were days I spent every second trying to analyze why things had happened the way they had. Why my mother and fathers had made the choices they did. Why I had reacted so dramatically to the loss of my fathers. Why it had taken so many years for me to realize how I had permitted the absence to misdirect my life.

I must have agonized for weeks and months after my trip to New Orleans about all of these things. One day, and I don't know what caused this, my relentless self-examination ended. I understood that I would never know the "answers." It was time for me to "accept the things I cannot change." Time to acknowledge them and move on.

In the summer of 1998, I made my final break with fatherlessness. I was consoling a young woman at American University. We had met days earlier when I presented a lecture to her class. As I was leaving, engaging in closing chitchat with a couple of students, she walked up to me and began crying. She had thought herself alone in her fatherlessness. Speechless and deeply moved, I put my arms around her and hugged her for several minutes. Days later she called me.

"How do you move on?" she asked. "How do you let go of the pain?"

"Forgiveness." I said the word without even thinking about it.

As I put the finishing touches on this book, I realized I had given that young woman a secret gift that I had not consciously given to myself. Although I had cleaned out my wound, removed the bandage, and could not fathom reinfecting it, the answer to the question, "Was I, in fact, healed?" was always no.

Why wasn't I healed? The answer I had given Helen was also meant for me. Forgiveness.

I remember that final epiphanous moment as if it were yesterday. Ten years after meeting my biological father for the first time, I sat, with the warm sun bathing my face, watching the birds skipping from branch to branch. I leaned back, with my eyes closed, and I suddenly cried out my father's name. I called out Noel's name. I called out Bill's name. I knew I had been graced with the ability to forgive. Then I opened the Barq's Root Beer soda I had purchased earlier, raised my bottle to the sky, and saluted my fathers and myself. At last, I could accept the hand dealt.

Later, when I arrived home, just as I crawled into bed, something came over me. I felt as if a heavy burden had been lifted. I cried. I cried for days. Those tears baptized me. I was reborn.

Is there a scar left by my father loss? Yes, but today it is a reminder of the healing that has taken place. My scars inspire and inform the choices that I make. Because of my fathers, I can now reach out to other women to show them the way. This is the gift that I gladly take from my fatherlessness.

"Whatever happened to daddy's little girl?" Today I can proudly answer. Daddy's little girl grew up and gave herself the wondrous gifts of self-acceptance and self-love.

References

Baldwin, Martha. *Self-Sabotage: How to Stop It and Soar to Success.* New York: Warner Books, 1990.

Barras, Jonetta Rose. *The Corner Is No Place for Hiding.* Washington, D.C.: The Bunny and the Crocodile Press, 1995.

Blankenhorn, David. *Fatherless America: Confronting Our Urgent Social Problem.* New York: Basic Books, 1995.

Bolton, Ruthie. *Gal: A True Life.* New York: Harcourt Brace & Company, 1994.

Coles, Robert. *Before Their Times: Four Generations of Teenage Mothers.* New York: Harcourt Brace Jovanovich, 1992.

Collins, Patricia Hill. *Black Feminist Thought: Knowledge, Consciousness, and the Politics of Empowerment.* London: Unwin Hyman, 1991.

Danquah, Meri Nana-Ama. *Willow Weep for Me: A Black Woman's Journey Through Depression.* New York: W. W. Norton & Company, 1998.

Dash, Leon. *When Children Want Children.* New York: Penguin Books, 1989.

Dawsey, Darrell. *Living to Tell About It: Young Black Men in America Speak Their Piece.* New York: Bantam Doubleday Dell, 1997.

Early, Gerald. *Daughters: On Family and Fatherhood.* New York: Addison-Wesley, 1994.

Edelman, Hope. *Motherless Daughters: The Legacy of Loss.* New York: Doubleday, 1994.

Erickson, Beth M. *Longing for Dad: Father Loss and Its Impact.* Deerfield Beach, Fla.: Health Communications, Inc., 1998.

Farris, Michael. *How a Man Prepares His Daughters for Life.* Minneapolis, Minn.: Bethany House Publishers, 1996.

Fishel, Elizabeth. *The Men In Our Lives.* New York: William Morrow and Company, 1985.

Friday, Nancy. *My Mother My Self: The Daughter's Search for Identity.* New York: Dell, 1987.

Goetz, Masa Aiba. *My Father, My Self.* Boston: Elements Books, 1998.

Harris, Maxine. *The Loss That Is Forever: The Lifelong Impact of the Early Death of a Mother or Father.* New York: Penguin Books, 1996.

Henry, Dewitt, and James Allan McPherson. *Fathering Daughters*. Boston: Beacon Press, 1998.

Hill, Robert. *Strengths of African American Families: Twenty-Five Years Later*. Washington, D.C.: R&B Publishers, 1997.

Horn, Wade and Jeffrey Rosenberg. *The New Father Book: What Every New Father Needs to Know to Be a Good Dad*. New York: Better Homes & Gardens, 1998.

Hutchinson, Earl Ofari. *Black Fatherhood II: Black Women Talk About Their Men*. Los Angeles: Middle Passage Press, 1994

Johnson, Ernest H. *Brothers on the Mend: Understanding and Healing Anger for African-American Men and Women*. New York: Pocket Books, 1998.

Klatte, William C. *Live-Away Dads*. New York: Penguin Books, 1999.

Madhubuti, Haki. *Black Men: Obsolete, Single, Dangerous? The Afrikan American Family in Transition*. Chicago: Third World Press, 1991.

Maine, Margo. *Father Hunger: Fathers, Daughters & Food*. Carlsbad, Calif.: Gurze Books, 1991.

Morrison, Toni. *Sula*. New York: Penguin Books, 1982.

Owen, Ursula, ed. *Fathers: Reflections by Daughters*. New York: Pantheon Books, 1985.

Parke, Ross D. and Armin A. Brott. *Throwaway Dads*. New York: Houghton Mifflin Company, 1999.

Pate, Alexs D. *Finding Makeba*. New York: G. P. Putnam's Sons, 1996.

Pittman, Frank. *Man Enough: Fathers, Sons and the Search for Masculinity*. New York: Berkley Publishing Group, 1993.

Popenoe, David. *Life Without Father: Compelling New Evidence That Fatherhood and Marriage Are Indispensable for the Good of Children and Society*. New York: Free Press, 1996.

Rabey, Lois Mowday. *Daughters Without Dads*. Nashville, Tenn.: Thomas Nelson Publishers, 1990.

Roiphe, Anne. *Fruitful*. New York: Houghton Mifflin Company, 1996.

Roth, Geneen. *When Food Is Love: Exploring the Relationship Between Eating and Intimacy*. New York: Penguin Books, 1992.

Rubin, Theodore I. *The Angry Book*. New York: Simon & Schuster, 1998.

Secunda, Victoria. *Women and Their Fathers: The Sexual and Romantic Impact of the First Man in Your Life*. New York: Delacorte Press, 1992.

Stack, Carol. *All Our Kin: Strategies for Survival in a Black Community*. New York: Harper & Row, 1974.

Stephens, Brooke, ed. *The Men We Cherish*. New York: Anchor/Doubleday, 1997.

Tavris, Carol. *Anger: The Misunderstood Emotion*. New York: Simon & Schuster, 1989.

Wade-Gayles, Gloria. *Father Songs.* Boston: Beacon Press, 1997.

Wakerman, Elyce. *Father Loss.* New York: Doubleday, 1984.

Wassil-Grimm, Claudette. *Where's Daddy?* New York: The Overlook Press, 1994.

West, Cornel. *Race Matters.* New York: Vintage Books, 1994.

White, John L. and Thomas H. Parham. *The Psychology of Blacks: An African-American Perspective.* Upper Saddle River, N.J.: Prentice Hall, 1990.

Williamson, Marianne. *A Woman's Worth.* New York: Ballantine Books, 1993.